Beyond Blood Oil

Explorations in Contemporary Social-Political Philosophy (ECSPP)

Series Editors: Naomi Zack (University of Oregon) and Laurie Shrage (Florida International University)

As our world continues to be buffeted by extreme changes in society and politics, philosophers can help navigate these disruptions. Rowman and Littlefield's ECSPP series books are intended for supplementary classroom use in intermediate to advanced college-level courses to introduce philosophy students and scholars in related fields to the latest research in social-political philosophy. This philosophical series has multidisciplinary applications and the potential to reach a broad audience of students, scholars, and general readers.

Beyond Blood Oil

Philosophy, Policy, and the Future

Leif Wenar
Michael Blake
Aaron James
Christopher Kutz
Nazrin Mehdiyeva
Anna Stilz

ROWMAN & LITTLEFIELD
Lanham • Boulder • New York • London

Published by Rowman & Littlefield
An imprint of The Rowman & Littlefield Publishing Group, Inc.
4501 Forbes Boulevard, Suite 200, Lanham, Maryland 20706
www.rowman.com

Unit A, Whitacre Mews, 26–34 Stannary Street, London SE11 4AB

British Library Cataloguing in Publication Information Available

Library of Congress Cataloging-in-Publication Data

Names: Wenar, Leif, author.
Title: Beyond blood oil : philosophy, policy, and the future / Leif Wenar, Michael
    Blake, Aaron James, Christopher Kutz, Nazrin Mehdiyeva, and Anna Stilz.
Description: Lanham : Rowman & Littlefield Publishing Group, Inc., 2018. | Series:
    Explorations in contemporary social-political philosophy | Includes
    bibliographical references and index.
Identifiers: LCCN 2018013054 (print) | LCCN 2018026504 (ebook) | ISBN
    9781538112113 (Electronic) | ISBN 9781538112090 (cloth : alk. paper) | ISBN
    9781538112106 (pbk. : alk. paper)
Subjects: LCSH: Petroleum industry and trade—Political aspects. | Petroleum
    industry and trade—Moral and ethical aspects.
Classification: LCC HD9560.5 (ebook) | LCC HD9560.5 .B468 2018 (print) | DDC
    338.2/728—dc23
LC record available at https://lccn.loc.gov/2018013054

Contents

Foreword   vii

1   Beyond Blood Oil   1
    By Leif Wenar

2   Bad Men and Dirty Trade   37
    By Michael Blake

3   The West's Energy Trap: Can It Be Broken?   51
    By Nazrin Mehdiyeva

4   Collective Resource Control and the Power of Complicity   73
    By Christopher Kutz

5   Does a Country Belong to Its People?   89
    By Anna Stilz

6   Why States Must Remedy the Resource Curse   105
    By Aaron James

Replies to Critics by Leif Wenar:

7   Reply to Blake and Mehdiyeva   119

8   Reply to Kutz   133

9   Reply to Stilz   143

10   Reply to James   149

Notes   157

Index   183

About the Authors   193

Foreword

Contemporary Social-Political Philosophy and *Beyond Blood Oil*

Now that my ladder's gone, / I must lie down where all the ladders start / In the foul rag and bone shop of the heart.

— "The Circus Animals' Desertion," William Butler Yeats

ABOUT THIS SERIES

From Plato through John Rawls, to Jürgen Habermas and Slavoj Žižek, philosophers have developed Political Philosophy as a stand-alone subfield in their discipline by focusing on political legitimacy, justice, and fundamental political institutions. The work of philosophers who focus on how societal practices and culture are related to politics or government is often subsumed under Social Philosophy, which has not been a strong, recognizable subfield. Nevertheless, scholars and students who critically examine social practices, traditions, and values, with the goal of improving the conditions of human life, are engaged with Political Philosophy—especially issues of inequality, oppression, and political power. For instance, philosophers who analyze racial and gender injustice have demonstrated how social norms and political principles can be productively investigated together. Such progressive or liberatory efforts have given rise to a number of questions, such as: How are social values and culture related to political power structures? How do social identities of race, class, gender, ability, religion, and ethnicity affect both individual status and power, as well as quality of life? Can justice be defined without close attention to actual oppression? The result of critical engagement with the questions of both social philosophy and political philosophy has been a new and growing body of method and content that is somewhat informally called Social-Political Philosophy. This hyphenated name signals an intent to address political issues in combination with social and cultural criticism, and/or to conduct social or cultural criticism with the goal of changing political structures.

The aim of this series is to present the best and most interesting work in Social-Political Philosophy at this time, for students, scholars, and general readers—in accessible and clear prose, and by authors who are transparent and self-critical about their methodologies.

Exploring Contemporary Social-Political Philosophy should not be equated with the *application* of theoretical philosophy to social issues. This is because new subjects often call forth and support new ways of theorizing and pursuing knowledge, as we hope will be evident throughout this series. That is, contemporary Social-Political Philosophy, as philosophy that evaluates the social and political conditions of human life, requires reassessing theoretical constructs and methods, as well as addressing practical issues. If the traditional, canonical works and ideas of philosophers could directly be applied to the realities of contemporary human life, then this series would not be needed. As a series of books, Exploring Contemporary Social-Political Philosophy will share important scholarly work and ideas with a multi-disciplinary audience, so that these ideas can be taken up to address some of today's most pressing problems.

—Naomi Zack and Laurie Shrage

ABOUT THIS BOOK

Over a decade ago, I watched the documentary "Darwin's Nightmare,"[1] which shows how a "natural" resource (in this case, an invasive species of fish) can contribute to the severe economic and political oppression of the human population that lives near that resource. Some of the most memorable scenes in the film are those of cargo planes on an airstrip in Tanzania, near Lake Victoria, which deliver weapons of war to local rulers, and then get reloaded with tons of fish. While the planes full of fish take off for Europe, we see that the local population is starving, and contending with the environmental and human catastrophes caused by the trade in fish in for arms. Unfortunately, the invasive fish is destructive to other lifeforms in and around the lake, and it provides local rulers with foreign capital to purchase sophisticated weapons that they use to maintain power over their subjects and engage in aggressive wars with their neighbors.

When I first came across Leif Wenar's book *Blood Oil*, the haunting images from this film came back to me. But I was very glad to encounter a philosopher who was thinking about how to interrupt the dynamics of power and oppression in oil-rich states. While other scholars have researched and described "the resource curse," which applies to rare minerals, petroleum, and other natural resources, Wenar appears to be the first to apply the analytical tools of moral and political philosophy to devise a solution. The solution relies on holding those who buy a natural resource accountable for both empowering politically corrupt and war-mongering elites and disempowering their exploited and immiserated political subjects. The solution is: Don't buy oil (or other raw materials) from despots who control the resource, but do not legitimately own it. We must and can find other vendors for the basic resources we consume, so that we do not enable aggressive wars, political repression, and human and environmental devastation.

Companies that buy oil from corrupt rulers enable autocratic and kleptocratic regimes that not only oppress their populations and invade their neighbors, but spread violence and xenophobia around the world. It is in our self-interest not to enter trade relationships that finance terrorist violence. Wenar also convincingly argues that such exchanges are simply immoral. His work forcefully challenges the skeptics, the cynics, and the indifferent among us who think that some interests and power relations are just too entrenched to ever be substantially changed.

Blood Oil was widely and favorably reviewed, and has become a subject of debate among political, economic, and legal theorists and policy analysts. Readers who understand the history, economics, and legality of problematic multinational exchanges that exist in our contemporary world can absorb Wenar's important analysis and proposals. However, if the very big and seemingly intractable problems discussed in *Blood Oil* are going to be adequately addressed, they need to be discussed in works intended for a wider audience. Many students and citizens think about the problems dissected in *Blood Oil*, or a film like "Darwin's Nightmare," and simply feel overwhelmed and discouraged. Fortunately, some of this sense of despair and defeat may be premature, and scholars and teachers can point to possibilities for bringing about more justice and peace.

Beyond Blood Oil distills the major insights from Wenar's earlier book and allows readers to see how his ambitious proposals are received and evaluated by other leading experts in the relevant fields. The commentators—Michael Blake, Aaron James, Christopher Kutz, Nazrin Mehdiyeva, and Anna Stilz—discuss alternatives to Wenar's proposals, and fill in the background knowledge needed to understand the theoretical and practical considerations behind different approaches to "the resource curse," and what is novel and promising about Wenar's proposals.

—Laurie Shrage

1

Beyond Blood Oil

Leif Wenar

Natural resources empower the world's most coercive men. Autocrats from Russia to Algeria spend resource money on weapons and repression. Armed groups like ISIS and the Congo's militias have spent resource money on atrocities and ammunition. For decades the West's worst threats and crises have come from resource-enriched autocrats and armed groups—and the ultimate source of their resource money is consumers, paying at the gas station and the mall.

The first part of this chapter analyzes the law, economics, and politics of the "resource curse." The deepest cause of this curse is an ancient rule that once licensed the slave trade, apartheid, and genocide. The abolition of this rule has marked humanity's greatest moral progress—yet the rule lingers in today's multi-trillion-dollar trade in resources, endowing despots and extremists with unaccountable power.

The first part explains why the resource curse is a systemic global problem, and also where the solution to it must be. The second part sets out national policies that can lift the curse. These peaceful policies will make us more secure at home, more trusted abroad, and better able to work across borders to solve urgent problems like climate change.

The third part of the chapter is intended for readers who are interested in more abstract issues, such as the nature of the principles that should guide the reform of global institutions, what is most important in distributive justice, and what values are ultimately worth pursuing.[1]

ANALYSIS OF THE RESOURCE CURSE

In 2014, Iraq became a war of oil against oil. The Kurds and the Iraqi government both controlled large oil fields, and ISIS, which fought both,
became "the world's richest terror army" by selling up to $1 million of
crude a day.[2] ISIS spent its oil money on genocidal assaults against the
Yazidis, a horror-filled global propaganda campaign, and the military seizure of more oil fields in Syria.

Meanwhile, Syria's oil-funded autocrat, Bashar Al-Assad, ordered the
barrel-bombing of his own people, worsening a refugee crisis whose defining image became the photo of Aylan Kurdi, a three-year-old Syrian boy
lying drowned on a Turkish beach. By 2015, this refugee crisis was straining
the politics of Europe.

In 2015, Vladimir Putin—his coffers still full from years of high oil
prices—joined Assad in a more intensive campaign of urban bombing in
Syria. In 2016, television news worldwide was showing apocalyptic devastation in Aleppo, and Syrian civilians were still being killed by chemical
weapons in 2018. The Iraq-Syria conflict became part of the cold war between
two oil-rich religious blocs. Iran and its allies like Hezbollah fought hard-line
Sunni militants, who received funds from within oil states like Qatar.[3] At the
same time, the Saudi crown prince was intervening in regional politics from
Qatar to Lebanon, most dramatically with the bombing and blockade of
Yemen, which caused thousands of civilian casualties, a massive famine, and
the largest cholera outbreak in modern human history.[4]

Oil was not the only factor in these conflicts and crises—it never is. Yet
when we look back over the past forty years, we see oil behind so many
headlines. In 2011, for instance, the West took military action in Libya
against Muammar Gaddafi, who had for decades used oil money to finance
terrorists from the Irish Republican Army to the Lockerbie bombers.[5] Before
Gaddafi, it was the Darfur genocide in the oil state of Sudan. Before Darfur,
it was Al Qaeda, which was behind both 7/7 in London and 9/11 in the
United States (seventeen of the nineteen 9/11 hijackers were from oil-
exporting countries).

In 1990, Saddam Hussein launched his invasion of oil-rich Kuwait, trig-
gering a Western invasion, then sanctions, then another invasion and an
occupation. In the 1980s, the West's biggest-ever existential threat, the
Soviet Union, used new oil revenues to surge ahead in the nuclear arms
race. And since the 1979 revolution, the Iranian regime has used oil money
to fund militant groups from Hamas to Islamic Jihad, while grasping at
nuclear weapons.[6]

Petroleum is the common element to these stories. All of these crises and
threats have come from countries that export a lot of oil. When we in the
West talk about these oil-rich countries, we often criticize the decisions that

our own leaders have made, perhaps under of the influence of the big oil companies like Exxon and Shell. Many of us, for instance, will complain bitterly about George W. Bush's decision in 2003 to invade and occupy Iraq. Others will deride Barack Obama's "red line" in Syria. Donald Trump's relationships with Putin and the Saudi crown prince have drawn much scorn.

All of these criticisms are correct. Western leaders have cost their countries dearly in terms of lives, money, and influence—and some of their decisions have simply been criminal. Yet there's a bigger picture about the context in which these choices have been made. Every Western leader has faced a problem of foreign power that has had no known solution—a problem that, as we'll see, now confronts the leaders of today.

And there is a deeper level to these stories as well, which involves each of us. The threats and crises above are not just disasters that we've watched—they're disasters that we've paid for. After all, the foreign autocrats and militants in the news have spent a lot of oil money on the bombs and the missiles and the propaganda. And, ultimately, that money has come from us—the world's consumers—buying oil. In a recent year, for instance, the average American household sent $250 to authoritarian regimes and armed groups, just by filling up with gasoline.[7]

What consumers pay at the pump has also gone to grim places that never make the headlines. The president's family in Equatorial Guinea, for instance, has for decades spent the country's oil money on itself—buying private jets, supercars, luxury residences in Paris, Washington and Malibu—while most Equatoguineans live in severe poverty, and half have no access to clean drinking water or adequate sanitation.[8] The country's president (whom a former U.S. ambassador called "a kleptomaniac without a scintilla of social consciousness") has used "fierce political repression" to quash resistance to his rule, including having his guards tie down political prisoners, slice their ears open, and smear their bodies with grease to attract stinging ants.[9]

So the money we've paid at the pump may have bought torture tools in an obscure African dictatorship, or textbooks that teach children to wage jihad against the infidel, or bullets that have been shot at our young soldiers. Somehow, our money is going to fund suffering and injustice, threats and crises, all over the world. Understanding our unwilling complicity with disasters and dangers overseas is essential for understanding the deepest flows of global power and the rules that run the world. As we'll see in the second part of the chapter, the rules that are making us complicit are also the rules that we can now change.

Oil Is Everywhere

To appreciate the depth of these problems, we need to grasp how intimately involved our daily lives are with oil. Because of climate change, it is urgent that we get off oil as quickly as possible. But that will still take many years, because oil is humanity's largest source of energy. Today oil supplies 33 percent of the world's power, while all of the renewables combined supply just three percent.[10]

The world uses a thousand barrels of oil—that is, 42,000 gallons, or 159,000 liters—each and every . . . second. Over 90 percent of the world's transportation runs on oil—that's nearly every car, truck, ship, and plane there is.[11] In most stores, every product has been delivered by oil-powered vehicles, and those vehicles deliver most online shopping too. It's not unlikely that everything that you can see right now—including the people—has been moved to where it is with oil energy.

The reason that oil is so present is that—leaving the environment and the geopolitics aside for a moment—it has been the best engineering solution to the challenge of moving people and goods. Oil fuels are light and stable, and pack lots of power: a gallon of oil contains about the same energy as ten pounds of coal, seventeen pounds of wood, and fifty days of slave labor.[12] Trying to fly a 737 using today's best batteries instead of jet fuel would mean loading batteries that weigh many times more than the plane itself.[13]

And oil is not just for transportation. Most of the food in our stores was grown with nitrogen that was extracted from oil. Petro-chemicals are also used to make many everyday goods. Basically, if it's plastic, it's oil. And if it's synthetic, it's likely made from oil. Some common goods made with oil are aspirin, asphalt, balloons, blenders, candles, carpets, computer keyboards and screens, contact lenses, clothes, crayons, credit cards, dentures, deodorants, diapers, digital clocks, eyeglasses, furniture fabrics, game consoles, garbage bags, glue, golf balls, hair dryers, infant seats, lipstick, lubricants, luggage, newspapers, paint, patio screens, perfume, pillows, shampoo, shaving cream, shoes, tents, toothbrushes, toothpaste, toys, and vitamins.[14] It may be in your waistband, you may have smeared it on your face this morning, it may be helping your sex life. Oil is everywhere—and we buy it all the time.

So our situation may be worse even than we thought. Unless we're walking to buy organic food at an Amish farm, our shopping will be saturated with oil at every stage. We may be funding oppression, strife, and extremism whenever we check out, online or in-store. Some oil does come from "good" countries, but tracing oil through the world's opaque, ever-shifting supply chains is too difficult for most products. It's hard to see how one could even try to be a Fair Trade consumer of oil.

Better technology is slowly shifting the economics of energy toward renewable sources, and better policies on climate can help to speed that shift. Still, even the fastest transition away from petroleum will likely take many years, as the world replaces its huge oil-powered transportation fleet—and finds other chemicals to make ordinary goods like those above. Someday, our grandchildren may laugh at our primitive condition: humans propelling themselves across the planet by burning mud. But today, if that mud suddenly became incombustible, most of humanity would be dead within a year. Even as we transition away from oil, we will be buying a lot of it for years to come.

The Systemic Curse of Resources

For as long as the world uses oil, we should expect headlines about big oil exporters like Russia, Iraq, Saudi Arabia, and Nigeria. Oceans of crude will flow out of these countries, and rivers of foreign cash will flow back in return. But why does oil cause so much trouble? Why don't we see such crisis headlines about, say, big rice exporters like Thailand, or big tea exporters like Kenya?

Some of the reasons are geologic and economic. Natural resources like oil—as well as many precious metals and gems—are "point source" resources: concentrated sources of economic value that can be extracted from easily secured small areas. These commodities can be mined or gathered by relatively few workers—and sold to foreigners for substantial sums.

The deeper reason that these resources correlate with trouble is what might seem like an obvious fact. Outside of democratic countries, whoever can control resource-rich territory by force can make large profits by exporting those resources. Essentially, whoever can keep control over some holes in the ground will get rich.

When an authoritarian regime (like the one in Iran) controls a country's oil wells, it gets the money to buy the muscle and loyalty it needs to stay in power. When armed groups (like those in the Congo) control the gold mines, they get the money they need to buy arms and pay their soldiers. Money—and, with oil, a lot of money—will go to whoever has the most guns, and help them buy more guns.

More, coercive actors can export resources even when the people of the country are very badly off. Even if the population is uneducated, unemployed, and hungry—indeed, even if the country is in the midst of civil war—whoever can control the wells or mines will still make money. These authoritarians and militants don't need a productive population to get their revenues, and the people can't stop exports by going on strike. In these countries, when an autocratic regime or an armed group controls resource-rich territory, it's like they can dig out huge troves of buried cash.

The "resource curse" is what political scientists call the results.[15] As Michael Ross has shown, oil states in the developing world are 50 percent more likely to be authoritarian than non-oil states.[16] Since petrocrats get the money they need by controlling the oil wells, many of these countries are full of poor people: in Angola, for example, the elite lives in luxury while the country's impoverished children have been dying at the highest rate in the world.[17] Corruption, often on the grandest scale, also correlates with resource wealth.[18] And civil conflict is another dimension of the resource curse: oil countries are twice as likely to be at war with themselves.[19]

Repression, conflict, corruption, extreme neglect—oil curses countries across the world's main artery of oil, which runs from Siberia through the Middle East to Africa. This map shows the oil states that are either authoritarian, or failed, or both.[20]

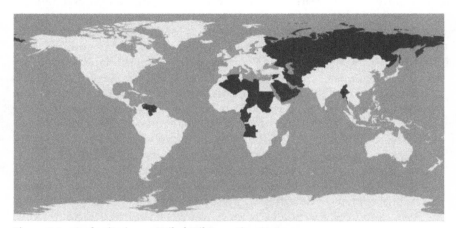

Figure 1.1   Authoritarian or Failed Oil-Exporting States.

Adding in the countries that are cursed by the money from metals and gems reveals an even broader resource curse.

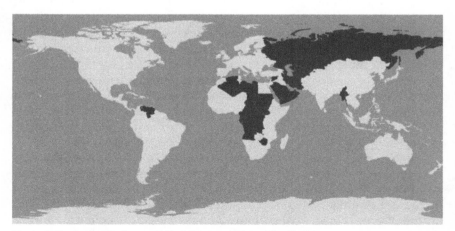

Figure 1.2   Authoritarian or Failed Resource-Exporting States.

Some of these resource-cursed countries suffered colonial exploitation by the Western empires, as well as more recent exploitation by the Western multinationals. Some of these countries have also been invaded and sanctioned. But the resource curse is a systemic phenomenon, which strikes countries that are otherwise quite different in their histories, geographies, and religions. (Compare, for instance, Russia and Iraq and South Sudan.) This systemic phenomenon calls for a systemic explanation.

The Political Economy of Resource-Cursed States

The root of the resource curse is that coercive control over resources yields *unaccountable* power. Controlling wells or mines is like controlling troves of buried cash—it's a bonanza that makes authoritarians and armed groups stronger.

Consider first an authoritarian, and how he can maintain his rule. The authoritarian might consider getting aid from a foreign ally, but that ally will want something big in return. Oil money is much better—it comes with no strings attached. The authoritarian might instead take out loans from foreign banks, but those banks will want the money back with interest. Oil money is much better for the authoritarian—it never has to be paid back.

The authoritarian might consider making his country's people more productive, to get more money from taxing them. But economically empowered citizens eventually demand political rights too. Oil money is much better for the authoritarian. Far from empowering citizens, oil money enables the authoritarian to divide and rule them. Striking oil is every autocrat's dream.

Oil money is like a huge funnel of cash that goes directly into the regime's hands. With this money, the regime can pay the security forces needed to crush dissent (as in, for example, Azerbaijan). The regime can create useless jobs in the state bureaucracy that keep citizens dependent for their livelihoods and status (Kuwait). The regime can play regions, tribes, or religions against each other, to prevent them from uniting against the state (Gaddafi was a master of this). It can flood the country with nationalist propaganda (as in Turkmenistan) or fund strict religious indoctrination (as the Saudis did for decades). If times get tough, it will have the money to distract the population with a foreign war (as Putin did with Ukraine).

Studies show that oil wealth lengthens authoritarian rule. The more oil a country has the less likely it is to democratize. No country with more oil income than Mexico has successfully become democratic since 1960. After 1979, non-oil states were almost three times more likely to make democratic transitions, which means that an ever-higher proportion of the world's autocrats are petrocrats.[21] In the popular uprisings of the past decade, from the Green Movement in Iran through the Arab Spring, the trend is that the authoritarians with large oil revenues survived, while the authoritarians with little oil fell. (Syria, which is running out of oil, is the intermediate case.)[22]

Oil gives authoritarians unaccountable power, which in turn enables them to keep the population away from the wells from which their power flows. *The Economist* lists fifty-two authoritarian countries, or 31 percent of all the countries in the world.[23] One might take a moment to ponder how many fewer authoritarians there would be in the twenty-first century—from Russia through the Middle East to Africa—if oil did not sustain regimes that can control some holes in the ground. One might also consider how different the politics of those countries, and of the world, would be.

Natural resources—and especially oil—are also prized by militants for the unchecked power they bring. Resource money enables armed groups to start or continue a conflict—and again, the money comes with no strings attached, it never has to be paid back, and it comes in regardless of the condition or the wishes of the country's people, who have to watch while the country's natural assets are sold off beyond their control. As Paul Collier quipped, "Diamonds are a guerrilla's best friend."[24] And oil-producing countries are the sites of ever more of the world's civil wars, and a growing percentage of all civil wars.[25] The unaccountable power of resources divides many countries against each other.

Studies report that resources increase the likelihood, duration, and severity of conflicts.[26] Oil and gems far from the capital make conflicts last longer.[27] The presence of oil and gems in conflict zones more than doubles the duration of the conflicts, and secessionist conflicts in oil-producing regions are the most severe.[28] Resources correlate with more violent rebels who attack civilians more indiscriminately.[29] In 2016, 25 percent of oil states were embroiled in a civil conflict, compared to 11 percent of non-oil states.[30] Recent oil-fueled civil conflicts have included not only Iraq, Syria, and Libya, but also Sudan-Darfur and Sudan-South Sudan.

The results of the resource curse are striking. Consider the remarkable progress that most developing countries have made over the past four decades—the economic growth in China and India, for example, or the great "third wave" of democratization across Latin America, Asia, and Eastern Europe. In marked contrast, the major oil states outside the West are, on average, no richer, no freer, and no more peaceful today than they were even in 1980.[31]

Resource-rich states have been falling behind for decades, producing a dramatic patterns in the statistics.[32]

1. Today most authoritarian regimes are in resource-rich states.
2. Today most civil wars are in resource-rich states.

3. Today most highly corrupt governments are in resource-rich states.
4. Today most refugees are from resource-rich states.
5. Today the highest rates of hunger are in resource-rich states.
6. Soon most of the world's poorest people will be in resource-rich states.

The resource curse is one of the world's most extreme dysfunctions. Because resources yield unaccountable power, they can curse the countries they should bless.

Effectiveness as a Systemic Cause of the Resource Curse

The deepest cause of the resource curse—and our own contribution to it—is that whoever can control resource-rich territory can get rich by selling the resources to foreigners. This appears to be a natural feature of the global economy, and most people accept it without much thought.

Yet, as we noticed, the "foreigners" who buy the resources are, in fact, us—the consumers of the world, who pay for natural resources whenever we buy anything that is made from or transported with those resources. We are the ultimate source of the unaccountable power of the violent and oppressive men in resource-cursed states, who use our money to dominate and attack ordinary people and enrich themselves. And why? Why does the money from our everyday purchases go to the violent and oppressive? Why are consumers unwillingly in business with these men?

The answer is an archaic law, a relic of the days of the Atlantic slave trade. This is the American law that makes it legal for Americans to buy natural resources from whoever in foreign countries can control them by force. This is in fact the default law of every country, which lawyers call "effectiveness." Effectiveness says that for the resources of other countries, "Might Makes Right."

For example, when Saddam Hussein's junta took over Iraq in a coup, American law made it legal for the Americans to buy Iraq's oil from the junta. And then, years later, when ISIS took over some of those same wells, all countries' law made it legal to buy Iraq's oil from ISIS.[33] Every country's default law for the oil of other countries is, "whoever can control it by force can sell it to us."

"Might Makes Right" has been the world's law for natural resources since the European empires were blasting each other's wooden ships with cannons. Yet, on reflection, this law makes little sense today. Say an armed gang seizes a gas station in Los Angeles. Should American law give Americans the legal right to buy the gas from that gang? No—such a law would empower criminals and cause chaos. But when Gaddafi took over Libya in a coup in 1969, American law did make it legal for Americans to buy Libya's oil from Gaddafi. And then during the Arab Spring of 2011, when rebels captured some of those same wells, American law made it legal to buy Libya's oil from the rebels.

The world pays over a trillion dollars a year for oil imports, which is why we see such an extreme oil curse—yet all countries' laws say "Might Makes Right" for other foreign resources too. Your smartphone, for instance, may contain metal that was plundered at gunpoint by one of the militias fighting in the Congo's civil war, who have used sexual violence as a weapon of war so extensively that the Congo has been called "the worst place in the world to be a woman."[34]

Yet even if your phone is made with metal plundered in the Congo, under the law of your country you own every molecule of your phone, and your rights to it will be enforced by your country's police and courts. Under your country's law, plunder abroad becomes property at home. The militants' violence turns into our legal rights—and our money goes back to the militants, to help them buy more bullets and bayonets. The alchemy of effectiveness turns the iron of coercion into the gold of legal title, and puts consumers everywhere into business with some of the world's most ruthless men. The resources they seize flow through the world's supply chains to us, trillions of our dollars and euros and pounds flow back through the supply chains to them. Combat-related deaths in Congo's long conflict are certainly over a million, and have perhaps reached Holocaust levels.[35] Today our laws make foreign violence pay, and, without change, our laws will continue to incite ever more violence tomorrow.

Whose Law Is Effectiveness?

Effectiveness, or "Might Makes Right," is the choice of every state—no ancient treaty requires it, no international agency enforces it. Every state has the sovereign right to decide its own rules on where its people can legally buy foreign natural resources—and from whom. Oil sanctions, such as those that the United States imposed on Libya when uprisings began in February 2011, are one example of this. By declaring sanctions, the U.S. government made it illegal for American persons (individuals and corporations) to buy Libya's oil from Libya's government.[36]

The United States then exercised its sovereign legal power in a more dramatic fashion. In April, it issued an order that made it legal for Americans to buy Libya's oil from the anti-Gaddafi rebels (so long, the order said, as no benefits from these purchases went to "the Government of Libya").[37] With this order, the United States authorized Americans to buy Libya's oil from a wholly unrecognized group that opposed the government, without heed to the laws of the state that it recognized diplomatically.[38]

Diplomatic recognition of a foreign state does not require commercial engagement with that state, or respect for that state's laws on who can sell its resources. Effectiveness only appears to be an international rule because today all governments choose effectiveness as their default for the resources of other countries. Governments choose effectiveness because they always have—and because effectiveness makes it easier to satisfy their consumers' endless demands for foreign oil and raw materials. No matter how desperate the situation in resource-rich foreign countries, effectiveness will draw the resources out. If an authoritarian controls a whole country, effectiveness allows your people to buy resources from him. If warlords control resource-rich regions, effectiveness allows your people to buy the resources that the warlords pillage.

Yet effectiveness insults the very idea of property rights: it turns raw violence into legal title. It is a rule that breaks the rule of law. Effectiveness also perpetuates the resource curse by incentivizing ever more authoritarianism and civil conflict.

To see those incentives, imagine for a moment that New York today declares "Might Makes Right" for all goods in New Jersey. Imagine, that is, that New Yorkers get the legal right to buy goods that have been seized by force in New Jersey, and that the resulting "property rights" will be enforced by New York's police and courts. One can picture what New Jersey would look like: crime kings, syndicates, turf wars, grand theft—similar to what we actually do see on a much larger scale in many resource-exporting countries today. When our laws reward brutality abroad with big money, the most brutal will rise to the top.

The Resource Curse on the West

The resource curse is a systemic phenomenon, driven by a rule that sends money from the world's consumers to repressive and violent actors in resource-rich states. Since this is a connected world, the violence in exporting states spreads back to affect importing states as well. This is where we began: many of the West's major foreign threats and crises for the past forty years have come from countries that export a lot of oil. Because effectiveness turns our money into unaccountable power, we see a second systemic oil curse: a curse on the West.

Iran, Iraq, Sudan, Libya, Syria, Russia—oil states have filled anxious headlines for a lifetime. As Jeff Colgan writes in *Petro-Aggression*, petrocrats with a revolutionary ideology like Khomeini, Saddam, and Gaddafi are three times more likely to start foreign wars.[39] Five of the seven states that have ever been on the U.S. State Sponsors of Terrorism list have been oil states.[40] When the State Department last drew up a list of whose nationals would require extra security screening at airports before flying to the United States, nearly two-thirds were oil exporters.[41] Putin's military campaigns and meddling in Western elections have been funded by the West's own money, paid for Russian petroleum.

The unaccountable power of oil is also responsible for the twenty-first century's greatest historical anomaly: the global spread of an Islamic fundamentalism that aims to re-create the politics of the seventh century. For over forty years, the Saudi regime spent billions of petrodollars to indoctrinate its own people with its intolerant doctrines, and many Saudis took up arms against the West or funded those who did. (For example, a 2007 West Point study found that over 40 percent of Al Qaeda's foreign fighters in Iraq were Saudis.[42]) More dramatically, the regime spent tens of billions of petrodollars to convert formerly tolerant Muslim communities worldwide to its extreme version of Islam in what Peter Maass has called "the most expensive information campaign ever mounted."[43]

The world has been proselytized by the past. Saudi-funded mosques and fighters have rooted down in Pakistan, sprung up in the Caucasus, further balkanized the Balkans.[44] In Saudi textbooks, Christians and Jews have been compared to pigs and apes. A twelfth-grade text explained the religious duty to wage jihad against the infidel to expand the faith.[45] A text recently found in a Saudi-administered school in Vienna teaches that birth control is part of a secret plot to spread Christianity.[46]

As Fareed Zakaria wrote recently, drawing on my research, "Almost every terrorist attack in the West has had some connection to Saudi Arabia."[47] Aggressive mutations of Saudi Salafism, like those of Al Qaeda and ISIS, have incited terrorist attacks not only in the Middle East and Asia, but also in Belgium, France, and Germany, and in Britain and America as well.[48] The global jihadi movement that we see today—and the fearful, angry Western response to it—would not exist had the Saudi absolute monarchy not spent enormous amounts, ultimately of consumers' money, to spread its medieval creed worldwide. The Saudis have recently started to turn away from the most extreme elements of their fundamentalism—yet even as they do so, the ideological pathogens that they have proliferated will still be killing for years to come.

The West's Failed Strategies

Oil money yields unchecked power, which has threatened the West in many ways. Once we see this, the West's foreign policies toward oil states make more sense. The West has been trying to check the power of oil from outside of these countries. Over the past four decades, Western leaders have used three main strategies to try to control the power of oil from outside:

1. Sometimes Western states have made *alliances* with oil-rich authoritarians, like the Shah of Iran, Saddam, Gaddafi, and the Saudis;

2. Sometimes the West has taken *military action*: Gulf War I, Gulf War II, the Libyan intervention, drone strikes;
3. Sometimes the West has imposed sanctions, as on Iran, Iraq, Sudan, Syria, and Russia.

These strategies have carried very large human and economic costs, and have had many unintended consequences. Several of the decisions of Western leaders now look foolish, immoral, or just criminal. And, simply in terms of geopolitics, the main question for Western leaders is this: how well are these strategies working? Beyond all of the deaths and expense and reputational damage, how should we assess the outcomes that these strategies have achieved in regions like the Middle East? John Brennan, when the director of the CIA, gave his verdict not long ago. Testifying before Congress, Brennan said that the Middle East is the worst it's been in fifty years, and that the region faces unprecedented bloodshed.[49]

What's notable across recent history is how negative the outcomes have been in oil states regardless of the West's strategies. Whether Western leaders have chosen alliance or intervention or neglect, painful dilemmas have been forced back on them. This is evident across today's strategic landscape, which contains a hostile petrocratic regime in Russia, an oil-fueled antagonist in Iran, an impulsive ally in Saudi Arabia, and active or latent conflicts across the Middle East and North Africa driven by the contending Sunni and Shia blocs and their respective extremists.

The unaccountable power of oil shrinks the West's choice-sets onto bad options no matter what posture it takes; the West's oil curse emerges whatever it does. The foreign policy lesson from the past forty years is that the power of oil cannot be controlled from outside these countries—by the West, or in fact by anyone. Our oil curse turns all of our options into lose-lose.

When we fund unaccountable power overseas, we shouldn't be shocked when we can't contain its violence. And the damage that we in the West take from the resource curse is not only from hostile authoritarians and reckless allies and aggressive extremists. Citizens of Western democracies also damage each other by fighting over which no-win options to choose. Iran, Iraq, Libya, Syria, Russia: think of how poisonous our arguments have been for four decades over whether we should take military action or not, impose sanctions or not, tighten our security against their terrorism at the expense of our personal freedoms. So much bad blood from our arguments, even between people of good will. The oil curse divides foreigners against each other, it divides foreigners against us—and it also, in the end, divides us against ourselves.

And, unfortunately, it looks like the world will now be getting even more oil-cursed.

The U.S. National Intelligence Council predicts that, because of climate change, the oil-producing countries in the Middle East and Africa will be getting hotter, hungrier, and thirstier—just as their youth populations bulge and they fill up with more powerful explosives and drones.[50] So these countries will likely become even less stable than they are today. More popular uprisings in these countries may be met with harsher authoritarian repression, leading to the further spread of violent extremism and, finally, more divisive dilemmas for the citizens of the West. If we keep choosing "Might Makes Right," our future may well be like our past, only more so.

Can Effectiveness Be Overcome?

Is there any hope for change? Could we possibly upgrade world trade so that it stops sending us these impossible threats and crises? It will be challenging. Authoritarian regimes and Western multinationals are invested in today's business as usual, and these are powerful global actors.

Yet there is hope for change. We know that effectiveness for natural resources can be abolished, because effectiveness has been abolished in other areas many times before. In fact, the abolition of effectiveness has marked humanity's greatest moral advances for the past three centuries.

Effectiveness was the main rule of the pre-modern Westphalian international order that solidified in the seventeenth century. In that violent time, "Might Makes Right" was the world's law not only for natural resources, but for nearly everything—even for human beings. Three hundred years ago, every country's law for Africans was "whoever can seize them by force can sell them to us." Under that rule, twelve million Africans were shipped through the gruesome Middle Passage where the survivors were bought legally as property in the New World.[51] Back then, might made right.

Even one hundred years ago, "Might Makes Right" made colonial rule legal. States that seized control over foreign territory gained the internationally recognized legal right to rule the people as their sovereign. Might made right.

Even in our own times, effectiveness made apartheid legal. A regime that kept coercive control over a population gained the internationally recognized right to enforce white rule. Ethnic cleansing, and even genocide, were also once allowed by international law.[52] Yet the good news is that now, in the twenty-first century, all of those laws of "Might Makes Right" have been abolished. The slave trade, colonial rule, apartheid, ethnic cleansing, and genocide: all of these are now violations of international law.

And, in fact, effectiveness has already been abolished for a single natural resource: diamonds. Twenty years ago, money spent by Western consumers on engagement rings and earrings went to fund vicious militias in Africa, who launched campaigns of amputation and mass murder to secure the stones.[53] Yet today, after a determined campaign by NGOs, every major importing country has made it illegal to buy diamonds that have been plundered by armed groups.[54] Diamonds that have been violently extracted in one country can no longer be bought legally in another.

Of course, in breaking all of these legal links between might and right, the world hasn't magically abolished power. Slaves are still secretly trafficked across borders; genocides still occur; blood diamonds still leak into global commerce. Still, the great progress of the past three centuries has been in turning what used to be taken-for-granted practices of violence into widely reviled crimes.

Public Accountability as a Structural Solution

This is where the analysis turns strongly positive. The systemic problem of the resource curse points to a structural solution. And the sources of our complicity in the curse—our own money and laws—can also be the locations of reform.

Under today's rule of effectiveness, coercive actors gain unaccountable power, and that power can't be checked from outside the country, by alliance or invasion or sanctions. So the source of accountability over resources must be inside the country—it must be the people of the country, who live there, on the ground, every day. From a political science perspective, the only reliable source of accountability over resources is the citizens of the resource-rich countries themselves.

One piece of evidence that an empowered citizenry is the solution to the resource curse comes from looking at the countries that have avoided the curse. Norway, for example, exports a lot of oil—and Botswana, "the miracle of Africa," is a major exporter of diamonds—yet neither has suffered authoritarianism or civil conflict. The main reason is that the governments in these countries were already accountable to the people when the resource money came in—accountable through fair elections, a free press, the rule of law, and more. Since the state was accountable to the people, the people made sure that the new resource riches were spent on public goods, instead of on coercion and patronage and corruption.

And there's a second reason for believing that public accountability is the key to lifting the resource curse, which specialists on resources and governance will appreciate. The many initiatives to fight the resource curse in recent decades have, without planning, spontaneously converged on one imperative. All of these initiatives have aimed to increase the power of the people of resource-rich countries to control their resources and resource revenues. Transparency reforms, for instance, aim to increase public control over resources by giving citizens more information about resource sales.

Anti-bribery laws try to keep officials from making deals behind the people's backs. Resource validation laws like the Kimberley Process aim to increase public control over resources that would otherwise be seized by militias. Oil-to-cash policies put resource revenues directly into citizens' hands, and so on. All of these reforms have aimed at the same goal: a more empowered citizenry in resource-cursed countries.

The Meaning of Popular Resource Sovereignty

Best of all, most people already believe in a principle that requires the power of resources to be accountable to citizens. This is just the principle that a country belongs to its people. On this principle, a country belongs to all of its citizens, and the country's natural resources start out in their hands. This is the principle of Popular Resource Sovereignty.

According to this principle, anyone who sells off a country's resources must be accountable to the owners of the resources—to the citizens. If a government decides to sell the country's resources to foreigners, then the government must be accountable to its citizens when it does so. And if a government privatizes the country's resources (as the U.S. government does with offshore oil), then again the government must be accountable to the people when it does so. No one should be able to transfer ownership of the property without being accountable to its owners.

To be able to hold their government accountable for its resource decisions, citizens must have at least bare-bones rights and liberties. Citizens must be able to find out what the government is doing with their resources and who is getting the money. Citizens must be able to discuss and peacefully protest what the government is doing without fear of losing their jobs, freedoms, or lives. And if a majority of citizens strongly disagree with what the government is doing with the country's resources, government policy must change to reflect this within a reasonable time. Not every oil-exporter needs to be Norway—to realize Popular Resource Sovereignty, a government just needs to be minimally accountable to its citizens (and according to current metrics even Kuwait is "above the line"). But this minimal accountability is lacking in all of the worst resource-cursed states.

If anyone sells off a country's resources without even minimal accountability to its citizens, then, by this principle, they are stealing the resources from the people. This is just like someone selling your property without your possible consent: a straightforward crime.

Popular Resource Sovereignty as a Global Principle

The idea that a country belongs to its people is already popular worldwide. National leaders from Bill Clinton and George W. Bush to the prime ministers of Britain and Australia to the presidents of Brazil, Mexico, and Ghana to the Norwegian parliament and even the Ayatollah Khamenei have publicly proclaimed that "the oil belongs to the people."[55]

This is a natural thing for politicians to say, because they are reflecting their people's beliefs. Large majorities of individuals in all regions of the world (including the Middle East) tell pollsters that they believe that citizens should be sovereign over their lands—that a country belongs to its people.[56] Insofar as humanity has heroes, they are heroes like Gandhi and Mandela, who won great victories for the people's rights.

And the language of Popular Resource Sovereignty is already declared in major legal documents. Both of the main international human rights treaties declare in their first article, "All peoples may, for their own ends, freely dispose of their natural wealth and resources." Both go on to affirm, "the inherent right of all peoples to enjoy and utilize fully and freely their natural wealth and resources."[57] Nearly every country in the world is already party to one of these treaties—in fact, 98 percent of the people in the world live in a country that has officially signed on to those words.[58] Many national constitutions and laws also speak the language of the people's resource rights. So the battle for the idea that a country belongs to its people has already been won.

The Principles Supporting the Abolition of Effectiveness

Nevertheless, the scale of violations of the principle of Popular Resource Sovereignty is immense. Looking around the world for countries where the people could not possibly be holding their governments accountable, for example, we find large Middle Eastern oil producers, such as Saudi Arabia, Iran, Iraq, the UAE, and Qatar, as well as major producers elsewhere, like Russia, Kazakhstan, Algeria, and Angola. That's already half of the world's proven oil reserves, and over half of the world's oil exports.[59] So, more than half the world's trade in oil today is literally trade in stolen goods.

Action to shift the global commerce away from effectiveness for resources will be action to enforce citizens' rights—their property rights. So this will be action to transform today's market in stolen goods into a market under the rule of law. To take a historical analogy, the transportation of captured Africans was once be thought to be "free trade in slaves," but no longer. The transportation of coercively extracted petroleum could once be considered "free trade in oil," but again, no longer. In both cases, the old "trade" is invalidated by coercion—in one case the wrongful coercion of Africans, in the other the wrongful coercion of citizens, and in both the forceful appropriation of a valuable asset. Against property owners, might makes wrong. Trade in resources will only become free trade when its foundations are secure property rights.

Reforms to enforce the people's property rights must be feasible, responsible, and respectful of the fact that the global economy today sustains the livelihoods of much of humanity. To withstand the rough-and-tumble of international politics, these reforms must also be grounded in robust principles that have earned the loyalty of powerful global actors.

The protection of property rights is such a principle—this is the mantra of every global business, as well as the world's largest investors. The rule of law, which requires that state officials be accountable, and that basic rights be secured, is another strong principle that supports reform. Human rights are a priority for determined international actors—and, as we've seen, the language of Popular Resource Sovereignty is already declared in the major human rights treaties.

Most importantly, action to reform the global economy must embrace the principle of peace. Peace is the word invoked by nearly everyone, and a condition genuinely valued by most. "Bombing for democracy" has not produced the intended results—and it is too much like the imperial campaigns of the past to build the trust that the West now needs.

Popular sovereignty and property, the rule of law, human rights, and peace. These are not ideas that the world needs to be converted to. These are the declared principles of the modern international system, and the ideals of the world's most important actors: individuals, firms, investors, and politicians.

By contrast, effectiveness is no one's ideal. "Might Makes Right" is the rule of coercive and corrupt actors who subsist on dead ideologies and the money that the world unwillingly sends them. Supporters of today's ideas will discover endless alliances to make with each other. Partisans of effectiveness will rally support mostly through fear and bribery—and will always be tempted to defect to the ideas of modernity and to the side of the majority. While effectiveness may hold out for a time, determined action on principle must win.

POLICIES TO LIFT THE RESOURCE CURSE

Peacefully and responsibly, resource-importing states can now change their own rules to abolish effectiveness and affirm all peoples' rights to their resources. Countries that choose these policies will stop importing resources from exporting states where public accountability is absent, and will support public accountability in exporting states where it is weak, by affirming Popular Resource Sovereignty as their basis for trade in natural resources.

This section first sets out policy tools: a Clean Trade Act and Clean Hands Trusts. These tools look dramatic—tapering off oil imports from the Middle

East, for instance, or imposing trade duties on China. Just as important as the tools themselves are the strategies for using them, which are discussed after. The power of these strategies is the power of democratic leadership—of free peoples changing their own laws, to align with their own principles, on behalf of the freedom of peoples everywhere. The challenges of leadership are significant: some policies will be costly, determination will be needed, and there will be setbacks before the goal is finally reached. So it has been with all movements for positive change.

A Clean Trade Act. By passing a Clean Trade Act, a country will make it illegal for its persons to purchase natural resources from disqualified states—those states in which citizens lack the basic rights and liberties to hold their government accountable for what it does with their resources.

Several respected metrics exist for measuring basic rights and liberties in every state—for example, those from the World Bank, Polity, Freedom House, The Fund for Peace, *The Economist,* and so on. These metrics tend to agree in their evaluations, and a transparent "index of indices" can be constructed to minimize bias and to protect against political pressures.[60] No metric can be completely uncontroversial—yet our current metric for deciding who it is legal to buy resources from is "Might Makes Right," and we can do better than that.

Solely for purposes of illustration, we can use a simple combined metric as a measure of political rights and civil liberties in resource-dependent states. This metric combines the ratings from Freedom House ("Not Free") with those of the Economist Intelligence Unit ("Authoritarian"), giving the following list of disqualified states:[61]

Algeria, Angola, Azerbaijan, Bahrain, Brunei, Cameroon, Central African Republic, Chad, DRC, Equatorial Guinea, Gabon, Iran, Kazakhstan, Libya, Myanmar, Oman, Qatar, Republic of Congo, Russia, Saudi Arabia, South Sudan, Sudan, Syria, Turkmenistan, UAE, Uzbekistan, Venezuela, Yemen, and Zimbabwe.

A Clean Trade Act will announce the end of resource imports from these states, for as long as their regimes remain unaccountable to their people. This will be a significant action in foreign policy, yet it will be less dramatic than other options. A country passing a Clean Trade Act will only be changing its own laws, on its own soil, for its people. Not a single bomber or soldier need be sent abroad to implement these laws.

Moreover, this legislation does not challenge any foreign government's legitimacy. A country enacting these laws need say nothing about the authority of foreign leaders, and need make no changes in the list of states it recognizes diplomatically. As above, diplomatic recognition and commercial engagement are legally distinct. Leaders of a Clean Trade country can say that who rules in, for example, Algeria is "none of our business," while also saying that today's unaccountable Algerian regime qualifies for "none of our business" in oil. Having thought about our own principles, we simply no longer believe that we have a right to buy that country's resources from that regime.

A Clean Trade country will end its resource imports from all disqualified exporters—yet it need not do so all at once. There are many options for sequencing. A minimal Act would disengage from a small, "worst-of-the-worst" oil exporter like Equatorial Guinea, leaving further action for later. A more committed Act would disqualify any country that remains below the line after a certain number of years (say, four years). A stronger act would match tapering to current consumption (for instance, the United States could give Saudi Arabia, which supplies 5 percent of current U.S. oil consumption, five years before disqualification[62]).

In late 2017, Senator Randolfe Rodrigues of Brazil made Brazil the first country to propose Clean Trade legislation, by introducing a strong Clean Trade Act to ban all authoritarian oil imports. This legislation also prohibits Brazil's national oil company, Petrobras, from signing any new contracts with authoritarian regimes. Brazil, the world's fifth-largest country, a leader of the global South, is showing the world that bold action to fight the resource curse is possible. Countries can choose Clean Trade right now.

Clean Hands Trusts. Passing a Clean Trade Act will publicly support the people's rights in resource-cursed states. It may not, in itself, stop resource money going to authoritarians and militant groups. Even if many countries enact a Clean Trade Act and stop buying oil from Equatorial Guinea, say, China may buy that oil instead. So the regime in Equatorial Guinea will be able to use China's money to resist reforms. And consumers will still be tainted with stolen oil when they import Chinese goods (it will be hard to know which) that are made from or with that oil. States need tools to encourage their trade partners to join them in respecting Popular Resource Sovereignty.

A Clean Hands Trust enforces the property rights of citizens of a resource-cursed state by collecting trade duties on imports from countries that buy resources from that state. If China buys $3 billion of oil from the regime in Equatorial Guinea, for instance, a Clean Trade country will put $3 billion of duties on Chinese imports. The money from those duties will be put in trust for the citizens of Equatorial Guinea, the owners of the stolen assets, and returned to them once a minimally accountable government is in place there.

A Clean Hands Trust will protect consumers in the Clean Trade country from the taint of stolen oil. It will also give the Chinese an incentive not to buy more oil from the Equatoguinean regime, since more purchases will mean more duties. And the people of Equatorial Guinea will know that a large sum of money will be theirs once they can replace the regime that is now stealing their assets. These trusts align everyone's incentives toward improving governance in Equatorial Guinea, simply by enforcing property rights.

Climate and Energy. There are many issues surrounding the policies above, such as WTO compatibility, which are discussed in detail elsewhere.[63] Climate change deserves special attention. For orientation on climate, we can recall two events late in 2015. The positive development was the Paris climate change agreement, which was at least more promising than what had come before. But in 2015 the FBI also began to raise the alarm on Russia's cyberespionage and information-warfare campaign to disrupt the 2016 U.S. presidential election.[64] Both of these issues have high priority—we must fight climate change at the same time as we try to reduce the aggressive power of oil-fueled regimes to undermine democracies.

Fortunately, the two efforts can go together. Clean Trade says that right now, on strict market principles, over half of the world's proven oil reserves must stay in the ground—these are "stranded assets" in the very real sense that they should not be legally purchasable. And Clean Trade asks that, out of the feasible paths to reach our climate goals, the paths that respect all peoples' rights should be chosen. One promising path is a national "Autocrats to Alternatives" plan to replace stolen fossil fuel imports with renewable sources of energy as quickly as possible. For instance, the United Kingdom gets about 15 percent of its oil from authoritarian countries. As it tapers off that oil, it should replace as much of it as possible with the renewable fuels of the future.[65] Clean Trade can be Green Trade—it can be "clean" in mutually reinforcing ways.

But then, will we have enough energy? Yes. Even today, Western states with low authoritarian import-dependence—such as the United States, the United Kingdom, Canada, and Norway—can switch away from authoritarian oil in a matter of months if necessary, with limited effects on the price at the pump. A transition for continental European countries, which are more dependent on authoritarian natural gas, will take more time and money: perhaps five years and tens of billions of dollars.[66] This is not trivial, but it is affordable, especially when put into context against military expenditures. The headline message on energy is that today there will be enough energy available; even on current demand, all the major Western importers could together stop importing authoritarian oil.[67] The West just doesn't need to buy oil from those men any more.

Strategy. A national campaign to "End the Tyranny of Oil" can unite a strong coalition behind Clean Trade legislation. Friends of free markets can support policies that enforce property rights. Those who prioritize national security will see measures that weaken hostile petrocrats, and that strengthen failed states where terrorism can incubate. Environmentalists can embrace an "Autocrats to Alternatives" plan. Protectionists will back the parts of the framework that insulate domestic industries from foreign competition. Humanitarians will endorse the empowerment of some of the most mistreated people on earth. Liberal, conservative, libertarian, populist, and progressive groups all have interests in supporting these policies.

Any state can claim global leadership by passing Clean Trade legislation. Brazil's introduction of a Clean Trade Act is promising, and as other recent reforms have shown, once one major state passes legislation, others may follow quickly. Even a country like China might willingly join in. That might seem optimistic; yet consider how many "impossible" political changes have happened in the past forty years.

Oil-powered autocrats and armed groups are a major problem that China and the West share. And if the West goes Clean Trade, the government of the People's Republic of China may not wish to take a public stand against popular sovereignty just as its own people are reaching the level of income where citizens usually demand more democratic rights. Most importantly, Clean Trade addresses China's greatest strategic weakness, which is high energy-import dependence on a destabilizing region—the Middle East—where China cannot project power. If the West adopts Clean Trade, and China does not, China will bear the brunt of tomorrow's oil curse. Will the Chinese leadership really see its national interest in buying oil from ISIS 2.0? More prudent would be for that leadership to announce that at some point in the future China will also be ending oil imports from disqualified countries. With this announcement, the game would be up for the oil-fueled authoritarians—at least, as authoritarians—as their power depends on their having future customers to sell oil to.

The great strength of these reforms is that they are based on an idea—Popular Resource Sovereignty—that most of the world already believes in. So Western countries can inspire change in resource-cursed states even if China mistakes its interests and decides not to join, and indeed, even if not all Western countries join. The real strength of these reforms is their soft power: the courage they give to others to act on their own convictions. Allow yourself to imagine the day that the United Kingdom, or Canada, or Germany passes a Clean Trade Act. The people of the enacting country would thereby declare that they are taking a stand for the people of resource-cursed countries, and that they will no longer buy resources from anyone not accountable to their citizens. This would greatly embolden the democratic reformers in resource-cursed countries (who live both outside and inside the palaces) to press for constitutional reforms that strengthen citizens' rights.

Imagine an American president declaring to the world that from now on America will be honoring the American principle—which Abraham Lincoln stated in his first inaugural address—that a country belongs to its people, and honoring Lincoln's principle not only in words, but in law, to show a proper respect for the peoples of all nations.[68] That will be the day on which a statesman addresses the root causes of tomorrow's problems.

These reforms are not magical. Even after they are successful, the world will still suffer war and tyranny and corruption and more. Yet removing the divisive anachronism of effectiveness from the world's rules will do much to heal its chronically inflamed conflicts, and to form the flesh of trust. How good in itself—and how good for the world—if, say, by 2028 the peoples of the Middle East could be sovereign, more moderate, and at peace with each other. Why not?

Supporting Accountability Above the Line. The policies so far define relations with resource exporters that are "below the line" of public accountability. Many exporting countries—like Nigeria, or Ecuador—are not so badly resource-cursed. In these countries, citizens have at least minimal powers of public accountability, yet resource exports still fuel grand corruption that degrades public services and that sometimes sparks armed violence. Today, the policies of importing states contribute to that corruption. With the second part of the Clean Trade framework, importing states can regear their trade policies so that they stop working against, and start working for, public accountability in exporting countries "above the line."

First, a Clean Trade country's Rules of Engagement will set uniform standards for all domestically incorporated and listed oil and mining companies. These standards will combine existing policies so that they reinforce each other to support public accountability in exporting countries. For example, an enacting country may combine a robust anti-bribery law with transparency laws that require disclosure of payments to foreign states and money-laundering laws that oblige banks to perform due diligence on foreign officials who may have embezzled resource money. Each Clean Trade country can set its own Rules of Engagement, with an eye to creating shareable standards that will level the playing field among all countries' firms.

The gold standard of Clean Trade is a country that holds its firms to the same legal standards whether they are doing business at home or abroad—and across the board on bribery, money-laundering, transparency, and human rights. Real leadership, from both political and corporate officials, would be on display in an announcement of a move to this gold standard. And the country that moves first on such reforms often leads other countries to follow to the new, higher level.

Second, a Clean Trade country's Public Power Spectrum will set policies that encourage the officials of exporting states to improve public accountability over resources. There are many options here. For example, foreign officials who receive bribes might face travel bans and asset freezes, while governments that implement resource transparency reforms or "oil-to-cash" programs might be offered more direct investment and diplomatic invitations.[69] With these kinds of trade conditionalities, importing states can support public accountability in exporting states, instead of ratcheting away from accountability as their policies now do.

Costs and Trust

In the early nineteenth century, Britain's elite was thoroughly entangled in the Atlantic slave trade, and slaving was a major part of the British economy. Over six decades of determined action, the British people finally forced their government to end the British slave trade, and to convince foreign governments to stop carrying slaves as well. Toward the end of this great movement for abolition, Alexis de Tocqueville wrote,

> Sixty years ago, if the foremost maritime and colonial nation of the globe had suddenly declared that slavery would disappear from its vast domains: what shouts of surprise and admiration would have broken out everywhere! With what concerned and passionate curiosity the eyes of civilized Europe would have followed the development of that immense enterprise! What fears and hopes would have filled every heart! This bold and remarkable task has just been undertaken and completed before our own eyes. We have seen something unprecedented in history. . . . Open the annals of all peoples, and I doubt you will find anything finer or more extraordinary.[70]

The British people's long campaign to end the slave trade cost thousands of jobs and lives. In one year, the British government spent 40 percent of its budget on the cause. In the end, abolition cost the British economy nearly 2 percent of GDP, each and every year, for sixty years.[71] Which politicians today would have the courage to back such reforms? Yet the British did it, and do we question whether what they did was worth it?

To transition away from "Might Makes Right" for resources, Western countries will have to bear costs: infrastructure expenses, somewhat higher energy prices during the transition, and political frictions and economic retaliation from old allies like the Saudis. The costs will be lower than the British paid to end slavery, and there will be many benefits in return. In fact, the biggest benefit will be something that the West can only gain by bearing costs—something that the West now needs more than it needs more soldiers or spies or autocratic allies.

People in the West may have some sense that the rest of the world views them with suspicion. The hard truth is that things are much worse than most Westerners (and especially most Americans) think. To take just two examples, in the most recent surveys, majorities in all Muslim countries said that Westerners are "selfish," "greedy," "immoral," "arrogant," "violent," and "fanatical." And majorities of ordinary Chinese agreed that Americans are "selfish," "greedy," "arrogant," "aggressive," and "violent."[72]

There are many causes of this lack of trust: the West's troubled history of militarism and its exploitation of foreigners' resources, the anti-Western rhetoric of foreign demagogues and extremists, and other causes too. There's enough blame to go around, if we're interested in blame. Yet even after we understand the past causes of this distrust of the West, we'll still need to know what to do to build trust now.

The strategic touchstones for Clean Trade are transparency, inclusiveness, and trust. Enacting states will say to other states: These are our principles, we think that you support them too. We'll show you why these reforms are in our long-term interests; we think that they're in yours as well. We're prepared to move first and to bear costs, to make these reforms and to build trust. We want to work with you to make this transition easier and quicker. We don't want to use these sticks against you—which, as you can see, will be bad for us too. But here are the sticks, so that you can predict what will come next. And even if you don't at first agree to move with us, our door will always be open.

Principled action is the best way for Western countries to counter the conspiracy theories and charges of hypocrisy that now echo all over the world. To take one important instance of this, principled action is the best way for Western countries to counter the jihadi victimization narrative that has attracted thousands of young Muslims toward radicalization and then extremism. Every Western killing of a Muslim abroad can be spun to strengthen this jihadi narrative. Western countries must create a counter-narrative that is more compelling. Only by showing that it is willing to bear costs for the sake of other peoples can the West drain the swamps of suspicion that mire it in its resource curse. Acting on principle is the best way to build trust.

These reforms also leverage the greatest shift in power in modern history. Europe's colonies, including the American ones, didn't win their freedom just because they had morality on their side. The people of the colonies fought for their freedom, and they won their freedom because they had become stronger—better armed, better organized, and more confident. As we've seen in the uprisings of the past decade, the citizens of resource-cursed countries also want to be free—and they are getting better weapons, better information, better networks, higher hopes. What's keeping them down right now is mostly the money that we consumers send to those who are oppressing and attacking them.

If we keep sending that money, those people will continue their struggle through uprisings and armed conflict. Some of them will, in frustration, turn to extremism and terrorism. The regimes that we empower will respond with more violence, more repression, more indoctrination. The peoples of these countries are getting stronger. Eventually they'll win—the question is how violent and chaotic this transition will be. We can ease the transition by getting onto the peoples' side.

Abolishing effectiveness for resources will preempt some of the threats and crises that importing states will otherwise face. And this will keep the international agenda clearer for states to work together to address urgent issues like climate change. Keeping foreigners from dividing against each other will keep them from dividing so violently against us, which will give the world more breathing room to work on the many problems that it faces. It will also keep us from dividing so bitterly against ourselves.

Faced with the endless foreign dilemmas driven by effectiveness, even well-meaning citizens in our countries will continue to fight each other over who caused the messes, and over what are now the least-awful choices. Our own entrepreneurs of division will then encourage our fights. Acting on principle will dissolve some of the dilemmas that will otherwise divide the citizens of our countries so angrily against each other. We can help to heal our own ruptured democracies by uniting to affirm our democratic ideals: by acting together to abolish "Might Makes Right," and to affirm the basic principle that all countries belong to their citizens.

PHILOSOPHICAL ISSUES

The West has a historic opportunity to build on the strengths of today's international system, while correcting one of its most disruptive defects. Western countries can change their own laws to align with the idea that a country belongs to its people, countering the power of violent and oppressive actors whose control over resources causes so much suffering and injustice and disorder worldwide.

Yet some cosmopolitan philosophers have said that the principle of Popular Resource Sovereignty is insufficient for justice, or even misguided. These philosophers have advanced a different principle as a basis for reform, which is that the world's natural resources belong to humanity as a whole. America's resources, for example, belong not only to Americans but equally to all humans. What should we make of this cosmopolitan principle of "the common ownership of the Earth"?[73]

More cautious philosophers deploy the principle of common ownership not as a replacement for national control over resources, but as a qualification to it. In Thomas Pogge's proposal, for example, common ownership of the Earth grounds an argument for forcing oil-extracting states to pay into a global fund whenever they extract resources, with that fund being used to meet the basic needs of the world's poor. Because all own the world's natural assets, he argues, all (and especially the poor) should benefit when those assets are exploited.

The cosmopolitan ideal of common ownership is undeniably attractive, expressing as it does a vision of human unity that transcends state boundaries. And for several issues—such as rights over the atmosphere and the deep seabed—this is a promising principle for guiding policy. As a principle for redistributing control over today's major traded resources, however, it is premature.

"A country belongs to its people" was the story of the twentieth century, a century whose main narrative was the struggle of peoples against empires. The triumph of peoples came in winning sovereignty over their land from the powers that had oppressed them, and in taking ownership of the resources that those powers were so shamelessly exploiting. In this context—in our world as it is now—attempts to weaken peoples' resource sovereignty with "the common ownership of the Earth" will not be well received.

Think of being a citizen inside a former colony such as Algeria or Indonesia or Zimbabwe, where the national identity hardened in bloody struggles to wrestle the territory and its resource wealth away from relentless empires that clothed their exploitation in the colors of morality. Westerners now come to you saying that you do not entirely own your country's resources, because the British and French, the Dutch and Japanese, and even the Americans partly own them too. However worthy are the derivations from this principle, the principle itself will be hard for many to hear. There just is not enough trust. More, the proposal would set resource-rich and -poor countries against each other. Many of the leaders of resource-rich countries are strongmen who still wear the clothing of the anti-colonial revolution. They would cry to their people, "The big powers want to take from us what we have won at such a price, and give it to strangers." And they would be right.

As a principle of political action, "the common ownership of the Earth" is parochial to the West, deployed most vigorously by Dutch, English, French, and American thinkers of the seventeenth and eighteenth centuries, who could draw on a shared biblical heritage as they opposed their kings. In countries like India and China, common ownership has never had that kind of resonance—and in countries that have recently escaped empire (including these), it may seem like a Western Trojan horse.

By contrast, Popular Resource Sovereignty is the principle that peoples everywhere have insisted upon across recent decades to counter the powers that have oppressed them, and it's the principle that can counter the powers that continue to hound them today. Its language is already in the treaties, elites and ordinary people already speak its words, and it already fits into the architecture of international principles. Policies to support Popular Resource Sovereignty will require the creation of no coercive world bodies, and are compatible with responsible national foreign policies. These policies work within the design constraints of the international system, which today secures the preconditions for moral progress of any kind.

The Costs of Cosmopolitanism

And yet, cosmopolitans say, isn't it just luck that some humans are born in countries rich with resources—like Norway—while others must wander the empty plains of countries like Paraguay? Doesn't justice demand the redistribution of resource wealth away from the lucky to the unlucky? No human is responsible for creating the Earth's mineral wealth, after all, so shouldn't our baseline be that every human has a right to an equal share of the world's natural bounty?

Philosophers have advanced several reforms based on the principle that the value of the world's resources should be distributed more equally to all.[74] For instance, Hillel Steiner recommends a 100 percent natural resource ownership tax, using the revenues to fund an unconditional global basic income or initial capital stake.[75] Such proposals are difficult to evaluate, because they remain incomplete—they specify an end, but not means to reach it. Many questions revolve around the agencies that will implement these cosmopolitan redistributions for major resources like oil. What is the nature of the power that forces states to redistribute the value of the resources in their territory? Does it have enough military capacity to coerce recalcitrant national leaders? Yet, if not, how does this agency require compliance—how does it make the petrocrats give away the power that sustains their rule?

At their least edifying, cosmopolitan proposals use a passive voice to insist on aggressive reforms. Something—something even quite difficult—must be done, yet who does this difficult thing, and how, remain hazy. Occasionally, a gesture may be made to some hypothetical body, like a widely trusted and incorruptible global panel of experts, or a world citizenry willing to accept majority decisions for the sake of humanity as a whole. Yet what is meant to happen when a powerful group—say, the Russians or the Saudis—rejects the implementation is left unsaid. If some pattern will be imposed across the planet, the power that does this cannot be passive.[76]

To put this another way, it's difficult to evaluate such cosmopolitan proposals because they don't much discuss the costs worth bearing to realize their principles. After a nod to the idea that, say, "equality is not the only value," they proceed as if pressing for global equality could not conflict with other values. Yet should we be willing to press for global resource equality if the cost is a global recession? Rich-world depression? Serious frictions between the West and China? Without some discussion of costs, it's hard to know what importance cosmopolitan principles are meant to have.[77]

A historical analogy may help. In antebellum America, many brilliant advocates demanded an end to chattel slavery. That was an achievement—yet eventually those advocates had to face squarely the real costs of abolition. For, by 1860, abolition and civil war were inseparable. Hundreds of thousands of deaths—including the deaths of many advocates—maimed men, bereaved spouses, children without parents, widespread deprivation, whole cities razed. Was it worth it to abolish slavery? What is it worth now to redistribute the world's resource wealth?

Cosmopolitans might attend more to the question of costs, simply because their ideals are so advanced. Rich-country academics sometimes don't grasp how little even basic universalistic ideas like human rights enter the reasoning of many people in poor countries.[78] And indeed, Western academics should see their challenge even more vividly, nearby. The recent populist victories in the West have revealed that many in these countries have weak allegiance to global norms like human rights and the laws of war—and that they seem willing to head backwards in history toward the pre-modern rules of "Might Makes Right."

In the world as it is, there is a decent consensus on principles for nation-states: principles such as each country belongs to its people, and that states should not seize each other's territory by force. What remains almost entirely absent are shared, substantive principles for how individuals should relate to each other across borders, as "citizens of the world." This means that the implementation of ambitious cosmopolitan reforms today would likely be impositions by a vanguard on an unwilling, even incredulous, human population—including a great many citizens in the West. Cosmopolitans might be more explicit about how coercive they are willing to be to realize their ideals.

One great advantage of reforms based on popular sovereignty is that this is already the world's ideal: peoples have won that battle. And the great promise of popular sovereignty is that self-determining nations grow together. Democracies are less likely to go to war with each other. They are also more likely to create and participate in international institutions and more likely to respect international treaties.[79] National democracy is also the best school that we know for educating people to be willing and able to cooperate across borders.[80]

To whatever extent a cosmopolitan future will arrive, it will require individuals who are willing to act together despite what divides them. For that to be possible, individuals in today's resource-cursed countries will need to become more democratically capable than they now are: more knowledgeable about the safe use of political power, more accustomed to the give-and-take of life within a self-ruling group. The surest way we know for these individual capacities to develop is within the institutions of popular sovereignty, which now exist in all regions of the world.

Moving power over resources away from authoritarians and militias, to sovereign peoples, will encourage the kinds of relations across borders that may eventually allow justice to emerge in some richer form. In the meantime, strengthening peoples will enhance humanity's ability to meet the challenges that will soon come. Those who wish to see power over resources spread still further can see Popular Resource Sovereignty as a stage along their way.

What Are Distributions For?

And what, at the deepest level, are the principles that should guide our efforts to better the world? Neither Popular Resource Sovereignty nor "common ownership of the Earth" are good candidates at this level. Giving control over a planet's rocks, mud, and gasses to groups of different sizes—these can only be mid-level principles, layers over more fundamental ideals.[81]

Some philosophers believe that the deepest principles will express the moral worth of all humans. Since all have the same moral worth, they say, we should arrange the world so that there's an equal distribution of what's really important. So, for example, all humans should enjoy equal well-being, or the opportunity to achieve equal well-being, or equal freedom, or some other such distribution of advantages.

It's worth noticing that all of these ideals only concern what individuals will get; they say nothing about what individuals will do with what they get. They say nothing, that is, about what kind of people there are, or how people relate to one another. These theories seem not to register whether men and women are shallow, hateful, thoughtless, and mean, or whether they are beings of integrity, generosity, conscience, and joy. These distributive philosophies are silent on much of what matters most to people in their daily lives.[82]

There is an older tradition of thought about institutions that's also concerned with distributions, but not only for their own sakes. What this tradition emphasizes is the effects that institutions have on people, and especially on their relations with each other. This is the tradition of Plato and Aristotle, of Montesquieu and Burke, of Rousseau and Wollstonecraft and Marx. In this tradition, institutions do more than distribute what people desire—they influence the desires that people have. As a contemporary author in this tradition writes,

> A country's social system shapes the wants and aspirations that its citizens come to have. It determines in part the sort of persons they want to be as

well as the sort of persons they are. Thus an economic system is not only an institutional device for satisfying existing wants and needs but a way of creating and fashioning wants in the future. How men work together now to satisfy their present desires affects the desires they will have later on, the kind of persons they will be.[83]

In this tradition, what is ultimately worth caring about is what kinds of people there are and how they relate to one another. Distributions of goods are important primarily because of their effects on "the kind of persons they will be." In *The Social Contract*, for instance, Rousseau requires that "no citizen should be so rich as to be capable of buying another citizen, and none so poor that he is forced to sell himself."[84] This is one element of Rousseau's design for institutions that will engender citizens who prioritize the general will over their own personal wants.

It is sometimes thought that Rawls is the "distributive" philosopher par excellence, but this is a mistake. Rawls's just distribution is a means to more profound ends: it gives public assurance to each citizen of their equal worth to society, so supporting the self-respect that everyone needs to pursue their plan of life "with zest and to delight in its fulfillment." Rawls's just distribution also enables an especially intense form of social unity—in this society, citizens "share one another's fate" in a very close-knit way.[85]

In this effects-of-institutions tradition, the best institutions form human environments that foster positive identities: identities that are more integrated, open, tolerant, cooperative, and uniting. This is the tradition that will be the most rewarding as we orient ourselves toward reforming institutions over the longest term.

Unity Theory

The Clean Trade reforms should be attractive from many philosophical perspectives. Liberals and conservatives, humanitarians and egalitarians, utilitarians and modern Kantians might all see their value. If I am asked the basis on which I recommend them, it is the free unity of humanity.

Going deep into one part of today's global economy, we find that it divides foreigners against each other. Unchecked power in resource-cursed countries creates more than human divisions—it creates divisive humans: the cruel despot, the corrupt official, the executioner with his sword, the drugged-up child playing war with a loaded gun. These divisive identities have been formed within terrains of power; they are adaptations, one might say, to specific human environments. Much of the war and oppression, the corruption and the extremism of our times are symptoms of these divisions. We also find that the unchecked power of resources sets foreigners and

Westerners against each other, and sets citizens in the West against themselves as well. If division is the problem, then unity must be the solution.

Unity is good: unity within ourselves, unity with the world, unity with each other. Our unity with each other is unity in our ends. Ends are less unified the more people have divergent goals, and want to thwart each other. Ends more unified the more people have common goals, and want to act together.

Everyone's evaluations of human relations track their degree of unity of ends. Cruelty marks maximally divergent ends—a person who is being cruel is acting on a desire to thwart the desires of her victim. Antagonism, rivalry, and competition are still divergent, but less bad. Forbearance, toleration, and cooperation mark relations of less divergence and increasing unification. Alliance, solidarity, and community are still more positive on this spectrum of valuable relations.

This unity of ends lives deep within human moral reasoning, and so within all moral traditions. The Golden Rule is a simple injunction to pursue ends that others likely share. Of the Ten Commandments, six regulate human interactions. Five of these commandments forbid having or acting on conflicting ends, and the sixth is an enjoinder to adjust one's ends to those of others (one's parents). In the Confucian tradition, unity is "harmony," which is the most cherished ideal.

At the positive extreme of the spectrum of value are other ideals of maximum unity, including Kant's "realm of ends": a "whole of all ends . . . in systematic connection."[86] Mill's moral ideal rests upon "a powerful principle in human nature": "the desire to be in unity with our fellow creatures." As Mill explains further:

> In an improving state of the human mind, the influences are constantly on the increase, which tend to generate in each individual a feeling of unity with all the rest; which, if perfect, would make him never think of, or desire, any beneficial condition for himself, in the benefits of which they are not included.[87]

What an individual thinks of, and desires, is a function of his identity. The perfect human identity that Mill describes is that of an individual who thinks only of self-benefits that are also other-benefits: an individual who only wants goods that are common goods. Such an individual pursues these common goods freely, not because of force; his actions toward unity express his identity. A community of such individuals is the end point of all ideals like Mill's, which are, with the appropriate sentiments added, nothing other than ideals of universal love.

How far human nature will allow the achievement of free unity has been variously imagined. In the Rawlsian well-ordered society, citizens raised under just institutions develop a strong desire to cooperate with their fellow citizens on fair terms. In the Marxist ideal of free social production, each wants to labor in ways that satisfy the true needs of others. Earthly utopias such as Thomas More's approach an ideal of spontaneous universality as closely as the constraints of human nature allow. With the constraints of human nature removed—in the scientific utopias by technology, in the Christian utopias by death—utopian ideals converge in describing beings who by their nature desire what others desire, all freely acting toward their universal common good. We can elaborate such visions of the free unity of ends to whatever limits our skepticism about human potential permits.

Unity theory says that utilitarians are correct to locate goodness in the satisfaction of desires. Yet there is more value in satisfying desires that converge with others'—and no or even negative value in satisfying desires that conflict. Kant's misstep in moral theory was to disqualify actions whose success depends on disunified ends (hence his rigorism on deception), instead of seeing greater unity of ends as a collective cause to be furthered, arduously and approximately, with whatever means are to hand.

Relations defined by hard power gravitate toward the negative pole on the spectrum of unified ends. Violence, threat, and manipulation are means for one party to achieve his ends at the expense of another's; so the exercise of such power has negative value. Both domination and indoctrination, for instance, are defined in terms of divergent ends, as are duplicity and fraud. Harassment, bullying, and intimidation again have divergence at their core, with their conceptual peripheries tailored to specific interpersonal contexts.

The use of hard power—which aims to achieve ends that others do not share—can be justified to the degree that this leads to a greater free unity of human ends. Otherwise, power should be countered. The domination by Hobbes's Leviathan can be justified by the great goods of peace—if the only alternative really is endless war *omnium contra omnes*. Yet Leviathan can also be condemned, as Locke and Rousseau condemned him, should a peaceful and less coercive commonwealth be feasible. The feasibility of peace without absolutism was a discovery of human social capacity: a discovery of a freer form of unity.

Where there is chaos, the cry is for order. Power can create peace, which is a species of unity and a step toward more. Where there is peace, the call is for freedom. Once order is established, counter-powerful campaigns will begin, promising that order can be preserved under conditions of greater liberty. The entrenchment of the rule of law, the abolition of slavery, the independence of the colonies, the rise of human rights and popular sovereignty—all of these movements reduced the negative value of the exercise of power, and established conditions in which valuable new free unities could emerge.

The freedom of unity is crucial. Demagogues always call for unity when enforcing their own (racial, religious, nationalist, class-based) ideology.

History forever replays this same move. As a result of this history, even those who know little of it will hear invisible klaxons whenever would-be leaders praise unity. Our ancestors, instructed in the dire lessons of demagoguery, have designed our minds to sound this alarm. Yet our resistance really reinforces the ideal. These mental alarms are themselves counterpowerful, and so can be guides toward a greater free unity of ends that, it deserves emphasis, always searches for less violence, coercion, and manipulation.

Unity does not mean uniformity; a unification of diversity may contain more value than a unity among sames. Diversity allows persons of various constitutions to pursue their favored ends. Different rites and styles will also suit different lives. Diversity itself allows citizens to enjoy and learn from each other, and so to have richer experiences than in a monoculture. And a more diverse community, like a more robust immune system, may also have more resources with which to meet the challenges that fate sends its way.

What is important is the actual achievement of valuable relations among real people, now and in the future. So what relations should be preserved, reformed, and rebelled against today depends on which rules are entrenched and what identities are present today. What matters for action is what relations of unity and disunity exist around us and how a greater free unity can be gained. The primary evaluation of every act, rule, role, trait, or identity—of every policy, treaty, office, and institution—is how it contributes, at its time, to promoting or hindering the achievement of freely harmonized ends over the long term.

Unity theory is consequentialist—it judges everything by its contribution to the maximum achievement of freely unified ends. The theory has many levels, including acts, rules, roles, policies, principles, and identities.[88] As in all consequentialist theories, here the ends justify the means. Yet to a great extent, the ends justify the principles that constrain the means. Principles solve collective action problems and prioritize long-term coordination. Supporting specific principles is especially promising when these principles have already gained widespread adherence, when their value has already been shown, when the mechanisms to enforce them already exist, and when coordination on their realization is as yet incomplete. These are our circumstances today with trade in natural resources.

As Mill nearly said, "It is proper to state that I forego any advantage which could be derived to my argument from the idea of abstract right, as a thing independent of unity."[89] The Clean Trade policies above are based on widely affirmed principles such as the rule of law, human rights, and especially popular sovereignty—which characterize the most successful forms of free unity that humanity has yet achieved on a large scale, and to which many already feel a strong allegiance. These policies also work with sentiments now strong within most people: an instinctive opposition toward concentrations of unaccountable power, and a repugnance at handling goods tainted with suffering and injustice.

The goals of these reforms are to reduce violence, coercion, corruption, and antagonism, to increase trust and so enable people to act more easily together, and, ultimately, to encourage identities closer to the Millian ideal of people who want goods for themselves that are also goods for others. The goal is for more people freely to pursue more goods in common.

Power is rightly praised above chaos, and partial unities are better than none. We will always prefer partial unities so long as no reasonable alternative is in sight. And we're only part way in a historical movement toward greater free unity. Humanity's capacity for collective reasoning remains poor; divisive identities are still widespread. Still, looking from the past toward ourselves, the scope of our current partial unifications is remarkable. Imagine what Rousseau—much less Aristotle—would have said of the chances that 65 million (United Kingdom), 320 million (United States), or even 1.3 billion (India) humans could unite in political formations that maintain civil peace, political rights, and personal liberties, as well as high levels of mutual identification. Philosophy is born in wonder, and we might be full of wonder at the unities that humans have already achieved— while also wondering how humanity itself can become more freely united.

Beyond Blood Oil

It may appear that today's rule of "Might Makes Right" for oil is just the way that the world must work, and that it will be too hard to change. On reflection, though, that's just how the slave trade, and colonialism, and apartheid seemed to serious people, before the reforms succeeded. Humanity has now abolished its old law of violence for all of those practices. The world is now ready to abolish that old law one more time. We can get ourselves out of business with violent and oppressive and corrupt men abroad, and look forward to a world beyond blood oil. We can create a greater free unity than humanity has yet achieved.

2

Bad Men and Dirty Trade

Michael Blake

There are few works of political philosophy that have a reasonable chance to change the world of political practice; there are even fewer that have a reasonable shot at changing that world for the *better*. Leif Wenar's *Blood Oil* is one of these latter, precious few. It describes, clearly and persuasively, the ways in which an economy built upon oil has incentivized brutality and atrocity throughout the world. It lays bare the relationship between oil use in a wealthy democratic state and the malignant governance of an African kleptocracy. It provides, finally, some hope, through tools that may guide us to a world in which we no longer use oil to incentivize political evil.

In this chapter, though, I want to focus my attention on that most important word: *may*. I share Wenar's conviction that oil exportation can explain the prevalence of atrocity and human rights abuses throughout much of Africa and the Middle East. I am less convinced that his policy instruments—including the use of Clean Trade Acts and Clean Hands Trusts—will actually make the world better for those suffering such atrocity and abuse.[1] My thesis in this chapter will be that, for his policy instruments to work, we must hope for both virtuous agents and fortunate circumstances; we need both good men and good luck, for these policy tools to achieve what we want them to do. Whether we can expect this, in the various contexts that collectively make up the real world, I cannot say. The field of development economics exists precisely because questions such as this cannot be answered by philosophers such as myself. What I want to do here, then, is simply to note the problem, and hand off the inquiry to others better suited than myself to find the answer.

To make this more precise, we might note that Wenar's book makes three key claims:

1. Extractive industries such as oil can incentivize and sustain malignant governance; those possessed of coercive power in an oil-rich society can simply extract wealth for themselves, while using some of that wealth to purchase security for themselves—without any particular concern for the rights or interests of the citizenry over whom that coercion is exercised.
2. A state that purchases oil from a malignant regime is part of a causal chain that perpetuates those human rights abuses performed by that regime.
3. If a state were to refuse to purchase oil from a malignant regime— through a Clean Trade Act, preventing acts of trade with such a regime—the result would be that such a regime would, over time, become less malignant.

I accept propositions one and two; those of us who purchase oil—which is to say, all of us in wealthy societies—are causally implicated in a chain that ends with concrete abuses performed on the bodies of the world's most vulnerable citizens. I do not accept proposition three—or, rather, I do not think that proposition three *always* holds.[2] We may be in a terrible situation: implicated in injustice, without any particularly good way to escape from that injustice. There are worlds, in short, in which a Clean Trade Act is likely to make things worse for the very people whose rights animate our moral concern. The act may make the poor more impoverished; the abusive government more abusive; the relationship between the West and the rest more fraught with resentment, misunderstanding, and violence. Again, I do not want to claim necessity for any of this; I hope Wenar can convince me that these worries do not hold, or at least do not hold in the particular contexts we face today. I am, however, still worried, and await his reassurances. I will lay these worries out in three contexts. What, I will ask, might the Clean Trade Act do for the country producing oil? What will it do for the country that purchases the oil? And what might it do for the relationships between the two, as well as for international relations more generally?

OIL-PRODUCING STATES

What will be the first reaction of a state facing the loss of a market for its oil? Bear in mind that this state still has possession of the oil; it is still there, in the coercive grasp of the state, ready to be sold. Bear in mind, too, that the demand for that oil has not gone down in any way; the oil is just as valuable the day after the act as it was the day before. So, what will the state do, given that it can no longer sell that oil to a particular market?

One possibility, of course, is that the state will clean its own house a bit; it will engage in reform, whether piecemeal or wholesale, designed to eventually bring it up to the standard required to reacquire market access. This is not outside the realm of possibility; South Africa, in particular, eventually abandoned apartheid, in part because of the force of economic sanctions.[3] There are, however, other possibilities, not all of them ethically problem-free. One possibility is that the capital that had been placed into the particular extractive industry moves elsewhere, simply abandoning the country that has been blacklisted under the Clean Trade Act. This is what happened after the passage of the Dodd-Frank Act, which prohibited the exportation of coltan from the Democratic Republic of Congo; those who had invested in Congolese mines simply moved their money elsewhere, with devastating results for over five million miners and their families.[4] This might be thought to be a precursor to reform; after all, if the miners are suffering, perhaps their suffering will motivate the state in question to reform itself. The problem, of course, is that we began with the simple fact that the state in question doesn't much care about the suffering of the miners, or those like them; if that state was independently interested in the rights and interests of the poor, we wouldn't be in the position of using Clean Trade Acts against it. Perhaps we might hope that the miners would simply take matters into their own hands, and engage in political activism —whether revolutionary or otherwise—designed to force change upon the recalcitrant government. This is, however, a fairly faint hope; the state, after all, has had the time needed to buy weapons to immunize itself against the threat of an uprising, and the miners are at any rate often more concerned with mere survival than with mass mobilization. More often, it seems that the result of the withdrawal of capital from extractive industries is simply a reduction in money flowing into the society in question. Wenar is undoubtedly right that the money that flowed into the country from extractive industries was effectively incentivizing political evil; the money stayed at the top, and gave those at the top the means to ensure their own dominance over those at the bottom. But it does not follow that the *withdrawal* of that money makes things better for those at the bottom. It might, instead, simply make the impoverished even more poor.

It's possible, then, that the withdrawal of a trading relationship doesn't lead to good governance, but to worse poverty. Other possibilities, however, are even more ethically unsavory. The oil, recall, is still useful; gasoline from a tyranny burns just as well as gasoline from Norway. So, if selling the oil is lucrative, would we expect that making the sale of that oil illegal will stop that oil from being sold? I think the answer is no—at least, not any more than the laws against the sale of marijuana have actually prevented people from buying and selling marijuana. (My own state, Washington, has recently legalized recreational marijuana; the use of marijuana among twelfth graders has actually gone *down* since legalization.)[5] Criminalization of drugs did not effectively prevent drug use; instead, it created a booming secondary market of smugglers, dealers, and money-launderers, all of whom were able to extract rent from those who produced drugs and those who purchased them. If a state refuses to buy oil from a given country, we might expect to see a similar market structure emerge: those who specialize in hiding the origin of the oil, those who arrange its covert entry into another state's legitimate supply, and so on. All these people cost money; the money they take will, of course, be factored into the profits of those who are already extracting the most rent from the oil. Whether we actually see such a black market will depend upon many factors—not least upon whether it is profitable for those who own the oil to pay black marketeers to bring their conflict oil to market. What is more certain, of course, is that the development of such a market will do very little to help the plight of those who labor to extract the oil itself.

All this, of course, depends upon the state using the Clean Trade Act having enough of a market share to make black marketeering economically viable. In the case of the United States, this may be true; but the presence of China makes it at least potentially false. A state facing a Clean Trade Act might, instead of reform, choose to sell its oil to China. Wenar is, of course, sensitive to this worry; he argues, though, that China has some incentive to stand alongside the United States, in defense of the principle of resource sovereignty (*Blood Oil*, 308; this volume, 22). As I will discuss in the third section of this chapter, I think this agreement is unlikely in practice. In the present context, however, I will note only that China's economic adventurism in Africa shows that it is much more willing to separate capitalism and morality than the United States is.[6] In fact, this might be China's defining hallmark, when it comes to foreign investment: Dambisa Moyo's advice to African states is to avoid entanglements with the United States, in favor of China, since the former wants to do good, while the latter wants only to make money—and profit, in the long run, is a more stable relational basis than virtue.[7] Whether Moyo is right or not, I cannot say. It is worth noting, of course, that she is not the first person of African descent to say similar things. Wenar notes (*Blood Oil*, 270) the public perception among non-Westerners that Americans are greedy. He might have added another stereotype: Americans are unduly willing to impose their own ethical values upon others—especially when those others are non-Western. The Nigerian-American novelist Teju Cole describes this well:

Feverish worry over that awful African warlord. But close to 1.5 million Iraqis died from an American war of choice. Worry about that. . . . I deeply respect American sentimentality, the way one respects a wounded hippo. You must keep an eye on it, for you know it is deadly.[8]

China, then, might well take the occasion to differentiate itself from the United States, simply in virtue of its insistence that commerce is not an occasion for ethical reflection. If it does so, then tyrannical oil exporters are unlikely to find a shortage of markets in which their oil might be sold. There are, however, structural problems even if China does not choose to differentiate itself in this way. The Clean Trade Act, I have suggested, will effectively prevent money flowing to a tyranny only if most states actually join up; otherwise, it simply represents a shift in location of sales. Once most states have signed up, however, there are standard game-theoretic pathologies that emerge; any one state can now gain advantages, from trading with the disfavored state. A group of states unified by a Clean Trade Act form a sort of cartel, even if it is a cartel of virtue rather than self-interest— and cartels are notoriously unstable things. Even if, then, the Clean Trade Act actually succeeds in making things difficult for the tyrannical government in question, it is not entirely clear that it will succeed in doing so for very long.

So: the Clean Trade Act may produce good results—it might produce reform, and eventually re-entry into global markets for a newly chastened government. But it might produce something else entirely. It might produce wealthy smugglers, increased trade links between oil-producing tyrannies and China, black market oil, and even more impoverished citizens. Do we have any confidence that the latter won't be produced, in the particular context of oil produced by (say) Nigeria? I don't see how, given the past century, we can avoid being rather worried. The United Nations (led, in this instance, by the United States) used the withdrawal of trading rights as a tool to make the Baathist government of Saddam Hussein reform itself in the 1990s. These sanctions did not result in a reformed Baathist government. They resulted, instead, in over 500,000 dead children.[9] Sanctions transformed an evil government with relatively functioning institutions of health, education, and infrastructure, into an evil government without any of these, while the lives of Baathist party members continued relatively unaffected, and infant mortality rates and the burden of disease skyrocketed for those who were not members of the inner circle. Economic sanctions—and the Clean Trade Act is, we should emphasize, a tool for economic sanctions[10]—kill people; indeed, they have killed more people since 1989 than have been killed by weapons of mass destruction throughout history.[11] I want to be clear, at this point, that I am not condemning sanctions full stop; unless one is a pacifist, one is willing to countenance death in the name of some overriding value, whether justice or democracy or something else. What I am saying, instead, is that we'd better be damned *careful*. Experience tells us that sanctioning bad countries doesn't always make them better. If we are to use this tool, we have to make sure that we are in the right sort of world—one in which we can expect the sanctions to actually produce reform, rather than retrenchment for the elite and misery for the poor.

One final note. It is worth asking how the tyrannical states will *use* the fact of sanctions. The Clean Trade Act, after all, is being placed into a world with a legacy of colonialism, in which there are resentments over acts of international injustice both historical and ongoing. Perversely, being sanctioned by a superpower can sometimes help a government get a bit of legitimacy in the eyes of its own citizens; look, the leader can say, I'm being punished by the United States, so clearly I'm on the side of the poor! Thus, the Cuban leadership has a habit of painting anything they don't like—any economic failure, any social problem—as a result of the American trade embargo.[12] The embargo provides an enemy; hardship is always portrayed not as the result of inefficiency or tyranny, but as the result of the outside aggressor, and thus a necessary part of a struggle for justice. Venezuela's leadership, similarly, has sought to create national unity through condemnation of the United States as an imperial power; Nicolás Maduro—like Hugo Chávez before him—justified any repression as a response to the imperial threat.[13] Thus, a sanction may end up producing almost precisely the opposite of what it is intended to do; it may impoverish the weak, while providing the strong with the tools they need to cling to power.

OIL-IMPORTING STATES

States that produce oil, then, might not respond to sanctions with sincere reflection and reform. They might, instead, simply look elsewhere—to other markets, to China, to smugglers—while clothing themselves as innocent victims of imperial aggression. Whether they will do that or not, of course, depends upon a great many things—not least of which is the moral character of those who are going to make the decision about how to respond to the sanctions. It would take a rather brave tyrant, however, to subject himself to the risks involved in opening up his society; opening up civil society, encouraging innovation, ensuring the rule of law—all of this makes it difficult for a tyrant to perpetuate his rule. People respond to incentives, as the phrase goes, and tyrants in particular have little incentive to be virtuous.

The same, though, can be said for the inhabitants of wealthy states. The Clean Trade Act, in particular, will not automatically produce virtuous agency on behalf of global human rights. Wenar knows this, of course; his discussion of the internalization of norms is unusual and welcome, precisely because it discusses how it is that what starts as a rule to be evaded becomes a rule for internal deliberation (*Blood Oil*, 140). What concerns me, though, is the extent to which this process of internalization can be interrupted; how a rule that starts as an alien imposition can *stay* alien, or gradually return to that status. (Think, for instance, of the cynical attitude among workers in the late Soviet Union; rather than producing the New Soviet man, selfless and able, Soviet propaganda became the subject of widespread derision and mockery.)[14] If the incentives are right, it's possible that the norms giving rise to the Clean Trade Act never develop the right sort of purchase on individual behavior that they need—and individual agents within the developed world never become the sort of people who actually take the lives of the global poor into account when they act.

What could we expect, then, if people in the developed world don't internalize the norm in question? Part of this would simply repeat what has been described above; networks of smuggling can be expected to emerge, much as they do for other illicit substances, in response to any sort of state interdiction. These networks emerged in the wake of the sanctions imposed upon Iraq, after its invasion of Kuwait; Iraq smuggled its oil to Turkey and Jordan, which turned around and sold that oil on the open market. (The U.S. government, it should be noted, quietly condoned this smuggling, so as to keep Turkey and Jordan as allies.)[15] What should be emphasized here is not that Iraq wanted to smuggle the oil; as discussed above, this is what we might expect Iraq to want. What we should emphasize is that the oil was sold around the world—including to Western companies and agents, who either didn't know or didn't care about its relationship to the suffering of the Iraqi people. If a Clean Trade Act were in place, the structure of incentives would unlikely be different. Those people whose livelihoods depend upon the flow of oil would ensure that the oil continue to flow. If this requires more complex shell games—such as moving the oil to a less-brutal third country prior to its importation—then that is the sort of game we can expect to be played.

What is more worrying, though, is what we can expect to happen if the sanctioning regime actually *succeeds*. Imagine, then, that the quantity of oil from foreign tyrannies is reduced. The same demand for the oil is in place; people in the wealthy country have not given up living in places that require one to have a car, nor have they begun to lobby *en masse* for an increase in public transportation. So, with reduced supply and a steady demand, we can expect an increased price for gasoline. The same agents who are in charge of making the oil flow can be expected to keep it flowing under these circumstances—most likely by an increase in oil exploration in domestic (or at least democratic) territories. The Athabasca oil sands, for instance, were for a long time economically unviable; it took too much energy to extract usable oil from the mix of oil, sand, and clay found in Northwestern Alberta. As demand for oil increased, however, the extraction of the oil sands became economically feasible. This extraction is environmentally unfriendly, with production emissions significantly higher than that associated with well production.[16] Canada, however, has been ramping up exploitation of its oil sands—a decision made prior to the recent reduction in oil prices. The use of Clean Trade Acts, however, might raise prices to the extent that the increased exploitation could be more profitable. One recent industry magazine raised the (rather breathless) hope that sanctions against Venezuela might be enough to make the oil sands economically viable once again: "If Venezuela's Maduro finally forces the Trump Administration's hand, Canada is an ideal position" to benefit from additional sales of oil-sands crude.[17] Once again, it's entirely possible that agents concerned with satisfying the demand of oil simply regard the use of the Clean Trade Act as a sort of market event, and find ways to satisfy that demand—not all of which come without environmental, and ethical, costs.

These agents, finally, have incentives to regard the Clean Trade Acts as tools with which to increase market share and increase competitive advantages. The evaluation of human rights abroad is never easy, nor free from controversy—both empirical and philosophical. We have seen, in the past, that the evaluation of human rights tends to be done in a not-especially-disinterested way; every state bemoans the human rights abuses of its enemies, while ignoring those of its allies. (The United States, after all, has maintained an embargo against Cuba for over fifty years, justified in part on the basis of human rights; by contrast, the Trump administration recently announced that it will be selling $110 million worth of weapons to Saudi Arabia.)[18] It would be too much to expect much more virtue on the part of oil executives than on the part of politicians. The oil and gas lobby is powerful; in 2011 alone, they spent $150 million in lobbying the U.S. government.[19] Some of that money is spent in an effort to increase freedom for the oil and gas industry as a whole; thus, ExxonMobil and Chevron joined together to lobby against sanctions against Russia after its invasion of the Crimean peninsula.[20] Companies can lobby, however, against one another just as easily as they can on behalf of their industries. The creation of a Clean Trade Act can create a new tool with which companies can seek to increase market share.

Wenar is aware of these worries, of course, which is why he wants an independent arbiter on whose human rights record is truly abysmal—Freedom House, perhaps, or *The Economist*. I am not sure, however, that this is sufficient. In the first place, corruption as a phenomenon can sometimes affect even nominally independent organizations. Given the sheer quantity of money involved, it isn't clear how we could guarantee that no effort to bias those charged with the evaluation here could succeed. (Both FIFA and the IOC, by comparison, began as independent bodies concerned with the promotion of sports; neither has escaped the corrupting effects of money in recent years.) More to the point, I'm not sure we can expect the government of a rich state to continue to *listen* to Freedom House, or to *The*

Economist, when so much money exists that will tell it to stop listening. The oil and gas industry, after all, has succeeded in the United States in getting one of the two major political parties to believe that climate change is a liberal hoax.[21] By comparison, getting the state to believe that a given human rights abuse is overstated—that it is "fake news"—seems comparatively easy.

INTERNATIONAL RELATIONS

I want now to discuss what I take to be the most difficult set of issues surrounding the Clean Trade Acts: its effects upon the relationships between states. Wenar is keen to portray these acts as simply bits of domestic legislative action; they do not tell foreign states what they have to do— they simply announce what *we* will not do, with our domestic legal systems (*Blood Oil,* 295). As such, there is no worry of the sorts of imperial overreach that might be felt to infect a global attempt to enforce justice abroad. We do not order you around, we say to the foreign society; we simply say that we won't take your title to the oil as sufficient, when we are not convinced that it respects the moral title of your people to that resource.

I think, in response, we might want to separate two distinct questions. The first is whether or not the refusal to engage with the nominal propertyholder of that oil counts as political interference with the foreign society. The second is whether or not that refusal will be *received* as a form of interference. The two questions are distinct; I will deal with them in order.

On the first question, Wenar notes that we are not saying anything at all about the nature or legitimacy of the state, when we refuse to allow it to sell the oil abroad; political recognition is distinct from commercial engagement (113–20). I think this is a mistake. To see why, note that the government selling oil abroad is wearing two hats at once; it is a (putative) property-holder, and a juridical authority. The former hat says: I own this oil. The latter hat says: in my capacity as domestic political authority, I determine who shall own this oil. The two are distinct. (The state might award itself the property rights; good states generally don't.) Wenar says that, when we refuse to recognize the government's authority to sell the oil, we are simply refusing to let our legal system be used to perpetuate an injustice abroad. But we are doing more than that. We are refusing the government the right to determine, on its own territory, the rules by which property claims shall be adjudicated. This is a fairly serious thing for us to do. Its seriousness is enshrined in American law under the heading of the Act of State doctrine, on which a domestic court is precluded from judging the validity of an official act of a foreign country undertaken within that foreign country's borders.[22] There are a variety of reasons for this doctrine's continued power—including the possibility of disharmony between the judicial and executive branches of the United States—but much of it comes from the fact that the refusal to show deference to foreign legal determinations is a refusal to recognize the political right of the foreign government:

> The refusal to recognize [a foreign legal determination] has a unique legal aspect. It signifies this country's unwillingness to acknowledge that the government in question speaks as the sovereign authority for the territory it purports to control.[23]

Imagine a parallel case, in which the foreign law of which we disapprove is not a law of property but a law of politics. An election happens in a foreign country, and we are convinced that the election was illegitimate; the choice of the majority of the citizens was the candidate announced as coming in second. We then decide to extend our diplomatic courtesies to that candidate, and not to the one announced as the winner; the second-place candidate shall be received by our government, given a state dinner, treated with the standard rituals of diplomatic life, and so on. Nothing in this is morally impermissible; we might imagine circumstances in which this is what we ought to do. But it would be hard for us to say, with Wenar, that our decision here is merely "putting our own houses in order" (xxviii) and not coercively interfering in another society's domestic government. We *are* interfering; that's the point of what we're doing. If that foreign state says that a given person has property rights in oil, and we say—no, actually, your laws giving that person these rights are invalid—we are doing much the same. We're interfering; we're standing in judgment of another society's domestic law. Wenar wants us to say that we are allowed to do that, because it isn't interference. I don't think this quite works. I want us to say that it *is* interference, but that such interference might sometimes be permissible.

I therefore want to pause for a moment to be clear about what I am not saying: I am not saying that we should not use Clean Trade Acts. If the pragmatic worries I describe above can be met, I believe we can and should use them, as Wenar describes them. What I am saying is that we cannot avoid thinking of these acts as attempts to dislodge, to a greater or lesser degree, the domestic political power of a foreign government. Sanctions are coercive, and the refusal to trade is not merely a refusal to act but a coercive (and often violent) intervention in a transnational supply chain. We might need to use them, if Wenar is right; but we should call them by their rightful name, and acknowledge that what we do here is very nearly an act of war.[24]

Even if these ideas are false, though, it seems unquestionably true that these sanctions will be received as (very nearly) acts of war by those against whom they are brought to bear. This brings us to the latter of the two questions I want to ask; namely, how these sanctions will be understood, both by their targets and by the international community more broadly. Wenar, as noted above, thinks we might expect China to stand with the West, and not take a position in opposition to the principle of Popular Resource Sovereignty. I think this is likely false, as a matter of prediction; but, more importantly, I think this response might confuse two distinct questions. The first is what the right principle is based upon which we might act to limit the commercial activity of other societies. The second is *who shall judge* what that principle is, and when it has been breached. A Clean Trade Act announces answers to both of these. The trade shall be prevented, when what is traded contravenes the principle of Popular Resource Sovereignty; and *we* shall be the judges, both of which countries have contravened this idea, and when they have restored their good names. China, says Wenar, will not want to stand against the principle that a society's people owns its natural resources. Even if that were true, it would *not* follow that China would welcome a world in which individual countries like the United States took it upon themselves to judge when that principle has been disrespected. Even if China likes resource sovereignty, that is, they can be counted upon to *dislike* Western democracies deciding to act unilaterally in its favor. There are a variety of reasons for this. One of these is that China has, historically, seen discussions of human rights as reflective of Western imperialism and moral hypocrisy; even if Chinese officials respect the idea of resource sovereignty, they can be counted upon to resent its use as a cudgel against weaker and non-Western societies.[25] Another reason is that what starts with violation of resource rights can easily be repurposed for labor rights. What happens if the movement that condemns stolen oil begins to focus on stolen labor? Much labor in China, after all, is performed in conditions that are (to Western eyes, at least) morally inadequate. Could we use these ideas to ground a refusal to trade in goods that are made under such conditions? Even if there are philosophical differences between stolen oil and stolen labor—and there are—it seems that the Chinese would be unlikely to appreciate any popular political movement that might ignore these differences, and bring pressure to bear upon both.

This brings us, then, to the broadest worry I have about Wenar's policy proposals: that they would involve the use of unilateral power, including power that seeks to dislodge the right of a given state to rule, by wealthy states against more marginal states. Even if this could work—and I am not sure, yet, whether it would, in the world we know—we need a theory of international relations that shows us why and when this pathway is morally open to us.[26] Not all pathways that might do the job are morally permissible. Take, for instance, a proposal parallel to Wenar's, by Paul Collier, who defends "over-the-horizon guarantees" of military force brought to bear against recalcitrant African states by wealthy Western ones.[27] The simplest way to describe this proposal is as a guarantee to kill the leadership of any country that falls below an adequate threshold of representation for its inhabitants. I take it that the permissibility of this methodology is not exhausted by an account of its likelihood of success. It might both work, *and* be morally prohibited, if only because of the ways in which it would reassert Western dominance over Africa as a continent. (As William Easterly notes in response: the word *neocolonialism* is overused, but faced with Collier's proposal, "I think one could drop the 'neo.' ")[28] Sanctions involve the imposition of risk: of malnutrition, of starvation, of death. We are not precluded from imposing these risks on others; at the very least, *I* don't think we're so precluded, and neither does Wenar. But more is needed, before we can rest easy. We need, at the very least, some account of how we harmonize the demands of an uneasy world of international relations with the demands of Popular Resource Sovereignty. We need, in short, to accept that the sanction both is and will be seen as a violent act—to face up to the effects using sanctions will have, upon those over whom they are used, and upon global relationships more generally—before deciding to deploy sanctions against even the most tyrannical government.

CONCLUSIONS

I want to briefly reiterate the virtues I describe above. Wenar's book is exemplary; it is courageous, wise, and combines skill in philosophy with skill in empirical analysis. If I have been negative in what I have said here, it is only because I want his tools to work; they are, at the very least, more appealing to me than any alternatives I have seen, as a response to the sorts of political evil so common in oil-exporting states. I am, however, convinced that evil is resilient. Even the best policy tools can be appropriated for malignant ends. For Wenar's tools to work, we would need to expect people to display certain sorts of virtues; they would have to choose to respond to these tools in a manner displaying thought, wisdom, and a will to forego market advantages in the name of others. Wenar is certainly right that we have seen these virtues in history; those who fought against the global slave trade looked as idealistic in their day as Wenar does today. I confess, though, that I am not sanguine about the extent to which we can expect virtue, not just from the activist, but from the statesman, the consumer, and the foreign tyrant. The world is a profoundly unlucky place, and there may be no policy path from where we are to where we need to go that does not involve the risk of failure and atrocity.

I will end, however, by invoking an idea I associate with Wenar himself: the thought that there is no way of doing good that does not involve the risk of doing harm. Wenar's earlier work emphasized that working against global injustice was, inherently, *dangerous;* dangerous because any intervention capable of remaking the world carried with it the risk of making that world worse. This, however, was not a reason to avoid doing the job; we need to accept the risk of harm as part of the price we pay, to be good people.[29] I have emphasized here the worry that tools such as the Clean Trade Act might actually make the world worse than the status quo. Wenar might emphasize—as he has done—that we should not therefore rest easy with the status quo; we have a reason to experiment carefully, but nonetheless to accept the moral risk involved in experimentation. What I have written here is, then, only an exploration of what these risks might involve. I do not mean them as a defense of the status quo; nor are they meant as a disproof of Wenar's arguments or his conclusions. They are, instead, worries that any proposal such as his will have to come to grips with. I look forward to seeing him do just that.

3

The West's Energy Trap: Can It Be Broken?

Nazrin Mehdiyeva

In his lucid book, Leif Wenar convincingly argues that international trade in oil and other resources is still marred by the rule of effectiveness where "might makes right" and where strong systemic incentives exist for the perpetuation of violence and corruption within the countries' borders. Wenar asks Western democracies to stop trading with resource-disordered states in order to break the cycle where the petrodollars that liberal democracies spend on importing resources contribute to the perpetration of authoritarian and corrupt practices, and, in extreme cases, to the killing and mass displacement of people. He asks Western governments and consumers to boycott the tainted goods and voluntarily bear the costs of that boycott, such as higher prices for natural resources, general inflation, and lower economic growth.

The argument is morally compelling. Heart-wrenching accounts of the brutalities committed in Sierra Leone, Nigeria, Equatorial Guinea, South Sudan, and Angola, to name a few, make a powerful case that the money paid by outsiders for these countries' resources finances the torture, killing, and subjection of their people. The impact of those petrodollars travels further as Western states that import resources from corrupt states put their own national interests at risk because the money sent to authoritarian or failed states returns as a blowback in the form of terrorism and other security threats.

Wenar's book is thus a call to action. He asks Westerners to take the moral high ground to end effectiveness-based trade in resources because it

51

is the right thing to do. This is a big ask. Wenar reasons that ending oil effectiveness today would be easier than at any time in the past because the United States has recently experienced a shale revolution; as a result, it has increased production and reduced its dependence on foreign oil. However, hydraulic fracturing, or fracking, as it is commonly known, which enables the extraction of oil and gas from shale, comes at a significant environmental cost as does the production of tar sands in Canada. Developing these resources on a scale necessary to make up the shortfall in supplies from authoritarian states, if those were to be sanctioned, would require the West to make sacrifices: these would include not only higher prices for hydrocarbons, recession, and changes to lifestyle but also environmental degradation and ill health of the people who live in proximity of the production sites. Wenar outlines the monetary sacrifices that people would have to endure as a result of boycotting authoritarian oil but it is the other, non-monetary issues that are unlikely to be most unpalatable to large segments of the public.

None of the analysis and concerns that I lay out in this chapter are to detract from the noble cause that Wenar has set out to achieve: to bring resource justice to the long-oppressed people in authoritarian energy-rich states. Benevolent kings, Wenar argues, are not much better than brutal despots because the former like the latter dispose of the resources to which they are not entitled (*Blood Oil*, 239). While in principle this is a powerful argument, my concern throughout this chapter is with the practical aspects of implementing Clean Trade. I worry that a selective application of Clean Trade sanctions against a handful of authoritarian states would be perceived by the target states (and many others) as a devious plot by the United States to advance its imperialistic interests. By contrast, imposing sanctions on all authoritarian oil states at once would annihilate a very large share of hydrocarbon supplies overnight and leave the West—and most notably, Europe—in a very vulnerable position. This chapter raises some difficult questions that need to be answered before the West is ready to adopt Clean Trade.

We live, in the words of one author, in a "hydrocarbons society,"[1] and, although Wenar does not use this term, he makes abundant references to the extent of our dependence on oil, gas, and oil products. The omnipresence of hydrocarbons in modern society is also what makes it so different to diamonds, which Wenar uses as an example of success in moving away from the rule of effectiveness. Diamonds are a luxury commodity that many can happily live without; oil hardly falls into the same category. The issue that Wenar glides over in his account is the psychological comfort that Western societies draw from knowing that they have access to abundant supplies of hydrocarbons. Energy security policies that the U.S. and EU governments have pursued for years have been driven by the need to

protect their societies from external supply shocks. The rise of energy consumerism in the United States was in different periods of history actively
encouraged by the government—for instance, between the 1930s and
1970s, energy consumption was elevated to an unspoken civic duty,
increasing by 350 percent, whereas in the Cold War, it came to symbolize
individual freedoms and exalt the prosperous lifestyle that U.S. citizens
enjoyed compared to the population of the Soviet Union.[2] Under Clean
Trade, a self-created and self-imposed supply shock that would result from
sanctioning authoritarian hydrocarbons would go against the grain of the
decades-long habit of energy consumerism that has been fostered in Western societies.

The ensuing international oil price increase would trigger demand
destruction. As the impact of the sanctions spreads, the question would
increasingly become whether large segments of voters will accept the self-
imposed restrictions on the resource that under normal market conditions
would be abundantly available. Would the U.S. voters want to sacrifice the
lifestyle that they have been accustomed to for the sake of instilling
resource sovereignty in Africa and Central Asia?

To be sure, the shock would be felt in Europe to a much larger extent
than in the United States, which is forecast to grow its crude production
steadily to 2020. Yet, despite growing production and exports, the United
States is expected to continue to import large volumes of crude: in 2016,
for example, it imported 7.9 million barrels per day, while in the first six
months of 2017 alone, imports rose by 300,000 barrels/day year-on-year.
Imports will remain significant unless U.S. refineries are reconfigured to
process the type of light "sweet" crude from shale that is produced in Texas
and North Dakota—an expensive and time-consuming undertaking.

On the level of principles too, it may be hard to justify the sanctioning
of authoritarian regimes under Clean Trade because it is highly probable
that the populations of the target states will be, at least initially, worse off
as a result of it. The end of slave trade, which Wenar uses throughout the
book, is an excellent example of human determination to end the rule of
effectiveness. But the question in my mind is whether this example is fully
applicable to oil in modern society. After all, when a sufficiently large number of people decided to boycott slave trade, demand for slaves dwindled
and laws were passed against slavery. As a result, the captured individuals
were set free while those who had not been captured no longer lived in
fear. By and large, the measures had an immediate benefit for the people
they were targeting.

By contrast, the lives of people who languish under the oppressive rule
of autocrats could get even worse following the passage of the Clean Trade
Act. It is undoubtedly true that the populations of the authoritarian states
are devoid of many freedoms; they suffer from endemic corruption, threats,

and occasional use of force by the regime. Yet they also, as Wenar explains, see some benefits that trickle down the clientelistic networks as the regime seeks to legitimize its rule. Wenar is spot on when he argues that "violence and clientelism are required strategies for all rent-addicted autocrats" (*Blood Oil*, 41). When oil money is available, autocrats use the combination of the two. For clientelism, in particular, they use "pipelines of state benefits [that] penetrate the population and hierarchize them along its nodes, the pipes becoming increasingly more articulated and smaller towards the bottom."

Thus, benefits trickle down to the people, albeit on a diminishing scale: more to those who are well connected, less to those who are not. During oil booms, high demand for hydrocarbons and high international oil prices swell the state's coffers, making the lives of ordinary people easier as more money streams down to the bottom of the pyramid. Meanwhile, during busts, ordinary people are the first to feel the impact. If sanctions were to be imposed under Clean Trade—and assuming they are well enforced—violence against people may remain the only strategy available to the autocrats under sanctions, worsening the plight of the very people that Wenar wants to help.

This chapter focuses on just how difficult it will be for the West to stop buying hydrocarbons from corrupt, oppressive, and authoritarian states. It starts by examining the concept of "sacrificial places" and the "Us vs. Them" divide between the West and the developing world, which could be inadvertently reinforced, instead of dismantled, as a result of Clean Trade policies—quite opposite to Wenar's intent. The chapter then turns to the examination of the options that the West has, thanks to the breakthrough in shale technology, to replace authoritarian hydrocarbons with its own domestically produced oil and gas. It considers the negative environmental aspects of large-scale development of shale in the West and concludes that, if Clean Trade is consistently reinforced over a prolonged period of time, then the brunt of environmental damage would be borne by those regions in the West that decide to raise production and help meet the supply shortage that would ensue from the imposition of sanctions on authoritarian supplier states.

Green energy is examined next along with Wenar's hope that the world would move away from fossil fuels and toward a more sustainable future. There is no doubt that the share of renewable energy in electricity production will continue to grow in the future and contribute to enhancing energy security. Yet in this analysis, I focus on the challenges of replacing fossil fuels with green energy. Specifically, I examine the problem with rare earth metals which are essential for producing key parts of green technologies. The environmental cost of extracting rare earths has been a deterrent to developing domestic production in the West, particularly as the international prices for the commodity have been low. But the strategic value of rare earths is on the rise, and China, which mines virtually the world's entire output of rare earth metals, could use its control of this market as a lever against the West. This scenario may play out if, for instance, China refused to join Clean Trade, as is distinctly likely, and the West responded by setting up a Clean Hands Trust to collect trade duties on imports from China.

It would be no exaggeration to say that shale has been the type of game changer that has given the West—and the United States in particular—an opportunity to implement Clean Trade. It has enhanced U.S. energy independence and given it the capacity to grow production to the level where it can export to Europe, at least partially compensating for the fall in supplies from the sanctioned authoritarian states. This newly acquired capacity, however, creates a politically charged issue of whether, by promoting sanctions against authoritarian regimes, the United States stands to benefit commercially from Clean Trade. The extraction costs of U.S. shale companies are higher than those of the Middle Eastern and Russian producers, which mine conventional hydrocarbons. As a result, the Clean Trade initiative risks running into the accusation that sanctioning low-cost suppliers would pave the way for increased U.S. exports of shale oil and liquefied natural gas (LNG).

The chapter also focuses on the question of political acceptability of Clean Trade to Washington's European allies and China. The fact that the United States stands to benefit commercially from banning a large percentage of hydrocarbons from the Western market and raising its own exports will significantly undermine the moral argument behind Clean Trade. Europe will see itself, and indeed will be, bearing the bulk of economic costs resulting from the ban of cheap authoritarian supplies (e.g., higher oil prices, recession). China is another international player that will be dissatisfied with the arrangement given its current energy consumption and forecasts for growth. It is unlikely to join Clean Trade because it has already invested billions in the economies of other states, some of which would no doubt be high on Washington's Clean Trade sanctions list. Beijing's strategic energy alliances with Moscow are highly noteworthy, as they demonstrate that the states which Clean Trade will target are not passive "policy takers." Quite the contrary, they are active international players, willing and able to pursue their own highly complex and well-coordinated policies with results that may change Washington's considerations when implementing the Clean Trade strategy.

US VERSUS THEM?

In her 2016 Edward Said lecture, award-winning journalist and author Naomi Klein argued that fossil fuels always require "sacrifice zones."[3] She staked her case on two key claims. The first was that fossil fuels are inherently dirty, so much so that until the 1970s scientists advising the U.S. government openly referred to certain production sites as "national sacrifice areas." Her second claim was that around the world, the constant need for fossil fuels has created "a system built on sacrificial places and sacrificial people" which has been underpinned by intellectual theories that justify the sacrifices. Orientalism, according to Klein, was one such theory that has enabled the West to satisfy its oil dependence by legitimizing the existence of sacrificial zones in resource-rich authoritarian or failed states of the Middle East and Africa. Supported by images of its peoples as "exotic, primitive and bloodthirsty," the theory of othering has made it far easier to legitimize the use of force against them when they suddenly decided to own and control their oil.

Wenar does not discuss Orientalism as such, but his analysis aligns with it in an important way. Up until now, it has been easy for the West to justify the existence of sacrificial places in remote foreign lands where no accountability to an empowered citizenry exists and where oil-rent-addicted authoritarians already plunder their own people using a mix of violence and clientelism. If the West knowingly perpetuates the status quo by continuing to trade with resource-disordered states, does such engagement in itself constitute an act of othering? By drawing mental lines between "Us" and "Them," do Western customers tacitly approve the existence of sacrificial zones because the people inhabiting them are deemed to be different, to be *other*?

So Wenar proposes to dismantle the mental lines and ban authoritarian hydrocarbons from the market. But this creates a distinct possibility that the Clean Trade strategy, despite its most noble intentions, may inadvertently deepen the divide between "Us"—Western, democratic, and prosperous— and "Them"—poor, underprivileged, and authoritarian. If the ban on the import of authoritarian oil were to be instituted, then it is plausible to suggest that the population in the target authoritarian states would come to believe—not least thanks to the mass media in the sanctioned states being under strict government control—that the aim of the sanctions is to impoverish and subdue their country to Western interests. The task of manipulating public opinion would be made easier by the cynical attitudes held by many in the non-Western world about the motivations and methods of the United States and its European allies in spreading democracy.

Thus, the sanctions imposed by the U.S. Treasury against Venezuelan president Nicolás Maduro fed right into his favorite rallying cry against U.S. imperialism that enabled him to take a publicly defiant stance against "Emperor Trump" and proclaim that he "does not obey orders from foreign governments and never will."[4] In another example, the Russian leadership has consistently diverted public attention away from the fact that Western sanctions were imposed on Russia as a result of its illegal annexation of Crimea in 2014. Instead, it has successfully steered the population toward the Kremlin's preferred message that the sanctions' true motivation has been the cynical pursuit by the United States of its own economic and commercial interests. These interests, Kremlin has argued, are focused on oil and gas, and the United States seeks to grow its own energy exports by restricting—through sanctions—Russia's access to Western funding and advanced hydrocarbons technology. The message that Russia is tending to its national interests and fending off competition resonates with many Russians: according to the polls, Russian president Vladimir Putin's approval rating jumped to 88 percent (from the low 60 percents) following the annexation of Crimea, with over 70 percent of Russians agreeing that Crimea's accession to Russia brought more good than bad.[5] Furthermore, most people (64 percent) thought that the sanctions would continue but that Moscow should disregard them and adhere to its own policy (72 percent).[6]

These insights are relevant to our analysis as they suggest that, if Clean Trade sanctions are imposed, then instead of improving governance, the authoritarian leaderships will find a way to use the sanctions to strengthen their own hand domestically. Indeed, they would also have to come up with a strategy to create new income streams once the West stops buying their oil, but the example of Russia demonstrates that it is already well under way in this endeavor. Given the context into which the Clean Trade strategy would be introduced, it may produce results diametrically opposite to its intent and accentuate the already existing—and in the non-Western world, acutely felt and frequently resented—differences between "Us" and "Them."

MOVING SACRIFICIAL PLACES TO THE WEST

Another unintended corollary of Wenar's analysis is that, with the adoption of Clean Trade, the sacrificial places in the West would multiply in size and number. If historically they have been dotted across the globe, the banning of authoritarian hydrocarbons would mean that production sites in the United States, Canada, Australia, and Norway would need to be expanded. The rising price for hydrocarbons would ensure that more resources become economically profitable to extract. This applies directly (though not exclusively) to shale in the United States and tar sands in Canada, the extraction of which has higher environmental costs than conventional hydrocarbons.

Indeed, any large-scale resource extraction is accompanied by risks and environmental costs. These can be managed and minimized, as socially responsible companies have done around the world and across the energy value chain. Nevertheless, the risks such as oil spills cannot be ruled out altogether—an obvious point but one that acquires greater prominence as production moves into the new energy provinces in which the industry has relatively little experience or where technology for cleaning up oil spills does not yet exist, such as the Arctic offshore. Moreover, environmental impacts vary with the type of production: for instance, hydraulic fracturing requires large swathes of land and millions of gallons of fresh water to develop a single well.[7]

The amount of water needed in hydraulic fracturing depends on the type of formation (shale, tight sand, coalbed) as well as the depth and length of the well, fracturing fluid properties, and so on. But there is no doubt that shale wells require significantly more water than, say, coalbed methane formations: in 2010–2011, the latter needed between 50,000 and 350,000 gallons of water per well; the former between 2 million and 4 million.[8] In 2011, when 35,000 shale wells were fracked across the United States, the annual water requirement hovered around 140 billion gallons. By 2015, the number of hydraulically fractured wells had grown to around 300,000.[9] Moreover, the amount of water injected has grown steadily over time as companies increased the size of the wells in order to raise productivity and stay competitive in the face of plunging oil prices. The amount of water used per average well increased from 3 million gallons of water in 2012 to 6.7 million in 2015 and 9.5 million in 2016.[10] Only between 10 percent and 40 percent of the water used during hydraulic fracturing is estimated to be recoverable after injection, and challenges remain with treating and reusing this water due to the high concentration of dissolved solids and other chemicals.[11]

Much of the U.S. drilling is concentrated in areas where water is already in short supply or where droughts have been recurrent, raising the risk of increased competition for this resource between the industry and other users. Withdrawals of large volumes of water have been a source of serious concern even at the levels of production witnessed in 2012–2017, with multiple studies addressing risk issues such as the volume and quality of water as well as the impact on geology. But in a Clean Trade world, augmenting shale production to the level where the United States would compensate for the sanctioned authoritarian hydrocarbons would not just exacerbate the problem of water scarcity but elevate it to a new level.

It is clear that the U.S. shale revolution and its newly gained energy independence have not come without environmental costs and risks. Some of the costs, such as methane leaks, are still poorly understood and fall into the category of major future uncertainties. For instance, until recently it was not even known that shale released methane in pre-production stage.[12] The analysis of the samples collected in Pennsylvania in 2012 revealed that methane release from hydraulic fracturing sites exceeded the EPA's expected rate from that stage of drilling between a hundred and a thousand times. As a heat-trapping greenhouse gas, methane is thirty-four times more powerful than carbon dioxide over a one-hundred-year time frame and eighty-six times more potent over a twenty-year time frame. The latest studies show that the impact that methane emissions will have on climate change is complex and difficult to predict, and at least one major study, led by an ecology and environmental biology professor at Cornell University, has argued that methane leaks must be treated in the same way as carbon dioxide because of their effect on climate change.[13] The results of the study, if true, are paramount because the increase in shale gas extraction would lead to the rise in methane emissions which, if left under-reported and uncaptured (as they are today), would exacerbate the earth's greenhouse gas problem.[14] Curbing exports of blood oil by increasing shale production many-fold may then not be the sustainable solution for the free world.

As a final note, it is worth stating that the implementation of Clean Trade would highlight that many Western stakeholders are not prepared to bear the environmental costs of shale production. In 2017, following an intensive grassroots campaign, the Australian state of Victoria permanently banned the exploration and production of shale oil and gas as well as coalbed methane gas. This is precisely the type of outcome that Wenar would applaud: a decision taken as a result of engaging with local communities where people who live on the land exercise their right to choose what to do with their resources. This is, in my interpretation of Wenar's analysis, what he hopes one day to achieve for all resource-rich states. Clean Trade is a means to get there. The complication arises from the fact that Victoria is not the only entity to have banned exploration and production for unconventional hydrocarbons. The list of places where mining companies have been prohibited from drilling is growing, and this heightens the risk that if oil and gas sanctions against authoritarian states come into force, democratic resource-rich countries will not produce the necessary volumes to pick up the slack in supply.

Just months before Victoria, the government of Canada's New Brunswick province announced that it would indefinitely extend the moratorium on hydraulic fracturing. Moratoria and bans on fracking were also introduced in Nova Scotia and Quebec after grassroots campaigns and several environmental studies, although the latter subsequently reversed course and approved drilling permits. The shale-rich state of New York became the first U.S. state to ban fracking on its territory in 2014, while internationally, France was an early mover when it passed the law banning exploration and production of shale hydrocarbons as early as 2011. France is believed to have some of Europe's largest shale reserves at 3.9 trillion cubic meters but, as not enough drilling has been done, these reserves remain unproven.[15] France's revocation of the exploration licenses of Total and Texas-based

Schuepbach Energy was intended to close the matter definitively. When Schuepbach disputed the fairness of the law in court, France's constitutional court upheld the ban, ruling that the legislation against hydraulic fracturing was a valid means of protecting the environment.[16]

The irony is that, having banned fracking on its own territory, France has been importing shale energy from the United States. This has not been lost on some industry observers who called France's actions hypocritical in that it is willing to damage someone else's environment but not its own.[17] A similar situation persists in the Netherlands where despite the moratorium on the development of shale until 2020, the port of Rotterdam, Europe's largest liquid bulk cargo hub, accepts shale cargoes from overseas. This raises an important question for Clean Trade: would the unwillingness of a growing number of democratic energy-rich states that refuse to bear the environmental cost of mining breed resentment among those Western allies that continue to produce hydrocarbons? A legitimate question that they may ask is why they should bear the brunt of the increased environmental burden that will result from the intensification of drilling—and particularly hydraulic fracturing—when demand for Western-produced hydrocarbons surges. Would they not become the new sacrificial places of the West?

One possibility, of course, is to stop drilling. Wenar would probably favor this option. He accepts that Clean Trade would come at a cost and that Western consumers should be prepared to bear it, but, after decades of energy abundance, little can prepare an average Western consumer for what would happen if authoritarian oil was to be sanctioned overnight and domestic producers found themselves unable—for any number of reasons, from legislative to technical constraints—to increase production quickly enough.

THE PROBLEM WITH GREEN ENERGY

Green energy is a key component of Wenar's solution to stop relying on authoritarian oil. He believes that major Western consumers should not just "taper off stolen oil"; they should also set reduction targets for the consumption of oil and gas (*Blood Oil*, 304). Indeed, with a growing number of governments adopting ambitious renewables targets, the move away from fossil fuels forms part of the solution. The problem with green energy is twofold. The first is the cost of implementation and the fact that any missed renewables targets, in the face of growing demand, would be covered by fossil fuels, creating a major alternative market for authoritarian hydrocarbons. The second is the current predominant position of China in mining and processing rare earth metals—essential for key components of renewable technologies—and the resultant political repercussion of increasing this dependence by switching to renewables at a faster rate.

In December 2016, the Dutch government unveiled a long-term energy plan to stop selling cars with combustion engines from 2035, replacing them with EV and hydrogen-powered vehicles.[18] The government also intends to disconnect all houses from the gas grid by 2050. The cost-benefit analysis of such a move conducted by McKinsey concluded that the changes would require capital and operational expenses of approximately 10 billion euros per annum—some 2.5 billion more than for a fossil-fuel reliant scenario.[19] This may be possible for a small and wealthy country such as the Netherlands, although McKinsey stated in their report that ensuring a transition of this magnitude would be a "formidable task" with limited precedents.

Technologically, the success of any major move away from fossil fuels would depend on three factors: the development of the system's renewable power generation capacity; demand management; and energy storage. The latter is fundamental because energy from renewables is intermittent and a smart grid capable of distribution to the extent that any location can be supplied with sufficient electricity at the time when demand arises is still some years away. To mitigate intermittency problems, deliver power into peak demand periods, and support transmission systems reliably, the grid would need access to significant electricity storage on a scale that far eclipses the capacity of existing technologies (e.g., batteries, supercapacitors, molten salt thermal energy storage). Today, such technologies are not yet sufficiently cost effective and operate only on a small scale or are still under development.

If it is challenging even for a small, developed state to abandon fossil fuels, then what about large developing states? India is a case in point. In May 2017, the Indian government committed to generate 40 percent of electricity from renewable energy sources by 2030.[20] India is a key international market which will generate, along with China, almost half of the world's energy demand growth to 2035. In fact, according to *BP Energy Outlook 2017* forecasts, India could overtake China as the fastest growing market for energy in the world by the end of the forecast period.[21] Expecting massive increases in demand, the government increased in 2015 the country's solar power targets from 20,000 MW to 100,000 MW by 2022. It has so far failed to deliver: the 2016–2017 target for grid-connected solar projects was 12,000 MW (to March 31, 2017); the actual performance (as of December 31, 2016) was a mere 19 percent of this target, indicating just how far the reality can lag behind aspirations.[22] If the targets continue to be missed while demand rises at the anticipated rate, then the difference would have to be made up with fossil fuels: coal, oil, and gas.

Energy developments in India are highly pertinent to our analysis of the obstacles that Clean Trade would encounter with its implementation. By virtue of its growing market, India is an emerging destination for oil and gas. It is to India and China that authoritarian states, such as Russia, will seek to send their hydrocarbons. The focus on these markets would intensify should states be banned from selling their production in the Western world under Clean Trade. Consequently, the effect of Western sanctions would be negated or greatly weakened by the presence of alternative Asian markets. By turning to Asia, authoritarian states would diversify the outlets for their hydrocarbons, ensure new revenue streams, and strengthen their grip on power.

The analysis in the next section will demonstrate that the pivot to Asia is already under way in Russia, accelerated by the sanctions that the West imposed on Moscow in response to its annexation of Crimea. Here, however, we turn to the examination of the second problem with green energy: rare earth minerals. I agree with Wenar that part of the answer to ending effectiveness-based trade in hydrocarbons lies in ensuring a faster transition to green energy. But the pace, trajectory, and, ultimately, success of this transition will depend at least partly on the dynamics of the current market. One reality that will affect the West in this area is its dependence on China in mining and processing rare earth metals. An unmanaged transition away from fossil fuels and toward renewable energy would risk deepening this dependence.

Today, all renewable technologies use rare earth metals for their key parts. This includes wind turbines, electric car batteries, and solar panels. Despite some investments in the West, China continues to control the lion's share of the world's production of rare earth metals—roughly 95 percent.[23] A recent Massachusetts Institute of Technology report highlighted neodymium (Nd), Europium (Eu), Terbium (Tb), Yttrium (Y), and Dysprosium (Dy) as particularly important rare earth metals "due to scarcity, high demand and criticality in much needed high-tech application."[24] Industrial demand for these rare earths is projected to increase by up to 2,600 percent in the period to 2025, highlighting their strategic importance to a world that seeks to transition to a more sustainable energy future. Both the U.S. Department of Energy and European Union have issued warnings of impending rare earths shortages.[25] Until the production of rare earth metals is geographically diversified, replacing fossil fuels with renewable energy will come at the cost of significantly greater imports of rare earths from China—hardly a politically palatable option for Western democracies.

It is notable that rare earth metals are not in fact that rare and can be found across the globe, with some of the largest deposits concentrated in Canada, the United States, Brazil, Russia, India, Australia, and Malaysia. Yet production of these metals is often unprofitable because rare earth elements do not tend to occur in sufficiently large concentration in economically exploitable ore deposits and extracting them comes at a high environmental cost. Transitioning to renewables without increased reliance

on China would require Western countries to make a choice: either stimulate production of rare earths around the world or mine them domestically.
If extraction is developed in authoritarian states, it risks creating the same
pattern of dependency on tainted products as currently experienced in
hydrocarbons—only this time in rare earth metals. Indeed, the experience
of China's rare-earth producing provinces demonstrates that this natural
resource is not immune to violent behavior from gangster miners, refiners,
and black marketeers.[26] Meanwhile, setting up large-scale production in
democratic countries is likely to be resisted on environmental grounds—
given the high risks of radioactive contamination, rare earth mining in the
West could encounter even more vocal and headstrong resistance than in
shale.

Processing rare earths is a remarkably dirty endeavor. Their ore is almost
always laced with radioactive materials such as thorium, which can form
into thorium dust, known to cause lung cancer. Other substances that are
either found in the deposits or used to process them are heavy metals, sul-
phates, ammonia, hydrochloric acid, and so on; for humans, they are toxic,
carcinogenic, or both. Over two thousand tons of waste result from the
production of one ton of rare earth oxide—the most common finished
product.[27] Wastewater is also a major concern in the mining of rare earths.
In 1998, the local water board in the United States fined Molycorp, the
only miner and processor of rare earths in the United States, over $400,000
after its Mountain Pass Mine in California repeatedly leaked wastewater.[28]
The company stopped its separating operations at the site that year to avoid
further leaks and fines, and ceased all operations in 2002. The following
decade was characterized by attempts to restructure and invest but, given
high costs and low international prices for the commodity, the company
was forced to file for bankruptcy protection in 2015. Prior to this closure,
the United States ranked as the number three producer of rare earths in the
world with the output of 5,900 tons. It was dwarfed by China's official
output quota of 105,000 tons; the actual production was estimated to be
considerably higher, at over 150,000 tons, due to illegal mining and
smuggling.[29]

Indeed, China's market dominance has been a notable source of concern
since July 2010 when Beijing briefly cut its annual export quotas by 37
percent on the previous year. Export cuts to Europe and the United States
were followed by a decision two months later to stop all exports of rare
earths to Japan, in a move widely seen to have been prompted by a maritime dispute.[30] The panic that ensued led to an unprecedented spike in
international prices for the commodity: the price of dysprosium, for example, increased by over 2,000 percent on the 2008 levels. Even though some
gradual reduction in Chinese export quotas had taken place prior to 2010,
it was the events that unfolded that year that made the West realize the

extent of its dependence on China for this strategic commodity. The episode is relevant for our discussion on Clean Trade as it raises the question of whether Beijing would be prepared to use the lack of geographic diversity in this strategic market as a political lever against the West. The use of the lever may become particularly tempting in a scenario where a Clean Hands Trust is set up, as outlined by Wenar, and the West decides to impose trade duties on Chinese imports in response to Beijing's refusal to join Clean Trade. The 2010 experience provides a glimpse of the reaction that would ensue in the West, laying bare the vulnerability of the importing states.

Thus, China's current monopoly in the rare earths market is an impediment to the West's ability to implement Clean Trade because a rapid transition to green energy that would be necessary to reduce imports of authoritarian hydrocarbons would come at an unacceptably high political cost. But a more gradual transition is possible and may even be aided by domestic developments in China. It is widely accepted that rare-earth mining and processing in China has caused severe ecological degradation, which has impacted the health of people living around production sites. To tackle pollution and bring supply under control, the government has initiated a clampdown on illegal mining and black market activities. This clampdown differs from the earlier government efforts in that it has progressed alongside the adoption in 2016 of the first Five-Year Plan for the Rare Earth Industry and has been concomitant with industry consolidation that envisage the creation of six state-owned enterprises by 2020.[31] The measures yielded first results by mid-2017, as the prices of rare earths surged: praseodymium-neodymium oxide, for instance, went up by 80 percent in the first six months of the year.[32]

Sustained high international prices would stimulate the development and reopening of rare earth metal mines around the world. While in the near-term perspective China will remain the preponderant player in the market, its ruthless exploitation of resources has led to their rapid depletion, with the Chinese share of world rare earth metals deposits falling from 70 percent to 37 percent.[33] At the right price, companies will become motivated to invest in Africa and in the United States—and the question of sacrificial places will arise once again.

MAKERS OF THEIR OWN DESTINY

In this section, I would like to discuss Wenar's claim that the Clean Trade strategy "should never presume enemies" and that, as a set of policies, Clean Trade is non-interventionist in character. I share Michael Blake's concern (in chapter 2 of this volume) that the sanctions envisaged under a Clean Trade Act will be "received as (very nearly) acts of war by those against whom they are brought to bear" (p. 46). Moreover, the states which will be targeted by Clean Trade will not be passive policy-takers but active international actors willing and able to respond to any measures imposed by the West, using significant resources at their disposal to mastermind strategies that would weaken the impact of sanctions. The case of Western sanctions imposed against Russia in 2014 in the aftermath of its annexation of Crimea provides insights on how target states are likely to interpret Clean Trade sanctions and how the leaderships of those states could attempt to turn the situation to their advantage.

Faced with Russia's blatant violation of the territorial integrity of Ukraine, the West presented a relatively united façade in its attempt to deal with the problem. The United States, the EU, Australia, Canada, Norway, Switzerland, and Japan condemned Russia's actions and imposed a series of measures including asset freezes, travel bans, and restrictions on capital and technology. Sanctions on capital and technology, imposed in the summer of 2014, were particularly important as they targeted the Russian oil and gas sector, and were specifically designed to disrupt the development of Russia's new hydrocarbons provinces, such as the Arctic, East Siberia, and the Russian Far East. It was well known, not least from Russia's official strategic documentation, that Russia assigned priority to the development of these hydrocarbons-rich regions but that it lacked equipment and expertise to drill complex wells, particularly offshore, in the icy waters of the Arctic. Russia also lacked the colossal funds required for the exploration, production, and transportation of hydrocarbons from those provinces, the task rendered significantly more difficult by the general under-development of infrastructure in the country's east. Investing in new oil and gas extraction and transportation facilities had been regarded as necessary because of the ongoing depletion of Russia's traditional production region of Western Siberia, but the financial burden became particularly onerous at the time of low international oil prices. These considerations led policy-makers in the West to conclude that the designed sanctions had a good chance of succeeding and making Russia reverse its policy course on Ukraine (and ideally, stem its aggressive policy vis-à-vis the West).

The results have not been encouraging. By 2017, Russia had diversified its markets to China and expanded its product range to liquefied gas, which has given it more flexibility to export globally.[34] Perceptions that underlined Russia's actions had been fundamental in propelling it to respond to sanctions the way it did—assertively and in a coordinated manner. Below we set out three clusters of perceptions based on the examination of Russia's strategic documentation and official statements.

First, Western sanctions were interpreted in Moscow as an attempt to limit Russia's future exports of hydrocarbons; this alone meant that they were seen as interventionist and hostile. Russia considers maintaining and strengthening its position as the world's leading energy exporter to be its top national priority because energy exports—and the revenue that they bring—are seen as an "instrument for conducting internal and external policy."[35] Designing measures to counteract Western sanctions became therefore paramount and a matter of national security.

Second, Russia understands the sanctions to be an instrument in the hands of Washington to compete with Moscow politically. Russia's growing sense of vulnerability and insecurity was revealed, for instance, in the National Security Strategy of the Russian Federation to 2020, adopted in 2015—soon after the imposition of sanctions. The Strategy asserts that pressure exerted through sanctions imposed by "the USA and its allies seeking to maintain their dominance in world affairs" is an instrument to "contain" Russia. It also emphasizes that a full spectrum of political, financial-economic, and informational tools is being used against Russia.[36] The sanctions were therefore perceived as hostile U.S. attempts to expand its political dominance as the world's only remaining superpower. Moscow's concerted determination to oppose the United States and, if necessary, its allies and build, in coordination with China, another pole of global power became known as "post-West."

Third, Russia regards the sanctions as a tool to promote U.S. economic and commercial interests in exporting its own hydrocarbons. Putin, for example, is on record stating that the United States is using its "geopolitical advantages in a competitive struggle with the aim of securing its economic interests" and is doing so "with particular cynicism."[37] Russia's initial disbelief about the impact that shale production would have on the international market gave way to the acceptance that the change was structural and thus would affect the global demand-supply for decades to come. This acceptance strengthened Russia's determination to compete against the United States in order to preserve and grow its share of the international oil and gas market. It also reinforced Moscow's perception that the sanctions were a hostile act aimed at undercutting Russia's competitive advantage in hydrocarbons and creating a favorable environment for American shale producers.

Two key developments highlighted the seriousness of the U.S. threat to Russia's export plans. The first was the lifting in December 2015 of the ban on U.S. crude oil exports which had been in place since 1975. It came months after the imposition of the Western sanctions and enabled the United States to ramp up its exports. Very significantly, Russia's key target market, China, became the number one customer for U.S. oil.[38]

The second development was the start-up and rapid expansion of the Sabine Pass LNG terminal, which in June 2017 began exporting liquefied gas from its terminal in Louisiana to South Korea under the terms of a twenty-year deal. Earlier that month, Poland received its first delivery of

U.S. LNG in what many Polish politicians, long keen to reduce their country's dependence on Russian gas, viewed as a historical moment. Days later, Lithuania signed a deal for the supply of U.S. LNG, and this was delivered in late August. Sabine Pass is the first LNG export terminal in the United States but another five are under construction and a further four have received government approval.[39] Indeed, President Donald Trump's personal vocal support for energy exports, coupled with a statement of the U.S. Commerce Department in May 2017 affirming that the United States "welcomes China" as a buyer of U.S. LNG, has reinforced Moscow's perceptions that the sanctions are commercially motivated and have used the annexation of Crimea as a convenient pretext.

What is the relevance of this analysis and indeed of this sanctions regime for Clean Trade? The answer is two-fold.

The first is that the willingness of the Western states to impose and adhere to sanctions will depend on the costs that they are asked to bear, which will have a material impact on the unity of the sanctioning coalition and will, in turn, determine the effectiveness of the sanctions. Wenar's analysis appears to assume that Western countries will, or at least should, act in unison. However, this is not a given, especially if allies regard the leading sanctioning state to be commercially profiting from the arrangement.

Post-Crimea, the West was agreed in principle that Russia had violated the territorial integrity of another state, but even so, in the words of the then U.S. vice president, Joe Biden, the United States found itself in a position of "oft times almost having to embarrass Europe to stand up and take economic hits to impose costs."[40] The end result was the imposition by the United States and the European Union of separate sanctions that differed in an important way: the EU, in the light of its dependence on Russian gas, deliberately avoided targeting gas production. If we extrapolate from this experience, and assuming Clean Trade sanctions will cover authoritarian oil *and* gas, then it is plausible to suggest that Europe will find itself in a precarious position. Sanctioning authoritarian hydrocarbons will raise the international price of oil which will benefit Western suppliers—most notably, the United States, Australia, and Norway. Europe, which forecasts show will grow more reliant on gas as its indigenous reserves are depleted, would be left to foot the bill, even if supply flows remain uninterrupted thanks to the United States making up the difference. As the leading state behind Clean Trade, the United States would be open to accusations by its European allies of acting out of self-interest and in pursuit of commercial gain. The moral legitimacy of Clean Trade would be undermined by the very circumstance that makes its implementation easier: the commercial advent of shale in the United States. Russia would no doubt exploit the schisms between the United States and Europe, which would be highly damaging for the unity of the West.

The second key point of relevance is that perceptions of the state under sanctions matter. Deciphering the true motives of the U.S. government behind the Russian sanctions regime is outside the scope of this chapter. Our main concern is with perceptions, the examination of which has revealed that the Russian government regards the sanctions not as a response to Moscow's violations of the fundamental principle of international law but as a pretext used by the United States to circumscribe Russia and further its own geopolitical and commercial interests. The conclusion relevant for Clean Trade is that if the target state believes that the sanctions are motivated by greed and self-interest, it will not reform.

Quite the opposite, as the Russian case demonstrates, the state may seek to mobilize its resources and take action to counter the sanctions. The significance of energy exports to Russia's national security led the government to undertake coordinated efforts to design and implement a strategy of diversification. Whereas prior to the imposition of sanctions, diversification referred only to Russia's commitment to bypass transit routes through Ukraine, following the sanctions, the strategy has come to encompass the expansion into LNG and, geographically, into Asia. The strategy is designed to give Russia the flexibility to send its cargoes globally through LNG and access the high-growth Asian market through dedicated pipeline infrastructure. In line with this thinking, Russia constructed the $27 billion Yamal LNG project, and pre-sold all output to Asian buyers on long-term contracts thereby securing demand for its commodity. Given the sanctions limiting its access to Western capital and LNG technology, Russia made a concerted effort to attract Chinese funding and did so with considerable success. Pipeline diversification also proceeded at pace, with Russia set to expand the capacity of the eastern oil pipelines to China and of the Pacific port at Kozmino Bay (from which cargoes are transported to Japan, South Korea, and Malaysia) by 2020. In fact, China became the dominant purchaser of Russian eastern crude already in 2016, but with the expansion, Russia can be expected permanently to displace Saudi Arabia as China's largest oil supplier. In gas also, Russia ended years of procrastination and disagreements with China, and moved promptly in 2014 to sign a major agreement to build a $55 billion Power of Siberia pipeline to north-eastern China, with the first gas flows expected between May 2019 and May 2021 (the exact dates are under negotiation). It has been confirmed that China will annually purchase 36.8 billion cubic meters of gas over a thirty-year period.[41]

The fact that the Russian state under sanctions has been successful in working with Asian stakeholders to finance large-scale projects at the time of low international oil prices and has secured demand through long-term contracts illuminates the high level of coordination at the highest level of government. Not only did the sanctions fail to make Russia reform and adhere to international law, but they have incentivized it to find new outlets for its strategic commodity sooner than would have happened in the absence of sanctions, under the business-as-usual scenario, where the majority of exports were orientated toward the West. Should Clean Trade sanctions be applied to Russia in the future, their effect would be severely undermined by the existence of oil and gas infrastructure to the east. Western sanctions would not carry the necessary weight as Russia will have already secured multiple outlets for its oil and gas and, with them, new revenue streams. Having invested billions in various hydrocarbons projects in Russia (as well as Africa and Central Asia) and signed binding long-terms deals, China is highly unlikely to join Clean Trade. China's failure to participate would further reduce the effect of sanctions aimed at ending the rule of effectiveness in resource trade.

A FUTURE FOR CLEAN TRADE

Wenar's thinking on how to reduce global injustice is extraordinary and thought-provoking. His empirical work is remarkable. He builds his analysis on a strong and well-argued claim that in countries where people and institutions are weak, resources are taken away from citizens, yielding no or minimal benefits to them and instead benefiting ruling regimes, which are often corrupt and violent. Wenar supports his claim by drawing on a plethora of examples from across the world through which he portrays the rule of effectiveness in the twenty-first century and the West's contribution to sustaining it. His book is a call to action and one that has the potential to change the world for the better.

What I have sought to achieve in this chapter is to highlight some of the areas where Clean Trade—the strategy that Wenar has designed to help restore resource sovereignty—may produce results opposite to intent. Several scenarios have been considered where a sanctions regime could leave the West short of hydrocarbons but without tangible benefits for the oppressed people of the energy-rich states. Scenarios have also been considered where rapid transition to green energy could make the West vulnerable to Chinese pressure, and those where high demand from Asia would galvanize energy-rich states to send their resources to this large alternative market, thereby enhancing the options of the ruling authoritarian regimes and reducing those of the West.

I support Wenar's conclusion that Chinese cooperation would be essential for Clean Trade to succeed but remain pessimistic that Beijing would be interested in breaking off its hard-won partnerships and deals with autocratic states. On the one hand, Beijing has invested billions in the economies of Africa, Central Asia, and Russia to guarantee future hydrocarbons supplies and the results of these efforts have only recently started to pay off. On the other hand, the reticence of China to engage seriously with the International Energy Agency is evidence that energy continues to be seen in national rather than multilateral terms.[42] Faced with the need to reduce coal consumption and find sources of gas (which is a cleaner fuel), Beijing has followed a self-help policy in energy and de-ideologized its energy relationships. As such, it would be unwilling to join the West in its quest for greater energy justice in the world. Moreover, as the above analysis shows, the fact that the shale boom has made the United States an exporter of oil and gas will make many, including China, question the sincerity of U.S. motives should Washington officially pick up the mantle of promoting Clean Trade. Indeed, as the analysis in this chapter has demonstrated, making up the shortfall in supplies to Europe and China that would result from an energy embargo on authoritarian states would be a very mixed blessing for the United States. Ruthless exploitation of U.S. shale reserves that would be required to compensate for the sanctioned hydrocarbons and meet Western and Chinese demand could cause profound damage to the environment and is likely to be opposed by U.S. voters.

There is nonetheless hope for Clean Trade. It lies in the development of new technologies which would enable the world to reduce reliance on oil and gas from authoritarian states without putting excessive pressure on Western producers. Nanotechnologies may be part of the solution: a breakthrough in this area could increase efficiencies of, say, solar cells beyond what is feasible today. In fact, research in this area shows great potential, especially in the utilization of nanotechnologies for the enhancement of electrical energy storage like batteries and super-capacitors.[43]

Furthermore, investment in research could lead to innovation that would enable a faster transition to green energy without exponentially increasing the West's dependence on rare earth minerals—and on China. Indeed, reports suggest that some nanotechnology-enabled technologies may not even require rare earths. For instance, nanocrystals of magnetic elements such as iron, nickel, and cobalt have been used to make rare-earth-free magnets. In other laboratory experiments, nanoparticles of a rare earth metal were mixed with iron nanoparticles to manufacture higher-performing magnets for generators and electric motors than those currently in use. These examples demonstrate the potential of nanotechnologies that could revolutionize the renewables energy sector and stimulate the West's transition away from fossil fuels.

A faster transition to green energy in Europe would not, of course, preclude China from buying authoritarian hydrocarbons and Beijing may well continue to refuse to join Clean Trade. However, a breakthrough in the application of nanotechnologies in the energy sector would significantly enhance the chances of success for Clean Trade for three reasons. First, it would enhance renewable electricity generation and storage in the West, meeting part of the domestic demand and reducing the cost of sanctions for the West. Second, it would stimulate the development and use of renewable energy technologies without dramatically increasing reliance on China for rare earth metals. Recycling and reuse of rare earths, which is currently low, would also stimulate transition to green energy. If nanotechnology-enhanced green energy production proves to be commercially viable, Beijing will almost certainly be keen to adopt similar technologies in order to lower its reliance on imported oil and gas, and reduce the ecological impact on the environment. If adopted on a large scale, nanotechnological innovations in renewables could permanently reduce demand for authoritarian hydrocarbons.

There is also some scope for ground-breaking discoveries in hydrocarbons that could prove to be game-changers. For instance, in May 2017, China announced a major breakthrough in the extraction of gas from an ice-like substance under the South China Sea. The substance, known as methane hydrates, or "flammable ice," is thought to be the world's last abundant source of carbon-based fuel. Producing it is difficult, energy-consuming, and prone to a greater climate change risk than from carbon dioxide. Yet if extraction can be made safe and commercial, the reserves will not disappoint. Found in sediments under the ocean floor and underneath permafrost on land, methane hydrates are estimated to be ten times more abundant than shale—and that is on conservative estimates.[44] Commercializing these reserves would drastically cut China's import dependence on hydrocarbons, which may lead Beijing to change its stance on Clean Trade.

A joint effort by the West and China to end the rule of effectiveness and restore energy sovereignty would stand a far greater chance of succeeding. The answer then hinges on a technological breakthrough, which would reduce reliance on oil and gas from authoritarian states and open new frontiers for Clean Trade advocates.

4

Collective Resource Control and the Power of Complicity

Christopher Kutz

Leif Wenar's chapter in this volume, like his book *Blood Oil*, from which it is drawn, is an example of public philosophy at its best, especially in its role of making the unobvious obvious.[1] In this case, the unobvious obvious is the First World consumption of petroproducts, in complete indifference even by self-described progressives, to the conditions of their extraction. As a life-resident in Berkeley, California, I know whereof I speak: there are few consumers in the world as concerned, to the point of ethical narcissism, with the ethical genealogy of their consumption. I don't believe I could buy a cup of *unfair* trade coffee if I wanted, nor an unethical chicken egg; and I am reasonably sure the diamonds in the jewelry shops have not emerged from civil conflict. But while environmental concerns about petroleum versus electric are ubiquitous—SUV drivers receive dirty looks—I have never heard anyone even express the mildest concern that the gasoline they put into their Priuses has returned a profit to murderous oligarchs.

Given existing concerns with the ethical sourcing of our consumption, Wenar's argument that we should extend those principles to petroproducts would seem incontestable or rather contestable only because of moral cowardice. It is a further virtue of Wenar's approach that it intersects tightly with more straightforwardly pragmatic concerns about the negative effects of current global petroleum markets, insofar as they feed domestic and international terrorism and repression. The combination of a clear moral principle and a strong consequentialist argument can appeal across a range of both philosophical and political positions: a sanctions regime for Putin's

Russia and Saudi Arabia is something that both left and right can probably
be brought to rally around. But a reader might worry that the intersection
of principle and consequence is too easy, and rests too much on empirical
predictions. If there is a vulnerability in Wenar's argument, it lies at the
level of mediating principle, a way of connecting the evil of the source to
the wrongness of consumption, and of connecting the political value of
accountability for natural resources to the claims that inhabitants of the
resource rich territories can claim. My aim, therefore, is not so much to
dispute Wenar's general conclusions, nor even his premises, but instead to
offer an alternative philosophical path between the two.

I thus aim to explore the following three points. First, can Popular
Resource Sovereignty be secured by arguments directly from principle, and
not only as instrumental, welfarist claims? I will suggest that it can, modi-
fied to protect residents as well as citizens, by working through the moral
status of a people understood in terms of collective political agency. Second, is the relevant concern popular control over natural resources, or popular access? I will argue that choosing control threatens to make Clean
Trade more interventionist than Wenar might like. Third, what are the kinds
of motivations that can best secure the success of a Clean Trade program
that can come at a cost to the state imposing it? I will argue that shame and
guilt, the emotions constitutive of complicity, are less likely to be reliable
motivations for Clean Trade than more positive emotions, associated with
human development.

I should say at the outset that while I offer criticisms, at the level of
principle, of some of Wenar's claims, those criticisms are mixed with admi-
ration for the straightforward pragmatism of his approach, and his remarkable success in translating a set of widely shared but diffuse concerns into
a genuinely viable path for political action. Whatever the abstract merits of
founding a political philosophy position on a commitment to cosmopolitanism, nation-based Popular Resource Sovereignty is, relative to the moral
status quo, a defensible and attractive improvement. Even without commitment to Wenar's particular form of consequentialism, I believe that anyone
can profit from his exploration of how we should think about relations of
dominance and inequality in our commercial relationships.

Begin with Wenar's principal philosophical question: who should own the
natural resources of a nation-state? By "own" Wenar is engaging a public
form of the traditional bundle of private property rights: ownership con-
sists, in his sense, of the right to control, in the name of the state, the
conditions of consumption or transfer of the resources in question. Call
this a principle of resource allocation. Wenar contrasts three possible models of resource allocation. The first is the status quo, which he calls, rather
contentiously, "Might Makes Right" (MMR). This name accurately describes

the effects of contemporary practice, according to which, in the absence of sanctions, international buyers need pay attention only to who actually controls a resource in order to establish a right to purchase (and hence a right to sell). The second model is his preferred alternative, Popular Resource Sovereignty, according to which the control of the resources is exercised effectively even if indirectly by the citizens of the country where the resource is found. The third alternative is Cosmopolitanism: that all the earth's resources should be treated as belonging to all the world, and thus that their benefits must be distributed globally on something like an egalitarian per capita basis.[2]

Wenar's argument for Popular Resource Sovereignty is principally pragmatic or consequentialist, as the last, best theory standing after considering the other two, and given what he sees as widely shared values of political unity in diversity, or diversity in unity.[3] The effects of the status quo, MMR model, speak for themselves: unless a country already has robust institutions of democratic self-rule in place prior to the discovery of oil (or any other natural resource), the MMR system generates powerful incentives for looting by internal power-seekers and exploitation by external powers. The follow-on effects of fueling international terrorism and armaments add additional power to the indictment.

Wenar, unsurprisingly, does not attempt to supply a prima facie basis for the MMR argument; he develops it as an uncharitable but not implausible interpretation of current international practice. With respect to the citizens of the resource state, there can of course be no principled argument that allocates all resources to him or those who can most effectively capture them. At best, one can construct a wobbly, pragmatic, Hobbesian argument that, in the absence of already present democratic institutions, a prize system will create proper incentives for state-wide consolidation of power, and resulting stability for a populace. Indeed, with respect to citizens, one might well dispute whether MMR names a normative principle at all—any more than the thief who pawns my stereo has a right to do so. Internally, MMR simply delineates physical control over a resource. The fact that someone occupying a position of power has seized and then sold the resource gives a citizen no normative reason to respect the claims of the sale.

Externally, with respect to other states, MMR is perhaps more like a normative principle, though not understood in those terms. Foreign buyers, not in contravention of UN or domestic sanctions, will come to hold a valid title to the resource, in the sense that they can defend their purchase (at least within a narrow, legal frame) from objectors. Thus, Exxon is within its legal rights to buy oil from Saudi Arabia and resell it to gas stations, which then resell it to you.[4] Because the legal title of the intermediate and end purchaser is regarded by America (and all other countries) as legitimate, we can say that something like MMR is indeed the operative principle. In fact, a better description of the operative principle would probably be "Sovereign-Determined Transfer Rights" (SDTRs). Were pirates to seize a freighter of Saudi oil en route to the United States and try to sell it, their right to sell would not be recognized—even though the pirates had physical control over the resource. Unless and until the seizure is cloaked with the garb of national sovereignty, no right can be found. Title to resources thus rides, normatively, on the back of the Realist principle of sovereignty with which the international system operates. By default, a nation is deemed sovereign with respect to international actors just so long as it has a government effectively wielding control over a specific territory and people.[5] Such sovereignty is anything but absolute—it is routinely pierced overtly and covertly by international organizations and foreign powers—but it has the normative effect within the international system of regularizing certain acts and transactions as representing the state as a whole. MMR is one strand in the rope that comprises the incidents of sovereignty: the capacity of the state to make its goods and resources available for export on the global market.

There is an obvious instrumental argument for a system of sovereignty in some form—roughly a Realist version of the argument made by Immanuel Kant in "Perpetual Peace" and echoed in Rawls's *Law of Peoples*.[6] A system of sovereignty, which entails domestic control over fundamental property relations and structures of justice, enables a people to engage in collective self-government on equal terms. In brief, statelessness under-protects human interests, while world government would tend to oppress (and to stifle diversity in forms of human governance). Indeed, Wenar himself asserts such a rationale for his preferred view. And there is a general value to stability in international markets, especially with regard to commodities as sensitive as petroleum. If sellers might come to be excluded from the international market because they will be deemed in violation of substantive norms concerning resource sales, then prices across the market might well rise, as the attendant uncertainty is internalized. The costs of market uncertainty can therefore be added to the costs of international instability, as part of a provisional case for SDTRs.

But of course the argument for a system of sovereign nation states with robust powers of self-government does not entail that the privileges of sovereignty should be conditional only upon the state's capacity to maintain order. Even modest contemporary normative accounts of sovereignty condition it on respect for basic human rights. From the perspective of external actors, then, a further justification is needed for the exceedingly weak practice of SDTR, by which any transaction authorized by the resource state is legitimate. And here the functional argument for SDTR becomes much shakier. While international stability may be a good to states external to the resource state, it is an evil to those suffering under a longstanding autocrat.[7] Put positively, if there is a consequentialist case to be made for SDTRs, it would need to net out the costs to local populations against the gains to outsiders of stable affairs and stable markets. Hence the strongest case to be made for something like an SDTR principle rests on a presumption that the sovereign states are minimally human-rights respecting, as in the Rawlsian model; only with such a presumption could a consequentialist argument for SDTR plausibly go through, I believe.[8] Such a restriction would still be weaker than Popular Resource Sovereignty. Imagine a target state that is a more human rights compliant version of Saudi Arabia, whose rulers deliver a significant portion of its resource wealth to its citizens.[9] Let us call it Petrostan. Petrostan would count as "decent" in a Rawlsian sense even if its citizens (and non-citizen denizens) cannot depend on those resource flows, except as a bribe to keep the peace.[10] By any more robust normative metric of liberal democracy or republicanism, such a state would receive failing marks; but it would clearly stand within the much cruder constraints of international recognition. This, then, is the best case for SDTR: it is part of the package of sovereignty rights that are both normatively coherent, consistent with variation in democratic development, and internationally feasible.

It seems clear that a state meeting the minimum threshold for SDTR would not necessarily meet Wenar's Clean Trade standard, which imposes the stronger Popular Resource Sovereignty constraint. Wenar would prohibit oil purchases from "a state in which citizens lack basic rights and liberties to hold their government accountable."[11] By hypothesis, while Petrostan citizens enjoy basic human rights, such as freedom of conscience and freedom from arbitrary treatment, they lack electoral power to enforce accountability and may lack some of the further freedoms associated with democratic rights, including freedom of the press and of association. So we have a clear conflict between application of a human-rights sensitive SDTR and Popular Resource Sovereignty. And here is the rub for a pragmatic argument for Popular Resource Sovereignty: while it is superior to unrestricted or barely restricted MMR, it is not clearly superior to SDTR. Continue with the Petrostan example, and imagine that a Clean Trade Boycott becomes internationally effective. Petrostan's rulers may be able to draw down national savings for a time, continuing to buy the goodwill of their people. But a likely outcome, as well, is that they will engage, in the short term, in increased repression, and perhaps international adventurism, in order to distract from the state's new-found money troubles. A principled case for Popular Resource Sovereignty might be able to justify the case for sanctions, on the grounds that anything else is international complicity in theft. But it is hardly clear that a purely consequentialist analysis, even one as capacious in its theory of the good as Wenar's, can tip decisively for Popular Resource Sovereignty over a more modest claim. So it looks like the case

for Popular Resource Sovereignty needs to be strengthened, beyond a pragmatic case.

If Popular Resource Sovereignty faces a pragmatic challenge on its right
flank, it faces a complementary challenge from the left: the Cosmopolitan
alternative. Cosmopolitans claim that, in the first instance, natural
resources belong to all the peoples of the earth. While assigning property
rights in natural resources to those living within the artificial boundaries of
the state is preferable to concentrating those resources among an oligarchy,
Popular Resource Sovereignty still falls far short of justice. On a Cosmopolitan view, even Norway falls short of resource justice: though it is one of the
most generous states in the world in terms of foreign aid, its distributions of
aid in 2015 were about 18 percent of its government's oil revenues. Given
that Norway's population, on whose behalf it retained 82 percent of its
revenues, is only about .06 percent of the world's population, this is a dramatically inegalitarian redistribution, from a global perspective.[12] Presumably a Cosmopolitan would criticize any national claim to oil revenues so
far in excess of a state's population ratio—and indeed, a Cosmopolitan
might further insist on actual global control of natural resources.[13]

The moral argument for a Cosmopolitan principle of global resource distribution is transparent, and needs no elaborate theory of justice (even if
such claims are sometimes expanded by way of a Global Original Position).[14] There would seem to be nothing distinguishing the moral claims to
oil wealth of a citizen of Burkina Faso from those of a citizen of Nigeria,
save for the accidents of colonial borders and birth. Nor, more generally, is
there anything to distinguish claims in desert of a citizen of Saudi Arabia
from a citizen of Bolivia. Thus, reason the Cosmopolitans, there is no rational basis for preferring a principle of national resource ownership over
international ownership, at least for resources whose existence predates the
state and in no way depend on it for their maintenance.

Wenar's argument against Cosmopolitanism is, as I have said, primarily
pragmatic: such principles rarely come with a plan for their realization, nor
with an accounting of their costs versus their benefits (pp. 28–29). He
points out that the rhetoric of global resource ownership is almost exclusively associated with progressive voices in states with imperialist traditions, and are poorly received by developing, de-colonized states, whose
principal national asset are liberated natural resources (p. 27). Wenar says,
entirely plausibly, that there is hardly any imaginary path whereby members of states housing resources would come to agree to a confiscatory tax
on those assets, or on institutions that would cause a major rupture with
even progressive, human rights–permeated conceptions of national sovereignty. By contrast, he says, Popular Resource Sovereignty fits within a generally recognizable model of sovereignty, is evidently attractive to any

citizen in a resource rich state who is not in oligarchic control, and would create a virtuous circle of democratic development.

As I say, I think Wenar's claims about the prospects of implementing Popular Resource Sovereignty relative to Cosmopolitanism are correct. But he does so at the price of effectively conceding the point of principle: at best one can say that Popular Resource Sovereignty is more just than MMR, and more feasible than Cosmopolitanism. But this still leaves Popular Resource Sovereignty relatively undefended, and vulnerable to critique on both fronts. If its main argument against Cosmopolitanism is practical, not principled, then Popular Resource Sovereignty would seem at best defensible as a middle ground, instrumental principle, and so operating always in the shadow of the intrinsically more attractive global justice principle. Wenar's argument that Popular Resource Sovereignty better conduces to "unity" is, as I understand it, mainly relative to MMR: popular resource ownership better protects and promotes social and political interdependence than oligarchy. That point is inarguable. But it is hard to evaluate the claim that it better serves the unity of humanity than the alternative put forward by Pogge, Steiner, Beitz, et al., which is a state system with a confiscatory resource tax. Cosmopolitan resource ownership, coupled with democratic states in all other respects, would seem to meet both goals of state level and global level cooperation and reciprocity (pp. 34–35). Such vulnerability itself has a practical problem: if it were widely understood that Popular Resource Sovereignty institutions were a second-best to global justice, then it would be difficult to motivate citizens to fully support them; and citizens of resource-rich states might reasonably fear an ultimate trajectory of globalization. "Partial unities are better than none" is not much of a slogan for a movement (p. 35). Put another way, Popular Resource Sovereignty institutions will be vulnerable to popular under-commitment unless they can be shown to represent a preferred model of justice. Wenar therefore needs to put forward an argument of principle, even by his own pragmatic lights.

There is a second, key concern with Popular Resource Sovereignty as a self-standing conception. Although Wenar routinely uses the language of a country's resources belong to its "people" (and hence *Popular* Resource Sovereignty), his view is more precisely defined as a matter of *citizen* control of resources, by way of mechanisms of democratic accountability.[15] But, in a literal understanding of a "people" in a region, citizens are a subset. Indeed, in the most important real cases of petrostates, noncitizens are a substantial percentage of the population: in Saudi Arabia, notably, about one in three residents is a non-citizen.[16] While Saudi Arabia is an extreme case, most resource-rich states host many authorized and unauthorized guest workers, whose work is usually especially tightly linked to resource extraction.

The citizen/non-citizen distinction matters because, at the level of distributive justice, it is hard to articulate a principle of ownership that hews to the positive, contingent criteria a state uses for citizenship. While a distinction between residents and non-residents might form the basis of a principle of ownership (as I will suggest below), it is hard to see why a legal distinction, formulated by insiders for the benefit of insiders, should have moral sway. The issue is not, as Wenar tends to describe it, lack of democracy, for democracies are as capable as non-democracies of tightly restricting citizenship (even if there are more avenues for political pressure open for expanding the net of citizenship).[17] The issue is that the reasons underlying the citizen/non-citizen line are unlikely to coincide with many of the reasons that support Popular Resource Sovereignty. To continue with the Saudi example, Saudi citizens plausibly profit from its oil wealth through widespread employment in national oil fields—so that they receive its benefits as employees, though not as owners. It is hard to see why the formal condition of ownership *vel non* would be more significant than the formal characteristic of citizenship. While Saudi citizens have little control over the use of those fields, there is no reason to doubt that their de facto owner, the house of Saud, is doing anything other than maximizing long-term net revenue, and so the control deficit is not the issue. What does seem egregious in Saudi Arabia (apart from the use of oil wealth to fuel radicalism and conflict) is the condition of its guest-workers, who do not receive comparable benefits from the oil wealth. That concern would be untouched by the Clean Trade requirement of popular control.[18]

The upshot is that without more elaboration, Popular Resource Sovereignty seems relatively unattractive in two dimensions relative to Cosmopolitanism: it fails to state a convincing principle of Popular as opposed to Global control over resources; and it fails to state a convincing reason for preferring citizen claims to resident claims. I believe Wenar would do better to start again, with a positive theory of popular ownership that looks to the people of a territory—the denizens, to use a current term.[19] Such a theory might be able to make claim both to principle and to practicality. I cannot here do more than sketch a justification for a principle of Denizen Rights Sovereignty, but I believe the promissory note I offer here can be honored.

I begin with what I have argued elsewhere is the key normative value behind the ideal of democratic legitimacy: active democratic political participation, or *agentic democracy*.[20] The value of agentic democracy extends beyond the borders of functioning democratic institutions, such as voting and accountable political offices: it is the value that justifies at the temporal margins of those institutions, in times of revolution, resurrection, and national self-defense. Imagine a people, living together in a territory, and cooperating across a range of social and proto-political projects—defining for themselves systems of contract, social order, dispute resolution, cultural institutions, and economic cooperation. Such projects are essentially collective, in the sense that they typically reflect the agency of individuals who understand themselves as participants in a shared undertaking, orienting their own actions around the actions of others, in a familiarly reinforcing dynamic of cooperation. The work of players in a string quartet is a highly idealized version of this model: each plays her instrument, attentive to both the individual task of making the instrument sound right, at the same time fully attentive to the timing and intonation of the others in the group, and so ready to alter the performance so as to realize together the finest rendition of the quartet. Such collective acts typically take place as well amid a dense network of mutual claims and expectations.[21]

The string quartet is, of course, an ideal type, and its extension to the national scale is non-obvious. But I believe that it is possible to understand the overlapping patterns of social, economic, political and cultural cooperation that take place within the (historically contingent) borders of the state as more diffuse versions of the basic model. The normative point is that these networks of collective action are the basis for ascribing a we—a *moi commun*, in Rousseau's words—to what is otherwise a collection of individuals. Through collective actions, we each understand ourselves as participants in a group, positively responsible for its accomplishments, negatively responsible for its liabilities. The criterion for inclusion in the collective is, therefore, agency itself—a criterion that supersedes, rather than supervenes on, merely formal, positive criteria of membership. A guest worker who helps to pump a nation's oil, or to harvest a nation's crops, is no less a member of shared collective agency than the citizen who enjoys a white collar sinecure in Aramco, or at Archer Daniels Midland headquarters. Indeed, by many informal moral metrics, the roughnecks and farm laborers are much more central contributors than the back-office staff whose salaries dwarf theirs.

The denizens of a state are not, to be sure, fully co-extensive with the contributors to its social, economic, and political projects. Some are too young to count as meaningful contributors, some are past the point of contribution, some have no access (for external reasons) or no desire to engage in the collective projects of the people. And in an increasingly globalized economy, there are many non-denizens whose work and efforts also play a role in the domestic productions of the people, and many denizens whose primary affective orientation is around external ties (for example, through remittances). But, as Wenar says, even in a post-Westphalian age the modern state is a rough but useful unit of normative analysis, and it is the center of the densest overlap of collective agency. There is, therefore, an empirical weight behind the normative claim that the world is composed of peoples inhabiting discrete territories, where "people" is understood as a collective composed of individuals mutually orienting around each other.

To say that a nation has a people, understood as a collective, is not yet to say anything about that people's claims to natural resources. There are, however, at least two promising routes by which an argument for the people's control of resources can be made. The first route is effectively procedural or general: a people acting together is the agent of its territory's politics. Territorial order can, to be sure, be imposed externally, as under colonialism; or internally, as under despotism. Under such conditions, a people is not constructing a shared political order at all. But when there is a collective political agent, whether or nor the conditions of institutionally realized democracy are met, the basic rules of property ought, morally, be a subject for specific collective decisionmaking. Historically, private property rules accumulate in fact through accretion, transnational borrowing, and more local forms of oligarchic control of the national legislative process. But the normative default must be that the rules are subject to determination of the collective agency of the people—an agency that extends beyond the border of citizenship. With respect to natural resources in particular, this presumption operates to secure Popular Resource Sovereignty as a baseline. (Think of this as a non-formalistic version of Wenar's thesis.) In particular, anyone defending an entitlement scheme to natural resources that vests control on some basis other than Popular Resource Sovereignty— whether finders-keepers or oligarchic control—has the burden of showing why a people might reasonably have acceded to such an order.[22] In the absence of such a justification, members of the international community can justifiably assume that oligarchic control is a result of subverting that collective agency, not recognizing it.

A second route from collective agency is substantive, and works by analogy to private property claims. In Hegelian property theory, the strongest argument for private property rights to land and resources in general is that such rights allow individuals to self-realize; private property provides the means by which we can securely realize and externalize our personal ends.[23] This is what H. L. A. Hart calls a general right: all individuals, by nature of an embodied will and equal worth grounded in their rational capacity, have a claim to the means sufficient to realize their wills.[24] The legitimacy of any particular property scheme depends upon satisfying the general claim. While the analogy between individuals and collectives fails at many points (in particular, the value of collective goals depends, in my view, on the value of the individual goals they collect), the analogy may hold with respect to natural resources. A stock in natural resources is, when available, one of the chief means by which a people can realize its collective political goals. A right to natural resources is a condition of respect for the capacity of a people to self-actualize by achieving collective aims. A principle that accords such resources only to a minority—and, arguably, a principle according resources on a global scale, without any corresponding collective—fails to respect the rational agency of the people as a collective agent.[25] Note that this argument, too, draws what force it has from a conception of collective political agency understood organically, in terms overlapping individual intentions and actions; it makes no reference to a post-political criterion of citizenship. Indeed, it makes no claim to a juristic, institutional understanding of property at all. As a claim on resources, it is satisfied when members have effective access to those resources (or the income stream into which they can be converted). Effective access is not the same as effective control, although control is a standard way of controlling access; a beneficiary of a trust, for example, has effective access without control. (I will return to this point below, in relation to the risks of Clean Trade as a way of seeking to guarantee popular resource access.)

A conception of Popular Resource Sovereignty anchored in collective agency therefore achieves the aim of anchoring resource ownership at the level of the state, without being vulnerable to a concern about the denizen/citizen distinction. All those participating in the national project have a claim on its resources, guest-workers and citizens alike.[26] This is thus revisionary, but not radically so, and is consistent with various forms of institutionalization, including most obviously, durable residency requirements. What it does not permit are criteria of control engineered to exclude some social cooperators from sharing in the bounty of the territory. But why, it might still be pressed, do I accept the contingency of the border as a boundary of resource claims, given that cooperation frequently spreads beyond the border? The answer is that the contingency of a shared border tends to lead to denser forms of cooperation and mutual dependence, and provides a frame through which large-scale collective projects are pursued. Put another way, the coincidence of a nation and a people is not a tautology, but an empirical truth. The relative density of intra-national cooperation may not be sufficient to block all trans-national justice claims, as some critics of cosmopolitanism maintain.[27] But it is sufficient, I believe, to give priority claim to natural resources to denizens over non-denizens.[28]

I have argued that grounding a denizen-inclusive Popular Resource Sovereignty in a conception of a people as a collective agent can secure Popular Resource Sovereignty better against the pragmatically attractive alternative of human-rights conditional SDTR, and against the more normatively ambitious and transparent alternative of Cosmopolitanism. The special claims of denizens on each other, and on the resources through which they can realize collective aims, occupies an attractive middle ground. But this is only to state a principle of access, not a program. One of the many virtues of Wenar's analysis of the problem is that his Clean Trade program, which I discussed above, in connection with assessing the pragmatic justification for Popular Resource Sovereignty over SDTR, offers a clear program of implementation: using a metric of resource accountability, a Clean Trade state will decide on what conditions it will conduct trade, rejecting trade with any state falling below a certain threshold.

The question I now pursue is whether a boycott-based program really is adequate to Wenar's goals of cultivating popular accountability. Return to the imaginary case of Petrostan, which honors human rights and returns some significant portion of resource wealth to its citizens, but which is non-democratic and non-transparent. Wenar's proposal would seem to entail denial of trade with Petrostan, because of the lack of accountability. I would not want to deny that Petrostan's citizens are fundamentally unfree in an important dimension. I have mentioned above pragmatic worries about whether denial of trade with Petrostan is net positive in welfare terms for Petrostan's denizens, or the world as a whole, given the instability such a boycott would create, and the risk that it will put purchaser states less attentive to human rights in a favorable strategic position.

But there is also a deontological concern with blocking trade in a case like this, stemming from the respect owed to decent but not democratic states. In particular, I worry that an application of Clean Trade constraints, if done without the active participation of target state civil opposition, looks more like external value imposition than the fostering of democratic agency abroad. As I have argued in *On War and Democracy*, I believe that democratic values impose deontological limits on the kinds of pressure one state can impose on another. The chief demand on a democratic state is that it respect the political agency of other peoples. This means that a democratic state must understand democracy abroad as something to be nourished but not imposed.[29] I am thus inclined to stand with John Stuart Mill and Michael Walzer, in worrying that too interventionist and belligerent a politics of democracy disrespects and ultimately undermines the political agency of the people we aim to support. While trade sanctions against what is likely a state's most valuable export are qualitatively different from the sort of military or covert engagement targeted by a non-interventionist principle, they nonetheless are a major form of coercive pressure.

I do not mean to suggest that Wenar is promoting the sort of coercive democratization agenda associated Bush-era neo-conservatism. To the contrary, a value of the Popular Resource Sovereignty-conditioned approach is that it can be consistent with respect for the political agency of the target state's denizens, by reducing some of the internal coercive advantages of oligarchs. Ideally, it empowers civil society actors by disempowering resource-controlling elites. Cases of raw petroleum theft, through civil war or crude autocracy, are easily analyzed. We already have sanction systems targeting rogue states and systems, grounded in a range of concerns about corruption and anti-democratic policy. But sanctions against major oil states have principally been implemented in response to direct national or international security concerns. The real challenge for Wenar's view, it seems to me, lies in justifying the boycott approach for Petrostan and its real-life analogs—states lying closer to it than Equatorial Guinea.

In the actual case of Saudi Arabia, Wenar is right that we cannot infer from domestic peace to popular legitimacy, much less accountability. But the bargain its rulers have struck with its people is in significant part by pacifying them with the profits of resource sales. The Saudi oligarchs return a relatively high ratio of national income to human development.[30] And that fact, of human capital investment even in the absence of democratic rights, differentiates the Saudi case from the Guinean. If the principal direct concern underlying Popular Resource Sovereignty is securing a people's access to natural resources, then it is hard to see why lack of control over those resources would be sufficient to justify sanctions. No one disputes the desirability of Saudi Arabia moving along a path of democratization, nor of the difficulty of a democratic opposition in Saudi Arabia arising. But the prospects for long-term success of a highly democracy-sensitive trade policy are not promising.[31]

A last concern on this note is that making the Clean Trade program a salient part of political discourse implicitly suggests that the wrongs it targets are especially egregious. But how to weigh the wrong of resource theft against other wrongs? The issue is building a case for scorning normalized resource theft, without the additional human rights factors of mass displacements, slave labor, and civil war. Theft is, of course, wrong even when the scale of the theft or its material effects are relatively minor. If Denmark, say, had some petroleum resources, all of it claimed by the royal family, that would be a wrong relative to the Danish people. But if petroleum sales accounted for only a trivial portion of national income, while a high functioning material and service economy sustained an otherwise well-ordered society, the wrong of resource theft would seem to be of little international traction. And on the other hand, if another country, say Japan, had no natural resources to sell, but all of its agricultural production was tied to land held by a very few; or if all its industrial production came from factories owned by a single family, paying exploitative wages, then these other issues of inequality would loom very high. These quick reflections suggest that the central wrong of resource theft is not the theft itself, but the contribution of that theft to national inequality.

My point is not that Wenar ignores other forms of injustice. The point is that the very heavy weaponry, and heavy justificatory burden, of the sanctions-based Clean Trade program looks as though it is caught in a dilemma: either it is being irrationally selective in focusing only on resource theft, as opposed to other injustices; or that it risks becoming such a moralized system of trade regulation that it cannot possibly coexist in a world of imperfect states, each with incentives to abuse such a system, and where trade even with imperfect states has strongly positive human development consequences for the least well off in those states. While I generally reject a principle that if a policy cannot be applied everywhere, it must be applied nowhere, such a criticism seems apt for an argument that requires singling out one form of injustice for uniquely severe treatment in international relations. I raise these points to suggest that the threshold for a Clean Trade boycott should probably be set at a level less demanding of target states than popular control.

Let me now put aside the question of the threshold for intervention and address a remaining matter: how can citizens of Clean Trade states be motivated to implement such a plan, when it might cause substantial price inflation? Whatever threshold is picked, if it is meaningful it will impose direct costs on consumers. Why should they forgo cheap gas for abstract principle? The problem is one analogous to that of climate change policies, where the principal direct beneficiaries of such policies are not those paying the costs. Wenar notes that, in the case of slavery, the British accepted very substantial costs for the sake of abolition (p. 24); in *Blood Oil*, he powerfully invokes the example of the citizens of Manchester who, in 1862, let their textile mills stop because of their decision to boycott American slave-picked cotton.[32]

Abolitionism is a powerful but perhaps incomplete example. I do not think it is merely the perspective of time which makes slavery, and trade complicit in it, seem like an especially significant form of moral taint.[33] I suggested in the beginning of this chapter that even in Berkeley, California, there is no attention to concerns about petrocomplicity. I do not, of course, mean this as a criticism of Wenar's argument. But it is striking that in a community in which opinion is clear on boycotting goods made in the Occupied territories of Israel/Palestine, and morally appealing pedigrees of goods and services are heavily advertised, there is so little salience to the idea of consumer complicity in petroleum theft. This fact is all the more striking given how morally charged petroleum use is, in relation to climate change. Is the relative silence simply that the facts of petrocomplicity have not been made sufficiently clear to consumers, or because ethically clean and the dirty hydrocarbon molecules have been sufficiently mixed?

I suspect that the cause is not because American consumers, even sensitive ones, underestimate the amount of oligarchic oil they consume. I suspect, to the contrary, that most Americans overestimate the ratio of Saudi to, say, Canadian oil in U.S. imports.[34] It is certainly possible that a guilt-based campaign, such as the blood diamonds campaign, or more recently, the campaigns concerning marine park practices surrounding whales and dolphins, would powerfully affect consumer behavior. But the psychology of complicity makes the claim dubious in the case of oil, I believe. For consumers at the end of the supply chain, the original sin of resource theft is very distant—indeed, the apparent cleanliness of the consumer's purchase, based on the legal title by the original autocrat, is a central part of the problem. This renders the oil case unlike that of blood diamonds in a crucial respect: the original sin in petroleum has been normalized over decades into market practice, except in exceptional circumstances. Blood diamonds, by contrast, are the loot of a hot or recently concluded civil war. Conflict petroleum, such as that claimed by ISIS in Syria and Iraq, can be moralized into an analogous case. But this re-description of a resource as the fruit of a crime is harder when the original misallocation is rooted a century of accepting Sykes-Picot blessed oligarchs, or the cloudy but legalistic privatization of ex-Soviet resources. This makes it harder for consumers to see the oil as tainted by crime, and hence to develop the aversive motivation of guilt.

A second factor that distinguishes blood diamonds from blood oil is the luxury quality of diamonds. The moral cost of wearing a conflict diamond easily dominates the other values of the decision to consume a highly specific and salient luxury good—if a diamond is tainted, it is no good at all, because it can bring shame where one need not incur it, simply by declining to consume. But, again, the ubiquity of blood oil, its admixture into the general petroleum economy, makes its consumption seem both inescapable and morally tolerable, given that that petroleum is being used to get us to work, diaper our babies, grow our crops, and supply the other necessities of daily life. That dual context of necessity and ubiquity makes me wonder about the success of a complicity-based campaign, as Wenar presents the Clean Trade program.

By contrast, a positive Clean Trade campaign that centers on rewarding morally attractive actors, though probably less effective, would seem far more psycho-socially sustainable. Such a campaign harnesses the sense that consumers can, through market choices, actually increase their well-being through wise petroconsumption: consuming the products they want, while at the same time generating positive political externalities by voting with dollars for morally clean petroleum. Instead of a boycott-based strategy, whose virtue is its binary clarity, endorsing Popular Resource Sovereignty might support a more supple implementation program, building around the non-coercive promotion of access and accountability values. Since energy trade is not controlled by the WTO, there is room for a more conditional program of energy trading, reserving boycotts for extremes. Importing states could, for example, impose a duty indexed to the degree to which denizens of the export state benefit from the resource sale, or from metrics of public accountability and control, as in the Freedom House indices Wenar relies upon. A tariff-based program, assuming defensible criteria, would fit better with a scheme of positive association rather than negative repudiation.

But these are, in the end, mere quibbles around a core of agreement with Wenar's brave endeavor. Shifting the consuming, democracy-valuing publics of the West from dull acceptance of MMR to more ethically refined consumption would clearly be a marked step forward toward a more just world. I hope that Wenar's work will transform consciousness around a product ubiquitous yet morally invisible.

5

Does a Country Belong to Its People?

Anna Stilz

The central idea behind Leif Wenar's "Clean Trade" proposal is Popular Resource Sovereignty. On this view, a country—along with the natural resources it contains—"belongs" to its people. Authoritarian governments and militias therefore have no right to appropriate and sell off oil and minerals without popular authorization. When Western consumers buy resources from unaccountable governments under the principle of effectiveness, they are buying stolen goods. To avoid theft, Wenar urges Western countries to implement "Clean Trade Policies" that require trading partner regimes to meet basic conditions for popular accountability, including (1) citizens' access to information, (2) their ability to freely discuss and deliberate about the regime's resource management, and (3) their right to publicly express dissent.[1] Wenar recommends that Western countries should gradually make it illegal to purchase resources from authoritarian regimes that do not protect at least minimal civil and political rights, and that they should deny authoritarian rulers access to their markets, financial services, and legal systems.[2] If third-party countries—such as China—continue to buy resources from authoritarians, Western states should place tariffs on goods from these countries, putting the proceeds into a "Clean Hands Trust" to be used for the future benefit of their peoples.

My chapter examines a key plank in Wenar's story: the idea that a country and its resources belong to its people. Wenar finds support for Popular Resource Sovereignty in international treaties—especially in the two human rights covenants, both of which proclaim, in their first and last articles, that "all peoples may, for their own ends, freely dispose of their natural wealth and resources."[3] Popular Resource Sovereignty is also cited in many national constitutions and laws, in UN General Assembly resolutions, and in the rhetoric of world leaders and mass movements. As Wenar emphasizes, the principle scores high in terms of feasibility: it provides an especially workable basis for international reform because it is already widely accepted. What I want to interrogate here, however, is its philosophical plausibility. What, if anything, makes a people the original owner of resources on its territory?

In *Blood Oil*, Wenar does not say much about this issue. Here is his argument, as I reconstruct it: if the people are sovereign, they have the right to authorize laws valid within their territory. One important dimension of territorial jurisdiction is the power to define property rights, including rights in natural resources. Wenar suggests that this power makes the people the *original owner* of their resources: "Each country's people has original rights to their natural resources, and as they exercise their sovereign rights to dispose of those resources for their own ends, quite different ownership arrangements will result."[4] A country's property laws may specify that natural resources are privately owned, owned by the public, or held in mixed forms of ownership. The laws may allow an adjacent landowner to drain his neighbor's oil (or not), and so on. This authority to define titles, Wenar concludes, makes natural resources ultimately the property of the people.

Yet it is not obvious that because a sovereign people has *jurisdiction* over natural resources, it must also have ultimate *ownership* of them. Consider that a sovereign people also exercises jurisdiction over persons. Through democratic legislation, it specifies and regulates individual rights, defining what conduct constitutes an assault or battery, what acts count as rape, whether homosexual marriage is legal, and so on. One would not therefore say that a sovereign democracy *owns* the persons over whom it exercises this jurisdiction. So why draw the equivalent conclusion in the case of natural resources? It is true that in order for the state to define and adjudicate property rights, it must have control over the resources on its territory. But it need not have a strong claim to the full value of these resources.[5]

Here Robert Nozick suggests that

> those believing that a group of persons living in an area jointly own the territory . . . must provide a theory of how such property rights arise; they must show why the persons living there have rights to determine what is done with the land and resources there that persons living elsewhere don't have (with regard to the same land and resources).[6]

What arguments might we provide in favor of the people's title? I examine three possibilities: (1) natural property rights, (2) international conventions, and (3) respect for collective self-determination. Ultimately I conclude that none of these accounts can support an exclusive "property-like" entitlement, on the part of the people, to the full value of their natural resources.

Indeed, I am uncertain of the extent to which Wenar believes that natural resources belong to peoples, despite the prominent role this principle plays in his account. My guess is that he thinks Popular Resource Sovereignty is a good pragmatic principle or "intermediate generalization" as to how best—in our historical moment—pursue a more fundamental goal: the "free unity" of humanity. But if this is the principle's status, then I worry that it is exposed to challenges I articulate in the second section of this chapter.

Despite my skepticism about the people's title, I believe that even if peoples do not have full "property-like" claims to their natural resources, there are good reasons—grounded in the value of collective self-determination—for outsiders to refrain from interfering with the people's control and management of them, in most cases. Yet this may not rule out all efforts to advance reforms based on the idea of humanity's common ownership.

NATURAL PROPERTY RIGHTS

Classical natural law theorists typically theorized the origins of territorial rights in tandem with the origins of property. While Locke's first labor account is the most well-known, I set it aside here, since it doesn't seem very plausible as a basis for natural resource ownership. Typically oil and mineral deposits are the result of naturally occurring processes for which the people living on the territory are not responsible. To be sure, oil and minerals have to be extracted, transported, and brought to market, and the people involved in these activities may have a claim to be compensated for their efforts, insofar as these help to make the resource economically useful for others. But these claims will typically fall short of anything like title to the full market value of, say, a country's oil.[7]

Other natural law thinkers—including Grotius, Pufendorf, and Vattel—instead invoked a principle of *first occupancy* to account for a people's claim to their country. In occupying an area, Grotius held that the people could acquire two distinct rights: "There are two things that belong to nobody of which one may take possession: Jurisdiction and the Right of Property, as distinguished from jurisdiction."[8] The right of *jurisdiction* was a right to make and enforce laws, including property laws, within an area, whereas the right of *property* was a kind of supreme ownership over that space. According to Grotius:

A Country is taken Possession of, either in the Lump, or by Parts: The former is usually done by a whole People, or by him who is their Sovereign. . . . But if, in a Country possessed in the Lump, any Thing remains unassigned to private Persons, it ought not therefore to be accounted vacant; for it still belongs to him who first took Possession of that Country, whether King or People; such as Rivers, Lakes, Ponds, Forests, and uncultivated Mountains.[9]

Pufendorf similarly held that

when a group of men have together occupied some portion of land, this has usually been done either as a whole or by sections. . . . Regarding "occupancy as a whole," moreover, it is to be observed that it establishes dominion for the whole group, as such, over all things in that district. . . . Therefore, if anything be discovered in such an area that is still without a private owner, it should not at once be regarded as unoccupied, and free to be taken by any man as his own, but it will be understood to belong to the whole people.[10]

Broadly following Grotius and Pufendorf, Vattel coined the term *domain* (a term related to eminent domain), to refer to the supreme ownership that a nation held over its territory. It was by virtue of the domain, Vattel argued, that "the nation alone may use this country for the supply of its necessities, may dispose of it as it thinks proper, and derive from it every advantage it is capable of yielding."[11] According to Vattel, the domain also allowed the nation to exclude foreigners from appropriating anything in the area: "No one can form any pretensions to the country which belongs to the nation, nor ought to dispose of it, without her consent, any more than of the things contained in the country."[12] Thus, on the natural law view—much like Wenar's own—a political group possesses a kind of original national ownership, from which private and corporate ownership are derived.

Yet this theory faces a number of challenges. Perhaps the most obvious one is that few peoples can show a historically "clean" title to their lands. Difficult though this challenge is, I set it aside here, assuming that the occupancy view can be updated to accommodate claims of prescription or supersession of past injustices (as natural law thinkers typically held). If so, then sufficiently *longstanding* occupancy might be the source of a people's title to its country.

Instead, I focus on a different challenge to first occupancy theory: why should the fact that one was the prior occupant generate exclusive property entitlements that others are bound to respect? This question seems particularly difficult when it comes to exclusive property in the earth's natural resources.

As I argue in other work, it is plausible that a country might "belong" to its people in the weak sense that they have a right to use that area as a permanent residence and as a site for the economic, social, cultural, and political practices they value.[13] Inhabiting a particular geographical space plays a key role in residents' material subsistence and in their most important projects and relationships. Geography and climate may affect the economic practices people take up, making it difficult for them to reconstitute those in some very different place. Their religious, cultural, and recreational activities also often have territorial components. And people form personal bonds and enter work, religious, and friendship relations in part because they expect to remain spatially arranged in certain ways. We structure our daily activities and associate together under the assumption that current patterns of residence will not be massively disrupted. I call these situated goals, relationships, and pursuits our *located life plans.*

I believe this interest in located life-plans is sufficiently weighty to hold outsiders under a duty to respect prior inhabitants' occupancy of their country. An occupancy right includes a liberty to reside permanently in a particular geographical space, and a claim against others not to remove one from that area and not to interfere with one's use of the space in ways that undermine the shared social and political practices in which one is engaged.

But an occupancy right is rather thin: it does not include many of the incidents associated with full ownership, such as the rights to alienate, bequeath, or derive income from the natural resources situated in the area. These additional incidents are not so clearly linked to our interests in material subsistence or fundamental life-projects. And recognizing such claims might prove potentially onerous for others, who have an interest in sharing in the value of the earth's natural resources. Can the mere fact of being a prior occupant bear this much normative weight?

In response to this worry, Grotius and Pufendorf invoke a primordial agreement in favor of first occupancy as a rule for creating exclusive property in the earth's resources. As Grotius puts it:

> The Original of Property . . . resulted from a certain Compact and Agreement, either expressly, as by a Division; or else tacitly, as by Seizure. For as soon as living in common was no longer approved of, all Men were supposed, and ought to be supposed to have consented, that each should appropriate to himself, by Right of first Possession, what could not have been divided.[14]

Pufendorf similarly suggests that "dominion presupposes absolutely . . . an agreement, whether tacit or express."[15] An agreement works to counteract worries about the unilateral imposition of potentially onerous duties on others, by ensuring their consent to these duties.

Yet this consent theory of property is subject to devastating objections. First, the hypothesis that all humanity ever agreed that countries should belong to their peoples seems implausible: when exactly was such an agreement made? Second, if dissenters had existed at the time of the proposed transition, they would not have been morally required to recognize these rights; instead, they would have retained their claim to use the world in common. Finally, even if such an agreement were actually concluded, it is unclear how the consent of ancestors would bind their children. On this theory, each generation would have to continually consent to Popular Resource Sovereignty, again and again, for it to remain legitimate.

So while natural rights theory might at first seem to support the people's exclusive title to its natural resources, absent the background assumption of a global agreement, that theory is unable to bear the normative weight placed upon it. While it may be legitimate to *occupy* a country, the people's more "property-like" exclusionary rights—including claims to exclude foreigners from entering their territory and from the benefits of their country's resources—still seem to lack justification.

INTERNATIONAL CONVENTIONS

Natural rights theory seemed to fail because it required a background agreement. But perhaps we were too quick to assume that there is no global agreement (of sorts) on the principle that countries should belong to their peoples. Here I turn to a second possible source of the people's title to territory: international conventions. Perhaps states are bound to respect natural resources as the people's property because a convention to that effect has been established *among states themselves*.

The international legal principle of "Permanent Sovereignty over Natural Resources" is relevant here. This principle evolved after World War II, as the newly independent states created by decolonization sought to assert their economic independence. Of key importance was the ability of developing countries to benefit from their resources and to cancel or alter exploitative arrangements, dating from the colonial period, under which Western companies and investors had won concessions to develop them.[16] In 1962, the UN General Assembly adopted Resolution 1803 embracing the permanent sovereignty principle, and the principle was later given a prominent place in the 1966 Human Rights Covenants. Developing countries have consistently pressed their rights to permanent sovereignty, often over the opposition of Western states concerned about access to oil and other resources. Western states have also sought to protect their corporations' business interests, worried that permanent sovereignty might expose them to the uncompensated expropriation of assets via nationalization. Despite these reservations, permanent sovereignty won widespread support from the international community. In recent years, it has been broadened to include new claims to maritime and seabed resources. Under the 1982 UN Convention on the Law of the Sea (UNCLOS), countries have extended their territorial waters to 12 miles offshore, created new "Exclusive Economic Zones"

(EEZs) in which they enjoy fishing and mineral rights, and established a mechanism for claiming exclusive rights over extended "continental shelves."[17]

How might the international legal principle of permanent sovereignty establish the people's *moral* claim to the natural resources on their territory? A standard view of property sees it as a conventional right conferred by legal institutions or social practices. Hume, for example, argues that property is determined by conventions that assign ownership of objects and define the conditions for valid contracts and transfers.[18] Hume held that a convention establishing clear property rules serves the general interest of society, by making peace, stability, and prosperity possible. As each individual is aware of the benefit to society of these rules, each conforms to property conventions, provided that others are willing to do so, and eventually members of society acquire a disposition to approve of rule-conforming conduct.[19]

While Hume was primarily concerned with domestic property rules, we might offer a similar account of the international rules regarding territory. The existence of clear principles allocating territories to particular peoples serves peace, stability, and prosperity in our international system. In this vein, Wenar stresses the evolution, in the postwar era, of a rule of "force-proof" borders. Perhaps permanent sovereignty over natural resources is similarly justified because it conduces to these important values.[20]

To be complete, however, this view requires a perspective from which to assess the *moral validity* of existing conventions. This was something Hume neglected. He thought that what is most important is that we have *some* scheme of rules defining property, not which scheme in particular this is. But that is implausible. The law of coverture, for example, once decreed that women could not hold property separately from their husbands. And until the early twentieth century, the international law of territory held that it was permissible to acquire territory by conquest, a permission that applied with special force to territory occupied by "uncivilized" non-Western peoples.[21] These repugnant rules created no binding moral entitlements. Though they may have given rise to expectations for those who lived under them, those expectations were not legitimate. So the existence of an international convention in favor of permanent sovereignty over natural resources does not settle the matter: we need a further evaluation of the moral validity of this convention. Is permanent sovereignty a morally acceptable rule, or—like the rules of coverture and conquest—should it be rejected?

The idea of a hypothetical agreement is often brought in here, to provide a suitable perspective from which to assess the moral validity of conventional institutions. We ask whether hypothetical contractors, situated in an impartial choice-scenario, would agree to a particular property convention over feasible alternatives, given their fundamental interests. We could apply the hypothetical contract device to permanent sovereignty: would contractors, tasked with designing the structure of our international system, adopt this rule? If so, then the principle creates genuine moral entitlements. If not, it should be reformed.

If I understand him correctly, Wenar proposes a different criterion by which to evaluate the moral validity of existing property conventions. Conventional rules and institutions are morally justified, for Wenar, when they do better than feasible alternatives at fostering identities that will facilitate the "free unity" of humankind over the long run.[22] On this view, the people's permanent sovereignty over their resources is justified—if it is—because adopting this rule would most likely lead to a greater free unity of human ends, compared to other alternatives feasible under current historical circumstances.

Yet it is not obvious to me that permanent sovereignty can be justified, on either criterion. Take the hypothetical contract criterion first. Surely one fundamental interest hypothetical contractors would recognize is an interest in using the earth to meet their basic needs. The earth is valuable as a livable environment, a sustainable ecosystem, and as a source of non-substitutable goods like clean air and fresh water. And the fulfillment of basic needs is a prerequisite for almost any other goal contractors might wish to pursue. Yet a strong Popular Resource Sovereignty principle may jeopardize basic needs fulfillment. For example, if unqualified, the principle would allow the United States to pollute the Rio Grande for industrial activity, or to deplete it in order to irrigate golf courses, depriving Mexicans downstream of water essential to their survival and livelihood. Or suppose that in the future we discover a sustainable solution to climate change, but its implementation requires mining a certain mineral found only in Bolivia. Under an unqualified permanent sovereignty principle, the Bolivians would have the right to refuse to mine the mineral—for trivial or even for no reasons—forcing people in other regions of the globe to lose their lands to desertification and flooding.[23] Because it might jeopardize basic needs, hypothetical contractors would reject such a strong version of permanent sovereignty. Instead, they would opt for a more restricted principle that includes some responsibilities to outsiders.

It is harder to evaluate how permanent sovereignty would fare on Wenar's free unity criterion. Much depends on what would make for a sufficiently "free" form of unity. But it seems that a rule that would license the depletion, environmentally harmful, or wasteful exploitation of resources; or the hoarding of non-substitutable inputs to basic needs would not conduce to a future free unity. It is also difficult to predict what would happen, in the future, as a result of various possible institutional setups. Suppose that a world government were coercively imposed upon existing states in order to enforce every global citizen's right to an equal share of the earth's natural resources. No doubt the transition would be a rocky one, with much strife and resentment on the part of those subjected against their will. But Wenar allows that the use of coercive power can be "redeemed" if it facilitates a greater unity.[24] Perhaps after several generations those living under this global order would develop new identities and allegiances as egalitarian world citizens, committed to freely sharing their resource wealth with one another. If so, then a common ownership rule might be preferable, on the free unity criterion. If the coercive imposition of world government is resisted, I suspect this is because of our commitment to collective self-determination, about which I say more below.

So it is not clear to me that the permanent sovereignty rule is preferable to more qualified alternatives, on either the hypothetical contract or the free unity criterion. Let me briefly canvass some suggested alternatives to it. In line with our hypothetical contract experiment, Mathias Risse emphasizes that common ownership grants every human being the right to use the earth to meet basic needs. To be morally valid, he concludes that existing property and territory conventions must ensure that basic needs are met.[25] Along similar lines, Thomas Pogge proposes a global resource divided (GRD), which would require countries to pay relatively small surcharge on the extraction of natural resources, such as oil, with the proceeds to be used to finance global poverty relief.[26] Appealing to the luck egalitarian intuition that justice requires mitigating undeserved advantages, others have offered much more ambitious common ownership proposals. Hillel Steiner envisions a global auction in which societies bid competitively for the land they occupy, paying others for the opportunity costs of foregoing their preferred uses of the area.[27] Chris Armstrong argues for shifting the benefits of world's natural resources to equalize opportunities for well-being across the globe, through taxes on resource ownership, carbon use, and sovereign wealth funds, and through the reallocation of fishing, mining and drilling rights in the world's oceans.[28] In addition to resource taxes, Paula Casal proposes redrawing boundaries to afford landlocked nations equal access to the sea.[29]

What to make of these proposals? Wenar rightly raises the point that cosmopolitans say little about the nature of the power that might be used to implement their preferred policies. As he puts it:

> All of the important questions surround the agency that will implement any cosmopolitan ideal. What is the nature of this agency's coercive power? Will anyone suggest that it be backed by armed force? Yet if not, how does a global redistributive agency require compliance?[30]

If implementing these proposals requires a coercive world government, that might prove a decisive objection to them. One of the most important values to be safeguarded in the design of our international system is the value of collective self-determination. It is important, in this context, to note that the world's developing countries have generally been the strongest supporters of permanent sovereignty over natural resources, precisely on self-determination grounds. As Chile—which introduced the UN Resolution establishing the permanent sovereignty principle—argued: "Self-determination would be an illusion in a country whose natural resources were controlled by another State, and it would be farcical to give a country political freedom while leaving the ownership of its resources in foreign hands."[31] Can common ownership be made compatible with self-determination, or does it require alien political control?

SELF-DETERMINATION

To answer, we need to say more about self-determination. The ideal of collective self-determination, as I understand it, offers an account of political legitimacy. The idea is that in order to have the right to make and enforce law for a population, an institution must be *collectively authorized* by that population. This does not merely reflect a concern that in the absence of constituents' support, just institutions may be infeasible or unstable. Instead, it articulates an important *moral* requirement that constrains how we ought to coercively impose law and policy. It is wrong to forcibly impose principles of justice in the absence of a shared will that could legitimate that use of force.

While a theory of *justice* addresses the question "What scheme of rules about rights ought a political community (ideally) to adopt and enforce?" a theory of *legitimacy* addresses a different question, namely: "What gives an agent the right to decide the rules governing a particular community, and to coercively enforce those rules?" The principle of collective self-determination holds that only where an institution reflects the shared will of a self-determining population does it have a right to use political power to require compliance with its decisions. The use of force by agents who are not collectively authorized in this way is illegitimate, however correct their views about justice might be. To the extent that there is no shared will to support global institutions, then, the ideal of common ownership might face a legitimacy problem, at least if its implementation requires coercion.

Adherents of common ownership may reject the idea that political legitimacy is an important value, distinct from justice. As Wenar notes, global egalitarians traditionally focus on distributive justice, trying to figure out what precisely are "the right rights."[32] Why not hold that rules can be legitimately enforced if and only if they are just? After all, on a common view, justice refers to the enforceable rights of persons. So long as one has the theory of the "right rights," why does anything stand in the way of efforts to enforce it?

But legitimacy and justice are indeed different values, and possession of the correct theory of justice does not provide an answer to questions about the proper use of coercive power. Suppose for example that Rawls's theory of justice is correct. By any reasonable estimation, current property laws in the United States are very far from satisfying the difference principle. Noticing this, should I and my fellow like-minded Rawlsians arm ourselves with AK-47s and—taking to the streets—strip the rich of their goods and give them to the poor so as to satisfy Rawlsian requirements? Would there be any objection to our doing that?

I believe there would be an important objection. Though our views of justice are—*ex hypothesi*—correct, that fact is not sufficient to confer upon us the standing to force others to comply with our decisions. Instead, only collectively authorized agents may use force to implement their decisions. In the absence of such authorization it is generally not permissible to enforce even a correct theory of justice. Moreover, sometimes collectively authorized agents may permissibly implement political decisions that are not perfectly just. For example, I believe that all citizens have a right to basic health care and that the most just scheme is a single-payer system. Nonetheless, I also believe that the U.S. government has the right to require me to contribute my tax dollars to support the Affordable Care Act, because that is the system we have together enacted, even though it is not the most just system. So legitimacy and justice are distinct values: sometimes it can be illegitimate to impose a just policy (because the imposer lacks the proper standing to do so) and sometimes it can be legitimate to impose an unjust policy (because the policy, while not perfectly just, is not so unjust as to undercut the imposer's right to decide).

Much more could be said about the value of legitimacy, how it relates to justice, and why it requires collective self-determination.[33] But here, I simply offer one brief remark about the moral sources of our respect for a self-determining people's collective decisions. After all, if one fails to enforce the "right rights," something will be lost: the world will be at least somewhat less just. What value could support our acquiescing to a less just world?

I believe autonomy is the value that often supports this acquiescence. Part of respecting other people as autonomous agents is treating them as authentic rational deliberators, who can reason for themselves how they ought to think and act. But unilaterally coercing others fails to respect them as rational deliberators. It leaves them unable to act independently, on the basis of their own sense of justice, to establish and comply with a political order they can affirm. Instead, they find themselves subjected against their will to institutions that fail to reflect their judgments and priorities. They are likely to find life within such an imposed order highly *alienating*. And they are unlikely to experience their social world as a cooperative system where they enjoy valuable relationships with fellow-participants, or as a place where they can feel at home. These are significant harms. Avoiding these harms, in my view, tells in favor of recognizing collective self-determination. This gives us *pro tanto* reason to refrain from implementing justice over the objections of a subject population, instead respecting their right to decide the rules governing their common life via their own deliberative agency, even at some cost to substantive justice.

Alien coercion, in my view, was one of key wrong-making features of colonialism. Along with other abuses, like human rights violations and racism, colonialism involved the forcible imposition, onto a subject population, of a political order that bore no relation to their own judgments about how they should be governed. This produced lasting bitterness and resentment among subject peoples, a legacy that has still not been overcome, even today.

Yet not all political coercion is alien coercion. Unlike alien coercion, *collectively authorized* coercion is based on individuals' shared political will: their joint commitment to self-organized procedures that they accept as an appropriate way to establish justice among themselves. The object of a people's shared will need not be first-order policy decisions: it can be abstract ideals and political procedures, of the sort typically enshrined in a constitution. What is necessary for coercion to be collectively authorized is for members to endorse their participation in a joint political venture and to accept certain higher-order procedures and values by which that venture is to be guided. When political coercion is collectively authorized, rules are made and implemented in a way that the subject population broadly endorses, even when they do not agree with all political outcomes. This enables them to relate in a valuable way to their state and to the constraints it coercively imposes on them. Here, the state is no longer a hostile, alien power: instead, it reflects, in part, its subjects' own commitments.

While very important, the value of self-determination is not in my view absolute. Consider two exceptions to it. First, in some cases there is no moral loss in coercing people in ways that do not reflect their judgments. The reason it is important to refrain from alien coercion is that doing so respects others' autonomy. But some people—murderers, rapists, fascists, and theocrats—refuse to recognize any foundational requirement to respect others' autonomy, even in a minimal way. When people deny others' very basic rights, they release those others from the requirement to respect their autonomy in return, by refraining from unilaterally coercing them. No wrong is done when we deny political self-determination to those who reject the more fundamental requirement from which its value is derived.

Second, even where self-determination is important, sometimes its value can be morally outweighed. So long as people are committed to reciprocal respect for others' autonomy, it is *pro tanto* wrong to subject them to alien coercion. But perhaps a basic functioning legal order cannot be achieved unless we subject some dissenters to alien coercion. If there is no other way to achieve the essentials of justice, security, and public order, the wrong of alien coercion may be trumped by its strongly beneficial effects. So self-determination can be legitimately denied in cases where its recognition would threaten decent governance or entail enormous social costs. While self-determination is of very great weight, it is not the only value.

With this sketch in place, let me return to the common ownership proposals canvassed in the last section as potential alternatives to permanent sovereignty. Can common ownership be made compatible with self-determination, or does it require alien coercion? The most ambitious luck egalitarian proposals do strike me as incompatible with collective self-determination. As Wenar notes, an essential element of self-determination is the authority to define property rights within one's jurisdiction. To be self-determining, a community must have the power to organize their internal economic life in accordance with their shared judgments and priorities—making rules that favor collective ownership, or implementing *laissez-faire* policies; deciding to mine their uranium, or eschewing its exploitation—even if their decisions depart from the requirements of the correct theory of distributive justice. Collective self-determination therefore tells in favor of affording peoples extensive management and control rights to their natural resources.[34] It is generally wrong—because disrespectful of self-determination—for outsiders to interfere with a people's internal economic decisions. Since luck egalitarian proposals typically require preserving equal shares of natural resources over time, they are likely to require continually overriding economic policy choices that might impact this pattern, including policies concerning exploitation and development, environmental policy, population policy, and so on. This is difficult to reconcile with self-determination.

But what about more moderate common ownership proposals—such as a Global Resource tax that would provide minimum welfare provisions to the global poor, or environmental regulations that would prohibit a country from using its resources in harmful ways? These proposals typically grant peoples' rights to control and manage, but constrain the people's self-determination, by imposing duties to outsiders if they choose to exploit their resources in certain ways. I doubt that respect for self-determination rules out these proposals, at least if their implementation is approached in the right fashion.

It is not obvious that the only way to work toward more qualified national control over natural resources is for one powerful state to impose it, or for the world community to submit to a coercive global Leviathan.

Another method is to generate these reforms "from the bottom up," by creating a global consensus in favor of them. Indeed, this is how most important international reforms have been brought about so far. No world authority imposed obligations on states to respect human rights, to create "force-proof" borders, or to sign the Paris climate change treaty: states voluntarily committed to these principles, in an act of "self-binding." So why couldn't states commit, via treaty, to taxing the extraction of their natural resources and transferring part of the revenue to the global poor? Since the tax would be levied by domestic governments, no global coercive apparatus would be required. And presumably, if the treaty were ratified by domestic states, it would have some significant support in popular opinion.

Of course, a degree of coercion might be necessary to stabilize a tax scheme, to provide assurance and discourage defaulters. But this might only require "horizontal" sanctions, such as levying tariffs on imports from noncompliant countries. Wenar's proposed "Clean Hands" reforms rely on similar mechanisms. Further, civil society groups could seek to create momentum in favor of a global resource tax, by engaging in publicity campaigns, and organizing boycotts or protest actions. Once a sufficient number of countries had signed on, further incentives might become possible—conditioning membership in international organizations on paying one's fair share of resource taxes, or withholding preferential trade agreements or technology transfers from noncompliant countries. None of these implementation options involves bombing recalcitrant governments into submission. Nor do they envision the creation of a coercive world government. So I do not see why efforts to advance reforms based on the idea of humanity's common ownership should be ruled out, so long as their proponents are willing to *persuade* and *induce* self-determining countries to adopt them, rather than *imposing* these policies against the will of recalcitrant populations.

Consider further that though respect for self-determination is a weighty value, it is not absolute. This means that it will sometimes be permissible for those whose basic needs are at stake to use force to take another country's natural resources, or to interfere with their management, if that is the only way they can secure the means of subsistence for themselves. If the only way to prevent massive death from climate change were to force Bolivia to mine their prized mineral, for example, I believe this would be permissible, even though it involves disrespecting their self-determination. Likewise, if the only way to prevent Mexicans dying of thirst is to coerce the United States to stop using the Rio Grande to irrigate its golf courses, I think this must be done. I note here that even Grotius qualified sovereignty over resources by a right of necessity: he held "Men . . . have a Right to enjoy in common those Things that are already become the Properties of other Persons" if that was the only means to fulfilling their most basic needs.[35] This right of necessity is subject to several qualifications, such as not threatening disproportionate harm, and using force only as a last resort. Still, in sufficiently dire circumstances, it strikes me as plausible that one may permissibly interfere with a people's control and management of their resources, even at some cost to their self-determination. Popular Resource Sovereignty cannot be absolute.

To conclude, then: while regard for self-determination requires us to grant a people extensive management and control rights over its territory and resources, this does not rule out all common ownership reforms. These reforms may proceed via "self-binding" mechanisms that reflect, rather than violate, a people's collective self-determination. And in cases of dire necessity, self-determination may have to be overridden. If I am correct, then despite current international conventions, there is no *moral* right to the full value of a people's natural resources. What we ought to do is to work, in an appropriately respectful way, toward the eventual establishment of international conventions that constrain sovereignty over natural resources by duties of common ownership.

6

Why States Must Remedy the Resource Curse

Aaron James

Although Leif Wenar's wonderful work dwells soberly upon the resource curse, its central aim is to bring good news.[1] Yes, much of our stuff—our cell phones, our jewelry, the gas for our cars—is made from resources bought from corrupt elites in awful regimes. The trades in minerals or oil lack even the minimal consent required for them to be properly conducted in the name of the country's people. And yes, all this is done under the color of law, because the state system's "rule of effectiveness" allows a regime to sell the country's resources as long as it controls the use of force over a territory. Which is to assume, in effect, that might makes legal right. And to make matters even worse, this legal privilege creates powerful incentives for misrule, civil wars, and bloody coups, as rulers need only get their hands on the oil spout to be become fabulously rich and pay off their cronies, generals, and war debts, all while caring not about sharing the wealth or investing in the education or health of the country's people. And yet, if all of this can seem like the sad way of the world, which we must resign ourselves to, Wenar explains that the problem has a relatively easy solution.

What makes the cell phone I purchase in the United States count as mine, as legally my property? The answer is that we in the United States have made certain decisions about our own domestic property rules. Under U.S. law, I enjoy clean title to the object, no matter how awful its origin—even if it comes come to me by theft. But since that is a *domestic* decision, we can just easily decide to modify our property laws. We simply pass a law pertaining to certain transactions from certain places to the effect that that legal title won't come along with the supply chain that the brings the good to my hand. We pass a Clean Trade Act and collect duties on imports from third countries that continue to do business with the unsavory regimes (*Blood Oil*, 283–87, 288–91; this volume, 19–21). So while the problem does arise from the state system, the solution can begin here at home. Domestic political winds need to blow in the right direction, of course, but there's ample room for hope and labor toward a better future.

In its "Westphalian" version, the state system applied the rule of effectiveness almost indiscriminately. Our post-war version is very different; the rule holds by default only, and once a "counter-power" norm is adopted, the legal situation changes (*Blood Oil*, chapter 9). Slaves were once traded freely in international markets. By a change in the rules of property, persons could no longer count as owned. We can now do the same for stolen oil or minerals, by denying the kleptocracies of Saudi Arabia or Equatorial Guinea the legal ability of free exchange. We could do that by clarifying public international law, in new treaties or a change in customary practice. But we needn't wait for sufficient convergence in international opinion. Wenar's good news is that there's a more direct option: any trading country, whether the United States, England, France, or Australia, can decide of its own accord that legal title doesn't pass into its borders or to its citizens. It can do that with no assurances that other countries will do likewise and still chip away at the resource curse, if only because its own citizens prefer cleaner hands.

INCOHERENCE AND ITS RESOLUTION

Wenar hopes governments will actually do this, but he offers more than a policy argument. His larger claim is that current international law and practice is not fully coherent. For there is already an important "counter-power" norm, the one upheld in the human rights covenants that made the Universal Declaration of Human Rights into international treaty law, namely: a country's resources are owned by its people. So the regimes of Nigeria, Yemen, or Sudan do not, even now, have unqualified legal title to the resources they sell to the rest of the world, at their discretion and for personal profit, with little or no accountability to their respective peoples. The problem is that international commerce still proceeds as though they do, which comes to the same thing practically speaking. Officials who set or shape the rules of commerce haven't quite grasped that the norm of effectiveness no longer legally rules in resource trade. And the confusion is abetted by international lawyers that fudge the point by treating *states*, rather than peoples, as the bearer of resource sovereignty rights (*Blood Oil*, chapter 12).

Arguably the whole point of the post-war human rights covenants is to qualify the rule of effectiveness. State sovereignty comes with legitimacy conditions attached. A country's resource sales are to be accountable to its people, and so can't simply line the pockets of elites. If enough countries did redefine their respective domestic property systems, they'd deprive foul regimes of dirty business and clean their hands. But they'd also implement or enforce what is *already* public international treaty law, advance the human rights project, and, ultimately, make the post-war system more coherent.

Of course, mere coherence could be achieved in a different way: just double-down on the rule of effectiveness in resource trade and disqualify the post-war human rights project of limiting its scope. (In fact, at the time of this writing, the U.S. Trump administration is both relaxed about human rights advocacy and firm in its support for authoritarians.) As the clever international lawyer might argue, any talk of the rights of "peoples" in human rights treaties is "diplomatic" language and not law properly speaking. Or perhaps the covenants are admitted as treaty law but narrowly qualified, with the rule of effectiveness generally holding sway.

Wenar would reject these moves, but not ultimately by a narrowly legal argument. The rule of effectiveness should go mainly because it's a disaster, objectionable for many reasons, and unnecessary. The rule lies behind many of what John Rawls called the "great evils of past and present," and only modest domestic legislation in key rich world markets is required to significantly mitigate a persistent source of insecurity, violence, corruption, oppression, and poverty. If we consider the preponderance of such reasons—of humanity, rights, justice, democracy, human flourishing, security—the case for the rule's abolition is wildly overdetermined. Even the "America First" nationalist has something to gain. Oil has fueled the rise of Islamic fundamentalism and terrorism, and addressing the root cause would make the United States (and Europe) safer (*Blood Oil*, chapter 6; this volume, 12).

Wenar's appeal to popular resource ownership can look at first like a deontological appeal to property rights. Although Wenar is himself a property rights theorist, his account of resource rights is intentionally thin about what such rights might be like. It is enough, for his present argument, that international law and practice already affirms resource sovereignty as a counter-power norm against the unaccountable exercise of political authority, and that applying this commitment more concertedly would mitigate many great evils.

So we should give up the rule of effectiveness for a preponderance of reasons. This conclusion—Wenar's main point—doesn't depend on any particular moral theory that privileges certain considerations over others. Yet Wenar tends to favor consequentialism: we morally ought to make the world a better place, or at least mitigate its evils as we can. Because the rule of effectiveness is causally involved with so many evils, its abolition is a key means to this morally good end. (Wenar also proposes "unity theory" as a general way of assessing outcomes, following the ideal J. S. Mill called "unity with our fellow creatures" [*Blood Oil*, 357ff; this volume, 31-35]. But this is mainly attractive supplementation; it improves upon utilitarianism but isn't essential for his main consequentialist argument about resource trade.)

In this chapter, I rephrase Wenar's core argument in terms of a deontological, practice-based theory. This is meant to complement Wenar's already powerful case against the rule of effectiveness, but also to strengthen it, by helping to explain why states are obliged to clean up.

The problem is indeed one of incoherence—but of a deep sort that Wenar never quite fully elaborates. The rule of effectiveness is inconsistent with the very aims of the territorial state system. The system's basic legitimating aims, such as peace, security, collective self-determination (among others), are by now widely but unevenly achieved. But the regulative rules that implement those objectives, including the rule of effectiveness, are not sensitive to the profound risks faced by resource-rich, institutionally weak societies. The result is the grave evils that Wenar so vividly explains, but also a gross structural inequity in the system's treatment of nearly thirty existing societies (for a list, see this volume, 19).[2] To allow this, as we do, is to violate requirements of what societies owe to each other within a state system, seen as a decentralized political union.

The Saudi or Angolan regimes, for failing to meet basic conditions of resource accountability, lack the right to rule. In addition, I want to maintain, our own right to rule, in the United States, Germany, or Brazil, depends on whether we each do what we can—especially when we easily can—to remediate major dysfunctions in our common system, including the gross structural inequity that is the resource curse. For us in the powerful states to do nothing to weaken the rule of effectiveness when we easily can, if only by passing domestic legislation, is for us to fail associative obligations we have simply by virtue of claiming the right of sovereignty. The rule's continued operation is therefore *wrongful* in a way that goes beyond any consequentialist reasons we may have to make the world a better, less awful, place.

In what follows I'll sketch this associational perspective. I'll close by considering Wenar's suggestion about how best to do political philosophy.

THE STATE SYSTEM AS A SOCIAL PRACTICE

In the modern age, beginning with the Treaties of Westphalia, the kings and princes of Europe settled upon a political practice that divides authority over distinct territorial jurisdictions. Each authority was to enjoy a default right of non-interference from outside, for the sake of certain social purposes—especially peace, or at least the reduction of violence. With fresh memories of the Thirty Years War, the bargain stuck and Europe was gradually pacified. By now, centuries later, every existing society and every government has been deeply shaped by the territorial division of political authority. Although domestic developments such as the rise of democracy and human rights have also shaped the system "from below" in a process of co-evolution, the state system remains the world's basic form of political order.

The state system itself is defined by at least three kinds of "constitutive" social norm. (1) Each of many distinct but functionally similar political states is granted jurisdictional rights over a specified territory (i.e., a set of [Hohfeldian] powers to regulate its borders, set rules for the use of its resources, govern supremely over its population, and so on).[3] (These are often called norms of territorial "supremacy.")[4] (2) Each such authority is permitted to repel outside attackers, subject to default expectations of non-interference across territorial jurisdictions (which may be qualified by secondary norms that permit intervention, under specified conditions). (This is often called the "norm of non-intervention.") (3) Further rules or understandings specify what types of functionally similar "states" could qualify for membership in the system, as a bearer of its rights and subject of its obligations. (Such "membership criteria" may evolve, being shaped by international standards within a secondary practice for "recognizing" a political group as a member by other member states.)[5]

This makes up a "social practice," in contrast to a mere system of coordination, in at least this minimal sense: the conduct of different agents is more or less effectively coordinated by widely understood social expectations, as rationalized and adjusted by some shared, or at least presumed, purposes. Most people, most collectives, and most of their officials the world over understand the basic norms of the state system and assume they are widely accepted and followed. Most largely comply on the presumption that enough others are doing likewise. Such expectations are themselves governed and adjusted over time, as political actors rationalize or adjust norms of state conduct, whether through state policy, treaties, international administration, political argument, or trend-setting action—all without a global state. "Realists" doubt that states actually follow rules.[6] Yet states clearly do regularly invoke them as a public pretext for action, or basis for criticism, sanction, and occasional punishment. And such speech, even as "lip service," is all it takes to reinforce the public understandings that constitute the background system against which all international rules and state choices function.[7]

Being a sovereign state at all, properly speaking, depends on this larger association. As Hedley Bull suggests, a domestic state is to be contrasted with a mere "independent political community," which "merely claims a right to sovereignty (or is judged by others to have such a right), but cannot assert this right in practice." This, Bull suggests, "is not a state properly so-called."[8] Like states themselves, the right of state sovereignty is in part a legal or social construction of the larger territorial practice.[9]

If a constitutive rule is essential to a territorial state system, the rule of effectiveness is a mere "regulative" rule. It is not required by the division of political authority over distinct territorial units, or by the idea of foreign sovereignty (*Blood Oil*, 111). Each state can set its own property law for itself, in order to better serve the system's larger objectives.

Was the rule of effectiveness once essential for the system's basic functioning? Perhaps. Maybe the post-Westphalian pacification of Europe depended on it for a time. Perhaps property disputes in trade gave rise to war or strife and a bright-line rule promised peace. But if that ever was so, things have long since changed. The rule of effectiveness is now not only unnecessary for stable commerce, but a cause of great violence, and so inconsistent with the state system's own aim of peace.

THE SYSTEM'S AIMS

In what sense can the state system have "aims" or "purposes"? As suggested, they needn't be endorsed, widely or even at all. Mere "ideational" endorsement can suffice to coordinate conduct without genuinely shared aims, commitments, or purposes. That is, agents can more or less effectively coordinate around a presumed end if enough of the agents accept that *enough of the other agents endorse* a purpose—even if few or none of them *in fact* accept its necessity or value. The coordinated group can merely "presume" the end, in the ideational sense.[10]

The founding Treaties of Westphalia themselves suggest that the aim of peace, or at least of improved security, is generally presumed if not also widely supported. And for all its horrors, the territorial state system did deliver, at least eventually. It brought the virtual end of territorial conquest by the era of decolonization, and finally the "long peace" that continues to this day. The system now appears capable of advancing peace over the longer haul much as Kant once dreamed. Unlike "the practice of slavery," it is not so patently unjustifiable that it should be abolished rather than further improved. So we can tentatively presume its basic moral legitimacy, if only for lack of fundamental options, while hoping to revise it in many deep ways.

The state system can also be said to have further aims, especially in its post-war re-construction. Aside from creating greater security and peace, the

current system arguably aims to secure conditions: (1) for stable possession, the establishment of (individual or collective) property rights, and
the conservation of resources; (2) for societal economic development and
plenty; (3) for collective self-governance and self-determination; (4) for the
realization of basic civil, political, and economic rights; and (5) even, perhaps, for larger social justice (perhaps variously understood).

These aims are perhaps more controversial than the aims of peace and
security. Peace and security can be attributed to the system by a "catholic"
interpretation that defers to established social understandings, even when
or if they conflict with our personal moral or interpretive judgment as theorists. The post-war era and human rights practice offers ample materials for
moralized constructive interpretation of the state system's aims, which
might include all of the aims just listed. The more controversial among
them may require a relatively "protestant" interpretation, which defers less
to prevailing social understanding and relies more heavily on the interpret-
er's own understandings and evaluations in making sense of the state system as a social practice.[11]

Wenar operates in a catholic interpretive mode. Peace is "invoked by
nearly everyone," quite sincerely (this volume, 18). Popular resource sovereignty is an idea "most of the world already believes in," even beyond its
public affirmation in treaty law (22). What Wenar means to add, perhaps,
is just an elaboration of the idea's plain moral meaning, for resource
accountability, property systems, and trade policy. As he elaborates:

> History, through its cunning, has already given us the legal texts that should
> be law. All that needs adding is belief in their plain meaning. Our good for-
> tune with texts is captured by Hegel's famous *Doppelsatz*: "What is rational is
> actual; and what is actual is rational." What is rational is actual: the most
> plausible principle of popular resource sovereignty is embodied in the interna-
> tional legal documents that most states are already party to. And what is actual
> is rational: there is a natural, even obvious, interpretation of the international
> legal documents that explains popular resource sovereignty and integrates it
> with other priorities in the international system. The world already has the
> doctrine that it needs. (*Blood Oil*, 196)

A more protestant posture allows our ideas of what is "most plausible"
to lead us beyond plain meaning to deeper understandings of the system's
very aims, including its assumed values. These might pre-date the postwar
era, and indeed explain what the legal documents meant to codify. Wenar
might agree, so long as this deeper argument isn't said to be necessary; his
point is that that there is an "obvious" interpretation of key texts agreed
upon by most states, and that this suffices for his argument.

However they are justified, the rule of effectiveness thwarts each and every one of the state system's aims as enumerated above, for the reasons Wenar gives. The rule systematically undermines conditions for peace by incentivizing violence in resource-rich societies, and by fueling war and terrorism abroad. It undercuts conditions for stable possession and the establishment of individual and collective property rights by enabling unaccountable rule. It hobbles the conservation of resources, which are pillaged by elites. It profoundly stunts societal economic development and plenty. It undercuts collective self-governance and self-determination by encouraging authoritarian rule, which also hinders the realization of basic civil, political, and economic rights, and any aspiration for larger social justice. If some of these aims are relatively controversial from an interpretive perspective, any one of them is sufficient to justify the rule of effectiveness's rejection. Together they mount an overwhelming case.

ASSOCIATIVE SOVEREIGNTY

This is not yet to address a further question of "normativity," about the reasons of states. The internal critique just offered can be a moral and not merely a legal argument. This does not necessarily require "external," "ideal" goals; for moral reasoning can be sensitive to the kind of practice the state system is.[12] (The moral argument might be legal as well provided a constructive jurisprudential philosophy, e.g., à la Dworkin.) But even so, even if we agree the state system is unjust because of its creation of the resource curse, it is a further question what reasons for action states might have as a result: why would any state, their officials, and their publics in particular have sufficient reason to do anything about it?

Life is not fair, and the state system may never be fully just. There are plenty of good causes to promote. Why if at all must a given state assign any very weighty significance to an opportunity to improve the system, let alone sufficient reason to act? How if at all is inaction *wrongful*, such that the resource curse is to be rectified, in the face of competing priorities, with all deliberate speed?

One answer appeals to natural duty. Rawls's Natural Duty of Justice might be applied to state practice, for instance. Dworkin suggests a duty of states to keep themselves legitimate. As a necessary means to this end, states are required to actively support the legitimacy of the state system, which in turn requires complying with international law, including emergent customary practice.[13]

Whether anything beyond power and interest could or should matter in state choices is of course hotly contested. Here I merely sketch a further moral account that does without appeal to natural duty—what might be called an associative conception of state sovereignty.

In this perspective, each state that claims the right to rule under the state system's prerogatives also incurs obligations by association. Of necessity, the right to rule over a territory comes with "associative obligations," both legal and moral. For both the rights and the obligations are justified together or not at all for the state system in particular, in view of the distinctive kind of territorial political union it is. As Hedley Bull suggests, those normative relations in turn define what it is to be a state at all, distinguishing it from an independent political community or a mafia syndicate. By virtue of asserting the right to rule within the system that defines the rights of territorial sovereignty, as states do, their officials, and their publics are together bound to follow obligations. States, if you will, are obliged simply as states. No obligation, no rights. And unobliging states are mere "regimes."

Law itself being a remedial institution, these responsibilities include an obligation to remedy the state system's dysfunctions. It is usually a delicate matter what exactly a given state is obliged to do in particular circumstances. In resource trade, the case is relatively clear-cut. Let me explain.

In part for its politically decentralized and territorial nature, the state system brings a distinctive class of problems. These must be handled somehow, by war if not by law and politics. But war cannot, morally or prudently, be the normal order of business, and politics is too unstable without a supportive legal framework.

Yet there is no central legislature to guide world affairs. States are not only the subjects but also the *authors* of international law and practice. In that case each state bears legislative responsibility in its conduct. Its foreign or domestic actions are rightly received as proposals for what is legally either permissible or obligatory, and addressed accordingly by other states or public actors. They are met, for instance, with demands for good faith justification, competing interpretations of what the law is, and measures of accountability (including "jawboning" or "naming and shaming," if not economic or military sanction). The dysfunctions of a decentralized and territorial system are familiar.[14]

For their rival interests and competing domestic constituencies, states find coordination slow and difficult. Cross-border externalities, from trade or pollution policies, easily appear to be someone else's problem, or devolve into mutual "beggar my neighbor" policies and recriminations. Given the limits of effectively holding defiant states accountable, their populations are often left in the clutches of their sovereign at sharp risk of abuse. What people gain in being freed from wars and invasions from the reduction of international conflict, they may lose in domestic tyranny or oppression, persistent corruption or complacency in the design of economic policy, or political exclusion or underrepresentation. Enforced borders may exclude willing migrants from greener pastures. And whole societies may suffer unfavorable conditions for development—because of a worsening climate, poor geography, or weak institutions, all within international institutions that create perverse incentives for elites to reinforce just such unfavorable conditions.

The resource curse is prime example. Again, as Wenar explains in careful detail, the rule of effectiveness gives illegitimate rulers title for the legal sale of a country's resources with little or no accountability or benefit for their respective peoples. This creates powerful economic incentives for plunder, corruption, neglect, or outright violence, as society copes in destitution while the rest of the world profits at its expense. We get the oil and the diamonds, they get the kleptocrats and premature death.

This is odious or worse for many reasons. As suggested, one thing it means is that the current state system is failing its basic aims on a large if partial scale; the rule of effectiveness creates a gross structural inequity in the way the system advances its own aims. Even as many societies prosper under the territorial order, enjoying relative peace, stability, commerce, development, and self-determination, a significant portion of the world's societies languishes by comparison, in part as a consequence of the same system.

In general, an associative obligation of mitigation requires that each state do what it feasibly can, at a reasonable cost, to mitigate the major dysfunctions of the state system in a given period of history. Bearing even a high cost might be morally necessary; the nineteenth-century British paid dearly for ending the rule of effectiveness for slaves (*Blood Oil*, 268–69; this volume, 33). But as Wenar explains, in the present case reform is not costly on balance. The rule of effectiveness causes a gross structural inequity and a major dysfunction, but most societies will make considerable security gains by curbing its influence. While our very way of life depends on energy and oil in particular, it isn't threatened by the end of effectiveness (this volume, p. 24). Security being of great importance, gains in safety offset what would be at most small or modest economic losses in the aggregate. Wenar emphasizes this as a point of national prudence. In the present context, the upshot is that inaction is not simply short-sighted, but also without excuse—or at least without one kind of excuse a state might otherwise fairly offer, which is that the cost of action is too high, or that it has done enough already.

THE DEONTOLOGICAL CAST

This may be expressed in deontological terms of "what we owe to each other" as follows.[15] No government in power can reasonably insist upon being free from any obligations of association whatsoever, if only the obligation of non-interference. For the people involved can easily be free of them by simply giving up power, along with any claim to its rightful exercise.

Making a promise can saddle one with promissory obligations, in part because one was free not to make it. In a similar way, simply by virtue of a putative government's choice to take or maintain power, its elites are thereby saddled with the state system's responsibilities. To the extent the government fails its sovereign obligations in its foreign or domestic policy, its sovereign rights are increasingly open to question, with interference by force, coercion, or sanction increasingly appropriate. In extremis, it can be legitimately forced out of power, the way a mafia ring can be run out of town.

No political grouping or government or party is entitled by nature to rule over a particular territory; any claim to rule must be recognized by other states on the basis of a government's substantive credentials (including the way it compares with another party or grouping). For indeed, might does not by itself make right. And no natural right to rule over others, if there is one, prevails against the right of sovereignty in legitimate state practice.

Why, though, is mitigation also part of the associational package? Because all states have ample permission to serve their societal interests on behalf of their respective peoples. So no claimants to the right of sovereignty can reasonably object to being asked to do at least *something* to mitigate disadvantages created by the common territorial practice, at a reasonable cost to them, at least absent some special justification. At the very least, they can be asked to cease and desist in exacerbating a gross problem of clear general concern, for instance, the insecurity wrought by the resource curse.

In resource trade, members of "cursed" societies have powerful reasons to object on their society's behalf that the international system is achieving its legitimating purposes in a partial and grossly inequitable fashion, by permitting great disadvantages to them as compared to other societies. The advantaged states, by comparison, have especially weak objections to being asked to curb their support for dictators (beyond asking for an appropriate legislative time frame and so on). Gains in security partly compensate for any losses in commercial profits to any particular local or multinational firms and shareholders. And while certain kleptocrats and profiteers will be made worse off, the cost to them is either irrelevant or insufficient to justify the grotesque consequences for "cursed" societies.

Moreover, since curbing the rule of effectiveness would bring major collateral benefits for every country, nothing could justify inaction. For surely we cannot *reasonably* complain of being asked to mitigate a gross structural inequity in our common territorial practice if this would make us on balance better off as well. We now lack political will to do as we ought, in part for our short-sightedness. But that fact does not *justify* collective inaction; it merely explains it.

In sum, then, any of the major economic powers can unilaterally weaken the rule of effectiveness, make itself and the world safer. Inaction is not simply imprudent or short-sighted. It is without excuse, a wrongful failure to meet the remedial obligations that underwrite our own sovereignty.

The rule of effectiveness is also a source of unfairness in the practice of international trade, taken by itself.[16] It is *especially* objectionable that so many societies tolerate the evils of effectiveness while profiting from it economically. Yet the wrong of failing a remedial obligation does not depend on the receipt of economic benefit or bilateral trade relations. The associative obligations in question arise from the state system itself, which embeds trade relations as a sub-system. So even if a powerful state conducts little or no trade with a "cursed" society, it would still have an obligation of remediation, for instance, to initiate or join a multilateral agreement that finally abolishes the rule of effectiveness in the countries that do trade with it.

Here one might be skeptical: is the United States really obliged to mitigate the resource curse in a way that would undercut its very sovereignty? Perhaps it is obliged—but with its very right to rule at stake? Angola's corrupt elite do lack the right to rule. But surely there is no point at which U.S. officials do.

My answer is that U.S. neglect for a time would not undercut its sovereignty rights. It would mean that the United States is failing obligations it incurs by virtue of the rights of sovereignty it asserts. And that *is* one count against its sovereign status. The U.S. government's right to rule in the first place depends on various qualifications, substantive and procedural. Sufficient failure of enough of those obligations would indeed make the United States into a rogue state and no longer a proper sovereign power. (Though once it has gone rogue, there may be little to be done about replacing it, as with many such regimes.) The United States is not at any immediate risk of this given the relatively high quality of its institutions and its major contributions to the world. Yet these conditions are not guaranteed. According to many observers, they are presently in peril.

It is worth noting that an associational deontology perspective may also help Wenar's own appeal to collective ownership. The human rights covenants mean that popular resource sovereignty is a legal right; but it also has moral backing of some sort. But of what sort, if not, say, a natural right? Wenar nicely outlines what "ownership" requires for accountability for how resources are used (*Blood Oil*, chapters 13 and 17; this volume, 26–27). It may help to add that, whatever natural rights individual persons might have in a state of nature, the "rights of peoples" need be nothing more than "artificial" or practice-based claims justified in light of what the state system is like. Which is to say, they are *moral* claims based in relevant interests of persons who live in a society under a particular sort of political association. The state system divides political authority over different territorial jurisdictions, and the association itself defines its participants in terms of certain groups, in this case a set of persons who reside on a territory and make up a more or less functioning society (a "people"). Assuming a social order of this general kind can be justified, the members of a given society will have morally relevant interests in how their society will tend to fare under alternative versions in respect to natural resources on its territory. These interests furnish a significant "claim"—meaning a potentially decisive ground for reasonable complaint—to control the resources within their particular jurisdiction, by way of a sufficiently representative government.

Note, finally, that for all this says the burdens suffered by "cursed" societies can count as absolutely bad or awful. I have suggested only that those societies' claim against the state system is a *comparative* one of structural equity as well. Here I mean only to bring out one important, deontological dimension of the problem.[17]

DO WE NEED THEORY?

Wenar's work can be read as making a suggestion, if only by its own example, about how political philosophy is to be done. It is to be done for and with the public, building up from the grizzly realities of law, politics, and markets to a cumulative, "bottom up" case for revising what can seem given with gains for almost everyone. The argument should draw from the lessons and trajectory of history, the realities of political economy, and relatively uncontroversial moral and prudential premises. But otherwise, Wenar seems to suggest, it can or should travel pretty light on moral theory, ignoring conventional theoretical preoccupations. (Again, his aspirational appeal to a "unity theory" isn't essential for the main argument.)

This is a welcome corrective. Anglo-American political philosophy has become insufficiently world-historical. I'd say this isn't a beef with high theory as such, however; it is simply reason for theory to be practice-based, in a way that fits nicely with the substance of Wenar's account. His work serves up ample resources for a "bottom up/top down" blend of the interpretive and the moral, the specific and the general, the ugly realities of the Arab or American street and the intellectual palaces of high theory. It nicely tees up a practice theory of justice of the sort I favor—a theoretical philosophy that's attuned to the world.

As I understand it, a practice theory of the sort just sketched offers a general method for reasoning about the evils of past and present as well as other major moral issues, including those that world politics has only begun to reckon with. By this method, justification, at least for certain central questions of justice, is in the first instance sensitive to the best constructive interpretation of our basic social and institutional practices, as inherited from history, and as they could be credibly revised in the foreseeable future, even with generous idealization about political will and about conditions favorable for human civilization. Thinking this way, I fold Wenar's resource argument into my own grand practice-based story about how the world could eventually see equalized standards of living. Technological change, trade, and factor price equalization gradually become framed by a more equitable global economy and state system. And capitalism is adapted to climate change, by cutting back the global rate of growth, reducing the work week, and retooling social insurance, along with new reforms in international capital regulation, finance, and taxation and more. A key part of the story is about what it takes for a capitalist global economy to be fairer to the Middle East or Africa given the resource curse. Which is to say that Wenar's work nicely complements world-historical normative futurology of a sort that goes well beyond an appeal to national security and the great evils of past and present, Wenar's ostensible focus.

Wenar needn't disagree. But is even a practice theory too much theory— too much of what responds to the intellectual curiosities of theorists, rather than to the concerns of soil, vice, and money that get the blood flowing among the general public, which might actually effect a change in policy? Perhaps the philosopher should focus simply on the greater evils and articulate and defend, simply and credibly, the reasons that are most likely to cause public action.

I'm only suggesting that our options are not so limited. As I've suggested, our understanding of the resource curse problem is illuminated by a practice theory and a structural equity optic. Made well, this sort of argument might even be of popular interest, and indeed part and parcel of philosophy's proper public aspirations. In short, we can have theory for real practice. We can advance—just for its own sake—the intellectual integrity of philosophy, that part of human culture, first defined by Plato, with which we have been entrusted. But theory, even high theory, can shape and be the basis of how we do practical philosophy, even with and for the public. Wenar himself is a leading light in how we might rise to what may be our most important task.[18]

7

Reply to Blake and Mehdiyeva

Leif Wenar

I would like to express my sincere gratitude to the other authors in this volume, for their incisive, imaginative, and illuminating explorations of the ideas.

The chapters by Blake and Mehdiyeva are mostly consequentialist, engaged in the real work of thinking through, as best we can, what we can do to improve the future of those who live and will live in our world. I reply to their excellent essays on these crucial points.

Kutz's elegant attack is two-part: his *attaque a fer* first aims to knock my consequentialist theory aside and then extend his own position. My *derobement* attempts to avoid his blade, and my counter-thrust to win the point.

Since the chapters of Stilz and James are mostly about their own non-consequentialist theories, my replies focus on philosophical method—I criticize their impressive theories, in support of my outcome-oriented approach.

Imagine that you have early-stage bone cancer—or, if you prefer, that you are a young doctor caring for someone who does. Some treatments are available: chemotherapy, radiation, surgery. All of them have risks, and all and will be painful and draining. The decision of which course to take is weighty, the treatments must be closely vetted. As you mull over the worst-case scenarios for the treatments available, your initial response may be to reject all of them out of hand. But the reality that you come back to is that rejecting treatment of the cancer is accepting the progression of the disease.

When we wake up tomorrow, we will need a rule to determine from whom it will be legal to buy the natural resources of other countries. Our decision tomorrow isn't "Clean Trade or not Clean Trade." Our decision is between Popular Resource Sovereignty and effectiveness. If we reject the treatment, we are choosing the progression of that disease.

As I've gone around the world discussing *Blood Oil*, nearly everyone has agreed with its diagnosis of the oil curse. Effectiveness gifts unaccountable power to coercive men who use it oppress their people, fight wars, undermine democracies, and spread their intolerant ideologies worldwide. This power cannot be held accountable from outside the country through alliances, sanctions, or military actions. Power over resources can only be held to account by the people of the country—which we know by looking at the countries that have escaped the resource curse and all of the reforms that have been designed to fight it.

The questions around *Blood Oil* have nearly all concerned whether the transition to Popular Resource Sovereignty is feasible: whether the cure is worse than the disease. These questions are of the first importance, and Blake and Mehdiyeva, being extremely acute critics, have raised several of them powerfully.

What should always be present in these discussions is that the alternative really is the disease. The disease is the rule that has powered autocratic repression, grand corruption, international aggression, civil conflicts with large refugee crises, genocide, and the spread of extremism from oil states, now to be exacerbated by new technologies and climate change—that cannot be the right choice for tomorrow.[1] If there is a "non-invasive" alternative that offers good prospects for a real cure, should we not choose it?

Politics is like medicine: decisions are made between options, and all options come with risks. Blake worries that the Clean Trade policies may fail because "evil is resilient"—and this may be right. Yet our other option is to continue to fund evil when we shop, and indeed to incentivize ever more evil in the future. In politics, medicine, indeed in all of life, responsible decisions must be comparative: they must always turn on a vivid appreciation of the choices that we have. In our case, the choice is between fighting evil and fueling evil—or, to put it in more sober terms, between maintaining and replacing a law that channels unchecked power to some of the world's most coercive, violent, and venal men.[2]

Blake raises a few legal and conceptual issues that we can clear up before comparing these choices. Blake says, for instance, that

a government selling oil abroad is wearing two hats at once; it is a (putative) property-holder, and a juridical authority. The former hat says: I own this oil. The latter hat says: in my capacity as domestic political authority, I determine who shall own this oil. . . . Wenar says that, when we refuse to recognize the government's authority to sell the oil, we are simply refusing to let our legal system be used to perpetuate an injustice abroad. But we are doing more than that. We are refusing the government the right to determine, on its own territory, the rules by which property claims shall be adjudicated. This is a fairly serious thing for us to do. Its seriousness is enshrined in American law under the heading of the Act of State doctrine, on which a domestic court is precluded from judging the validity of an official act of a foreign country undertaken within that foreign country's borders.[3]

This is not correct: Clean Trade legislation says nothing about how any foreign government adjudicates property claims on its own territory. This legislation only suspends the rights of persons of the enacting state to buy resources—it doesn't concern any foreigner's right to own or sell. A quick way to see this point is to grant for the moment Blake's (mistaken) premise that Clean Trade imposes sanctions. If Blake's premise were correct, then his legal point would carry over to sanctions too. And sanctions clearly do not refuse a foreign government the right to determine the rules for adjudicating property claims on its own territory, nor do they "stand in judgment of another society's domestic law."[4]

Although Blake declares that his criticisms do not accept the morality of the status quo, he slips (perhaps unconsciously) into language that makes sense only if he does assume just this.[5] For example, Blake says that the Chinese in Africa are "much more willing to separate capitalism and morality." Yet in order to make such a claim, he must be assuming that what the Chinese are doing in Africa is buying legitimate title to resources, instead of buying resources stolen from the people.[6] So he must be assuming that "Might Makes Right" is right.

Similarly, Blake charges that Clean Trade would coerce foreigners or that it would interfere with their domestic affairs. Yet beneath this view is again an endorsement of the status quo. Blake must be assuming that the alternative to Clean Trade, the rule of effectiveness, is non-coercive and non-interfering. That is, Blake must be assuming that states today that choose to send hundreds of millions of dollars to empower repressive regimes, while simultaneously incentivizing the violent overthrow of those regimes, are not involved in coercing the people of those countries, or interfering in their affairs—and that only the states that choose *not* to do business with the repressive regimes are coercing and interfering. As argued in *Blood Oil*, this is not plausible.[7]

In philosophical parlance, Blake is relying on a "non-moralized baseline" for deciding when coercion and interference occur: coercion and interference are measured only against what *does* happen, not against what *should* happen. Using such a baseline we would, for example, have to conclude that the Mafia today is not coercing anyone on Sicily, nor interfering in anyone's life—and that coercion or interference would only occur if someone tried to stop the Mafia. Using non-moralized baselines cannot detect wrongs in progress; it can only condemn efforts, however laudable, to correct those wrongs. Blake accepts the badness of effectiveness, so it is surprising that he embeds it so firmly into his arguments.

Some of Blake's most dramatic language embeds a status quo bias in a different way. Blake says that Clean Trade is sanctions, and that sanctions "kill people." He blames sanctions, for example, for killing 500,000 Iraqi children during the 1990s.[8] Here Blake implicitly accepts the context of the sanctions as given, and focuses all of his moral evaluation on the outsiders who change the status quo trade relations.

Let us agree first that the West has committed many and extreme injustices in Iraq across several decades—that is not controversial. Still, can we endorse the pattern of reasoning beneath Blake's claim that sanctions killed half a million Iraqi children? How might this reasoning look in a parallel case?[9]

> Rancher Jones is a nasty piece of work. He often picks fights with his neighbors, and usually starts shooting to win them. He beats and neglects his children, sometimes keeping them locked in the barn for days. One night he leads an armed gang that chases out the owners of a neighboring farm, and takes this farm for himself. This is the last straw for most of his neighbors. They agree with each other not to buy Jones's cattle any more. After this, Jones still makes enough money to live the high life himself, but he buys less and worse food for his children. Two children weaken and die while locked in the barn.

Using Blake's reasoning, the conclusion is unavoidable: the neighbors killed Jones's children.

Such examples suggest that the status quo bias and the "outsiders only" focus in Blake's reasoning are leading his conclusions astray. Additionally, if Blake's "outsiders only" focus were correct in itself, Blake would have to reverse his conclusions. For outsiders choosing effectiveness has had much worse consequences than outsiders choosing sanctions.

For example, in the late 1980s, Saddam's regime spent its oil-export revenues to launch attacks (including chemical attacks) against the Iraqi Kurds that were so devastating that several countries have recognized this "Anfal campaign" as a genocide. If, as Blake implies, it was outsiders' choice of sanctions that killed Iraqi children in the 1990s, then we would be forced to conclude that it was outsiders' choice of effectiveness that paid for and so killed tens of thousands of Kurds in the 1980s. And, of course, outsiders' choice of effectiveness would also have killed very large numbers of people in other decades and other countries. If all killings in oil-cursed states should be attributed only to the choices of outsiders, then the death toll from outsiders' standing choice of effectiveness is many orders of magnitude higher than that from their relatively rare choices of sanctions.

Turning now from legal and conceptual issues to Blake's worries about the risks of efforts to improve on effectiveness, some of these worries look hasty. For instance, Blake asserts that the mineral-tracing law that the United States enacted in 2010 has had "devastating results for over five million miners and their families." Yet Blake's assertion is based on a single 2012 working paper from an NGO, which footnotes unattributed sources making unverifiable claims at a seminar in Washington.[10] While the U.S. law did cause disruptions in miners' lives, the 2017 report from the UN Group of Experts on the DRC is more positive about its effects:

> Concerning natural resources, the implementation of mineral traceability in the Democratic Republic of the Congo has considerably reduced instances of armed groups directly benefiting from the exploitation and trade of tin, tantalum and tungsten. In addition, opportunities for indirect benefits from such minerals are decreasing.[11]

A scholarly study shows that claims about unintended negative effects of the law have been exaggerated by foreign business interests. And, crucially, today highly respected leaders in Congolese civil society support the mineral-tracing reform, and are calling for its approach to be expanded.[12]

This should reassure Blake about the potential for Clean Trade reforms to improve on the status quo (and to do so without, as he says, "good men and good luck"). In the Clean Trade scenario that Blake describes for the Congo, no one can legally buy the country's minerals until the government becomes more accountable to the people. And here, the only way for both powerful insiders and powerful outsiders to make money from the Congo's minerals is for there to be better governance in the Congo. This aligns the incentives of the powerful with the interests of ordinary people. This must be a more promising scenario than continuing with effectiveness, which has for decades helped to keep the Congo extremely oppressive, corrupt, and poor, and funded conflicts that have caused millions of deaths.

Blake's other practical worries about Clean Trade can also be eased. For example, Blake raises the concern of oil smuggling. Yet oil in any quantity is big and heavy and easy to track—indeed the world's oil is already being tracked by several intelligence agencies and commercial firms. States with the political will to enact Clean Trade should have little trouble stopping significant smuggling.[13]

Blake also worries that Clean Trade states would need to form a "cartel," and that cartels are unstable. He is unlucky to be making this point within the industry that contains the longest-lasting international cartel in modern history (OPEC). And what Blake is calling a cartel is really just international cooperation of the usual sort, as we have seen, for example, with the spread of anti-bribery laws across the industrialized countries and with the spread of laws against importing blood diamonds around the world.[14] Nor has this cooperation required national leaders to be heroically virtuous—as *Blood Oil* explains, these reforms were made by national leaders looking to their country's and their own interests. So it will be with Clean Trade, which furthers so many national interests and political agendas that national leaders can further their own electoral advantage by championing it.

Both Mehdiyeva and Blake draw on the history of sanctions to evaluate the effects of a Clean Trade Act. While a Clean Trade Act is not sanctions, it is worth taking a look at modern sanctions before saying why a Clean Trade Act should work even better.

Like any other policy tool, sanctions cannot automatically or by themselves change the behavior of recalcitrant states. But the West's use of oil sanctions has become increasingly more potent, as a recent major case study shows.[15] In 2010–2013, the United States and the European Union imposed sanctions to pressure the Iranian government to scale down its nuclear program through a broad shipping blacklisting policy. Vessels carrying Iranian petroleum were thereafter banned from trading in U.S. and EU ports.[16]

The sanctions produced impressive results: Iranian seaborne oil exports fell from 2.5 million barrels per day in 2011 to 1.1 million barrels per day in 2014, a decline of 56 percent.[17] Relative to its oil-rich peers, during sanctions Iran consistently underperformed on major indicators such as oil production, oil export revenues, economic growth, and inflation.[18] Several experts have cited these sanctions as crucial to the Iranian regime's decision in July 2015 to make a deal on its nuclear program with the group of six nations led by the United States.[19]

The decline in Iranian exports during these sanctions was especially dramatic, given that these were "partial" sanctions, imposed only by Western states. China and India continued to buy Iranian oil throughout. Yet because of the Western shipping blacklists, Chinese oil imports from Iran still fell by 23 percent during the sanctions.[20] Properly framed, oil sanctions can be a powerful tool.[21]

As Mehdiyeva and Blake rightly say, being sanctioned can help an authoritarian regime to rally public support, by portraying the sanctions as another attack by the West. But what if instead of sanctioning, Western countries do something different? What if Western countries take a public stand for the rights of the citizens of resource-cursed countries, by getting out of business with those who (as those citizens know) are giving them a very raw deal?

Although a Clean Trade Act shares some features with sanctions, its public justification is entirely different. Sanctions are punishments, and Clean Trade does not aim to punish anyone. Rather, with Clean Trade a country aligns its laws with the widely applauded idea of Popular Resource Sovereignty. The people of the enacting country take a positive stand, affirming the rights of the peoples of all countries—an appeal to a principle that the people of resource-cursed countries also affirm.

Blake says that Clean Trade's reforms will be perceived as "(very nearly) acts of war by those against whom they are brought to bear," and that the Chinese will resent the United States' unilateral invocation of Popular Resource Sovereignty "as a cudgel against weaker and non-Western societies."[22] If this is how Clean Trade is perceived, it will only be because of a lack of skill among the politicians who present it. (Blake's worries sound a little like a drug dealer saying, "I can't possibly do the right thing. After all, who would ever believe me?")

If the problem of perception is unilateralism, then many states can announce Clean Trade reforms at once. If the problem is a perception of American imperialism, then perhaps Brazil or Norway can pass its Clean Trade Act first.[23] And consider how confounded Blake's doubters will be when Western states signal so clearly that they don't "just want the oil," by announcing even-handed treatment of traditional allies (Saudi Arabia) and enemies (Iran) alike. Clean Trade is the opposite of "business as usual": it is an innovative effort to solve a problem that all can see damages the interests of both the people "there" and the people "here." What statesman would not relish the opportunity to explain it to the world?

Mehdiyeva raises a related concern based on the prediction that the United States will export ever more oil to Europe and China. Asking these trade partners then to join in ending their authoritarian oil imports might look less like action on principle, and more like a means to promote American commercial interests in oil exports.

Let me first just note that in the past some have said that Clean Trade is impossible because American energy interests would oppose it too much. This new concern is that Clean Trade will face challenges because American energy interests would favor it too much. Having the support of powerful domestic interests for principled reforms seems not the worst problem to have, and Mehdiyeva's challenges seem manageable. If perception of U.S. commercial advantage becomes a problem, then the United States can offer to sell the Europeans and Chinese energy far enough below market prices that no accusation of profiteering could stick.

It's true that reforms such as these would require both America and Europe to bear costs. But as *Blood Oil* says, bearing costs is essential to Clean Trade's strategy—a strategy of integrity. People come to believe those who act consistently on their principles, and who bear costs for the sake of their beliefs.[24] America gained real credibility through the Marshall Plan in Europe and the PEPFAR program to fight AIDS in Africa. Imagine an Oval Office speech in which the president forthrightly sets out the economic costs that America will be bearing, finally to do right by the peoples of oil-exporting states, and the benefits of peace, security, and trust that will flow from doing so. (In international relations theory, this is known as "costly signaling.")

Nor need the costs be ruinous: Clean Trade reforms can be phased in so as to achieve whatever level of costs is politically feasible. For example, the average U.S. household spends around 3 percent of its income on gasoline.[27] If Clean Trade reforms gradually increase gas prices by 25 percent, so that they come closer to prices in Europe, this will not cause real hardship to any but the poorest Americans, who could be compensated by adjusting tax rules. Or, even better, an American president could say that reform will mean that gasoline prices will be going up by 15 percent, but that fuel efficiency will also be going up by 15 percent, leaving drivers no worse off at the pump, while the environment gets cleaner.

Mehdiyeva's discussions of both climate and China-Russia are penetrating, as one would expect from a first-rate energy analyst. These are the two most important issues for Clean Trade going forward, and adequately to address them would require more space than is allowed here. Here I can only make remarks of orientation, and draw on some of the solutions that Mehdiyeva herself generously explains.

The need for coordinated action on climate change should be apparent to all reasonable observers. Clean Trade aims to speed the transition away from fossil fuels by emphasizing the dangers of the oil curse for people in both importing and exporting states. Continuing the energy system that we have will be lose-lose for both the climate and peace; reforms can be win-win when they replace "blood barrels" with alternative energy sources. The best way to transition away from blood oil is to get off oil altogether.

One challenge for this "Autocrats to Alternatives" plan is geographical. In general, the oil in oil-cursed regions like the Middle East tends to be "cleaner" and cheaper, while the oil in stable democracies tends to be "dirtier" and more expensive. Tapering off imports of Middle Eastern oil, as Clean Trade does, may pressure toward greater exploitation of the Canadian oil sands, as Blake worries, or toward increased use of techniques such as fracking, whose risks Mehdiyeva explains.

The first point to make here is that problems like methane leakage and water use in fracking are not Clean Trade problems—as Mehdiyeva brings out forcefully, these are serious issues that must be addressed right now in the world as it is. Clean Trade would at most intensify the need to implement solutions to problems that we already face, and in most cases the solution must be better regulation of production. There's nothing technically difficult about this regulation, but Mehdiyeva is right that it must be firmly defined and implemented.

More, these problems, weighty as they are, should also be kept in perspective. For example, the International Energy Agency estimates that producing even a massive three million more barrels a day from Canada's oil sands instead of from conventional sources would increase global emissions by less than a single day's worth of emissions from China.[26] And when the costs of transition are raised, such as costs of improving regulation to protect the environment, the larger context should be kept in view. Energy analysts tend to think on the scale of energy costs, yet estimates of the military costs to the United States of protecting Middle Eastern oil supplies range from tens of billions to hundreds of billions of dollars annually. Even modest savings in this military spending would be more than enough to pay for better regulation and a faster energy transition.

And, as always, evaluations must be comparative. It is likely that continuing with effectiveness will create its own risks to the environment. As Michael Ross and Eric Voeten show, the more oil a country exports, the less likely it is to join intergovernmental organizations, like those that will be needed to coordinate future efforts to address climate change.[27] Historically (and not surprisingly) many areas that have suffered extreme environmental degradation from resource production, such as Eastern Siberia and the Niger Delta, have been in countries where governmental accountability to citizens has been low. And looking at the countries that engage in highly climate-negative practices like gas flaring, one finds that all of the highest-flaring countries are "below the line" of Popular Resource Sovereignty.[28]

In projecting the costs of transitioning away from effectiveness, we should also remain alive to the real possibility that—as Mehdiyeva helpfully suggests on rare earths—technological progress will reduce friction toward a feasible solution. Many projections of energy costs are simple linear projections and so are unreliable.[29] Progress on renewable power generation, batteries, and energy efficiency may speed progress away from fossil fuels, and so ease an "Autocrats to Alternatives" solution.

The key point is that, even without technological progress, Clean Trade is compatible with whatever climate goals we aim for. Even extremely ambitious climate targets can be combined with policies to taper off authoritarian imports, by extending the time of the tapering. As always, the greatest power of Clean Trade is the soft power of its announcement—how long the tapering of authoritarian imports will take is less significant. What matters most is whether we—the people and leaders of the West—will take a public stand for the right policy.

Like environment, the Chinese posture toward Clean Trade raises many large questions. Let me add a few remarks to the discussions in *Blood Oil* and chapter 1 of this volume.[30]

When considering geostrategy on a large time scale, it is important to start with the basics. China is rising, but it is not yet on top. By Western standards, China is still a poor country, with a GDP per capita around a quarter of that in the United States (comparable to Brazil or the Dominican Republic).[31] An aging population will increasingly slow China's growth through the medium term, while a youthful, democratic India overtakes it as the primary engine of Asian economic productivity.[32] And while the Chinese military has made impressive gains in its capacity to project force in its region, the United States will likely remain the only military superpower for another decade at least.[33]

In the big picture, China is rising but the West will remain dominant over China along nearly every dimension of hard and soft power for some time. The question of the next decades will be how the West will use its power as Asia rises—which norms and institutions the West will choose to strengthen as a legacy for the future, when power will be more evenly balanced between the hemispheres.

So far, China's support for the norms and institutions of the post-war international order has been steady. Indeed, on issues such as trade and climate, China has recently been a stronger supporter of the international consensus than has the United States. To take its relations with Africa as a major marker of this, China has mostly "played by the rules" in offering its own development model to poorer countries, while taking on increasing responsibilities such as providing more support for peacekeeping efforts.[34] While there have been inevitable frictions during China's big push into Africa, China is, much to its credit, today regarded positively by substantial majorities of Africans.[35]

This is encouraging, and it should encourage the West to consider how it wants to use its current advantage in power to influence China as it rises further. The West should welcome China's rise within the international order, while emphasizing the importance of popular sovereignty. And the best way to take this stand is through peaceful promotion of Popular Resource Sovereignty.

When Western states implement Clean Trade, they will gain trust around the world. While it may seem that China will get something even better than trust—cheap oil from the Middle East and other authoritarian states—this conclusion is much too quick. Clean Trade will give China's leadership compelling incentives to pivot smoothly toward supporting popular sovereignty, abroad and even at home. Several strands of reflection support this conclusion.

The first strand goes back to the basic analysis of the political economy of the oil curse in parts 1 and 2 of *Blood Oil*. If they keep choosing effectiveness, the Chinese will be gifting unaccountable power to violent and coercive men in the countries on which they will be heavily dependent for energy imports, with all the consequences for instability that we have seen over the past forty years. And in fact, the situation will be worse for China, because it cannot project force into the regions where there will be energy supply disruptions. China's leadership should consider its position when only a Clean Trade West—or no one—will have the means and desire to, say, deter Saudi Arabia and Iran from escalating a conflict.

The second strand again goes back to political economy. While petrocrats stay in power today by keeping their people weak, the Chinese regime has maintained its power by making its people economically stronger.[36] This will mean that the Chinese people will increasingly demand political rights. The Chinese Communist Party cannot resist these demands by pivoting away from its inbuilt ideological commitment to popular sovereignty.[37] And China will simultaneously begin to be overtaken in economic growth by its neighbor and peer competitor, democratic India. This will weaken the "faster growth" story that the Party has so far used to legitimate its authoritarian control over its own people. Popular sovereignty will rise with China, and Clean Trade gives its leadership a means to stay on top.

The third strand of reflection comes from the nature of the Clean Trade reforms. While Western states will take a strong stand for popular sovereignty by disengaging commercially from authoritarian oil exporters, they can do so without disputing the political legitimacy of the Chinese or indeed any other government. Indeed, the West can take China's customary "no politics, just business" mantra for its own, merely changing the basis on which it does business—while leaving it to China's leadership to consider how to explain to its own people why China is not respecting the rights of other peoples.

Faced with increasing risks to energy security, eroding legitimacy from slowing growth and a rising India, and domestic demands for greater political accountability, the Chinese leadership should see the advantages of announcing a transition away from effectiveness-based trade in resources. And China can make this announcement without giving up the energy that it needs to import. As with Western states, what will be most important is China's announcement and initial implementation of policies that signal respect for Popular Resource Sovereignty. With China's announcement of even a long tapering period, the sun will finally set for authoritarian control over oil.[38]

Indeed, while announcing its legal support for Popular Resource Sovereignty abroad, Chinese leaders may see the opportunity also to announce greater protections for civil liberties and political rights at home. Of course, China might not consolidate democracy overnight, or even in a decade, any more than the Middle East might not. But the West will, in taking a strong, public stand for Popular Resource Sovereignty, do as much as it can to encourage a peaceful transition to greater public accountability across the regions of the world where such accountability is now lacking, including in China.

Finally, as *Blood Oil* explains, Clean Trade is also an excellent way for the West to strengthen its own commitment to popular sovereignty. This brings us back to the most important question of all: whether we in the West do really believe in the idea of empowering ordinary people to hold their governments to account. The recent rise of demagogic populists in both Europe and the Americas has rushed some critics to the judgment that the value of popular sovereignty is overrated—or even to suggest that democracy is less desirable than elite rule in some form. Having this debate forced on us is uncomfortable, but it does provide an opportunity. This is a good time for us all to think through our politics at the most fundamental level, and to declare where we stand.

The thought that I offer is that—as always, and in fact more than ever—unaccountable power is the greatest threat to the human future. Our choice is now whether to strengthen or weaken the people as a source of accountability over power. While ridiculing or even demonizing democratic publics might seem clever, we in the West must consider carefully whether we want our generation's historical legacy to be a weakened commitment to popular sovereignty. For weakening this commitment is the same as strengthening the power of states and corporations to act without constraint. Anyone who has faith that governments and corporations will reliably act to benefit ordinary people without being accountable to those people might declare that faith now.

Politics is about choices, and all choices come with risks. For three hundred years, those who have chosen to side with power by affirming "Might Makes Right" have ended up losing their bets. The slave trade, colonial rule, apartheid, ethnic cleansing, and genocide: all of these practices have been replaced by rules requiring respect for the rights of ordinary people. Effectiveness for natural resources is one of the last remnants of that ancient regime, and it is now ready to be discarded. The winners that we celebrate over these three centuries have been those who have chosen to counter power, even when that power has at first seemed too strong. Imagine the doomsday scenarios and massive cost estimates that critics would have presented decades ago, in volumes titled Beyond Apartheid or Beyond Colonial Rule. Would we have chosen back then to bear the risks and do the hard work that was necessary for progress, despite the critics?

We might pause to wonder why the people have been winning over power for so long. I would venture that a desire for unity really is a powerful principle in human nature, and that long experience has taught us that unchecked power is a constant threat to that unity.[39] The principle of Abraham Lincoln's first inaugural address, that a country belongs to its people, has been so potent because it expresses the urgency of constraining absolute power, while also declaring the desirability of creating communities among individuals that define—in our time in history—boundaries of strong mutual identification and fellow-feeling. The principle of popular sovereignty feels right to most people in the world because it captures a unity that they know or want, and because it protects them against the powers that have always threatened when unchecked.

To choose effectiveness is to take a stand for the violent, coercive, and corrupt in a rotten status quo. Those who make this choice, by design or default, will have their conscience to reckon with as the future unfolds. The other choice is a strategy of integrity. The power of this strategy comes from bearing costs to build trust across borders, by standing for the rights of all peoples everywhere.

If we are still uncertain about which choice to make, we might measure our convictions with some more words of Abraham Lincoln. Lincoln spoke these words in 1860, when all his fellow citizens were facing a great choice. "Let us have faith that right makes might," Lincoln said, "and in that faith, let us, to the end, dare to do our duty as we understand it."[40]

8

Reply to Kutz

Leif Wenar

Christopher Kutz perceptively marks out different principles for the laws regulating international resource trade, and offers probing questions about the superiority of Popular Resource Sovereignty as the basis of that trade. The four alternatives to Popular Resource Sovereignty that he vets are effectiveness, the "Petrostan standard," trade based on denizen rights, and cosmopolitan principles. Kutz's wide-ranging discussions present a welcome opportunity to review and expand on why trade based on public accountability for natural resources is, of all of these, the best choice.

Kutz first attempts to provide a prima facie basis for effectiveness by recharacterizing it as "Sovereign-Determined Transfer Rights." It is important to see that this is not the correct way to conceptualize the current legal situation, and that it will obscure accessible solutions to the resource curse.

As chapter 7 of *Blood Oil* argues, the law of diplomatic recognition and of commercial engagement are distinct. The way that Kutz presents effectiveness, it appears to fit in the first category: sovereigns, who must be recognized as a matter of international law, must also have the right to determine what sales of resources from their countries will be legal.

But effectiveness is actually law that fits only the second, commercial, category. Think of effectiveness as how importing states define rights to *buy* resources. Each state determines what and from whom its own persons will have a right to buy. And this decision is not a bound by international law. It is within national law, a matter for the discretion of each state.

This distinction in law means that it is quite possible for a state to recognize another state diplomatically, but to ascribe to its own people rights to buy resources that do not correspond to the target state's laws on rights to sell those resources. As discussed in *Blood Oil* and chapter 1 of this volume, during the Arab Spring uprisings in Libya, the United States recognized Gaddafi's government diplomatically—but gave its own citizens the right to buy Libya's oil only from the rebels who were attacking Gaddafi's government, and who definitely did not have the right to sell Libya's oil under Libyan laws.[1] Nor is such a separation between recognition and commerce merely a temporary exigency during a wartime transition—indeed, it can go on for decades.

The U.S.-Taiwan case is especially instructive, as it reveals a long-standing separation between diplomatic recognition and commercial relations. On January 1, 1979, the United States announced its new "One China" policy, ending its diplomatic recognition of Taiwan (Republic of China) and starting its diplomatic recognition of China (People's Republic of China). As the State Department describes what happened on that day in 1979: "The United States changed its diplomatic recognition from Taipei to Beijing. . . . The United States recognized the Government of the People's Republic of China as the sole legal government of China and acknowledged the Chinese position that there is but one China and Taiwan is part of China."[2]

As it ended its diplomatic recognition of Taiwan, the United States also terminated official agreements such as the U.S.-Taiwan Mutual Defense Treaty. From the perspective of U.S. law, there was now no government in Taipei to have such a treaty with. However, Taiwan was in 1979 (and remains today) a significant trade partner of the United States, and the U.S. Congress did not want to grant the communists in Beijing the power to disrupt that partnership. The italicized terms in the 1979 U.S.-Taiwan Relations Act (which still provides what the State Department calls "the legal basis for the unofficial relationship between the U.S. and Taiwan") show how Congress got its way:

Sec. 3301. (a) The President having terminated governmental relations between the United States and the governing authorities on Taiwan recognized by the United States as the Republic of China prior to January 1, 1979, the Congress finds that the enactment of this chapter is necessary . . . to promote the foreign policy of the United States by *authorizing* the continuation of commercial, cultural, and other relations between the people of the United States and the people on Taiwan. . . .

Sec. 3303. (a)(3)(A) *The absence of diplomatic relations and recognition with respect to Taiwan shall not abrogate, infringe, modify, deny, or otherwise affect* in any way any rights or obligations (including but not limited to those involving *contracts, debts, or property interests* of any kind) under the laws of the United States heretofore or hereafter acquired by or with respect to Taiwan.

(B) For all purposes under the laws of the United States, including actions in any court in the United States, *recognition of the People's Republic of China shall not affect in any way the ownership of or other rights or interests in properties,* tangible and intangible, and other things of value, owned or held on or prior to December 31, 1978. . . .

(4) Whenever the application of the laws of the United States depends upon the law that is or was applicable on Taiwan or compliance therewith, the law applied by the people on Taiwan shall be considered the applicable law for that purpose.[3]

In the first paragraph, Congress says that it is using its authority over U.S. persons to continue commercial relations with the people on Taiwan. In the next three paragraphs, Congress declares that U.S. persons should define their commerce with Taiwan—regarding what they can buy from whom—according to "the law applied by the people on Taiwan" (note the lack of governmental language), and not according to any law passed by the government in Beijing. Congress pronounces that whatever Beijing says regarding the right to sell from Taiwan, this will not affect Americans' rights to buy from Taiwan. Nor is this American exceptionalism: the EU has an identical "One China" policy.[4] In most cases states' commercial laws mirror one another, but as these examples show, they do not have to.

Each state sets its own rules for its own persons on the right to buy, independently of the laws of other sovereign states on who has the right to sell. Indeed, states can (and do) give their persons the right to buy even when it's clear that *no one* in the target country had the legal right to sell those resources. Consider again the metals that may be in our tech. As chapter 1 in this volume says, there might be metals in your phone that were plundered by militants in the Congo. These militants did not have the rights to sell these metals under the law of any country—but nevertheless by the time the metals pass through the world's supply chains to you, the laws of your country gave you the right to buy them as a component of your phone. Those metals are now your unchallengeable legal property.

Clearly, whatever we call effectiveness, we should not call it "Sovereign-Determined Transfer Rights." If we relabel effectiveness at all, we might focus on the sovereignty of the *importing* state: we might rather call it "Sovereign-Determined Rights of Purchase." This is crucial, because it shows that solutions to the resource curse are easier than we might have feared. To fight effectiveness, we need not change the international law of recognition, which would pose existential questions for all states. We need only convince states to use their discretionary power to change their own commercial rules for their own people. Effectiveness may be entrenched in our minds, but it is not entrenched in international law—which makes it much easier to overturn.

Before leaving effectiveness, I will note that Kutz says that a consequentialist case for staying with this rule (which he says is shaky) would weigh its benefits for international stability against its costs for the people of resource-cursed states. Yet Kutz here neglects the costs of international *instability* (including market instability) that are so salient in our effectiveness-based world. Think again of Iran, Iraq, Darfur, Libya, Russia, Syria, al Qaeda, ISIS—not to mention the West's often-violent, often-failed, and always-costly efforts to contain the unaccountable power of oil for these cases and many more. As chapter 6 of *Blood Oil* argues, the resource curse is not only a curse on "them," it is a curse on "us" as well—which makes its replacement a matter of prudence as well as morality.

Kutz's Petrostan example is meant to define a standard to replace effectiveness that is less demanding than Popular Resource Sovereignty—and one that is, Kutz says, not clearly inferior to it on consequentialist grounds. As Kutz describes Petrostan, it is a more human rights–compliant version of Saudi Arabia, where citizens receive (close to) the full value of resource revenues in benefits, but where the government nonetheless remains unaccountable to the people.

Now it would be tempting to point out that Kutz is resorting to the imaginary example of Petrostan here instead of giving a real case, which might make us suspect that he is bypassing the analysis of the political economy of oil in part 1 of *Blood Oil*. If the world worked differently than it does, then a different consequentialist analysis might indeed follow. ("Imagine gravity is reversed—*then* what's the best way to get to Chicago?") It may be worth pointing out that, in our actual world, at the same time as the Saudi crown prince was imposing austerity cuts on the people of his country, he impulsively spent more than half a billion dollars of the country's oil revenues to buy a yacht for himself.[5] (With that amount, he could have bought 2,700 Lamborghinis for himself instead.) Surely, in the world as it actually does work, the Saudi people would be better off if they could hold the crown prince (and the rest of the hugely expensive royal family) to account for disbursements of the country's oil wealth.

Yet I want to grant Kutz's imagined example, and focus on his reasoning for thinking that a "Petrostan standard" may be superior to Popular Resource Sovereignty. Kutz asks us to "imagine that a Clean Trade Boycott becomes internationally effective. Petrostan's rulers may be able to draw down national savings for a time, continuing to buy the goodwill of their people. But a likely outcome, as well, is that they will engage, in the short term, in increased repression, and perhaps international adventurism, in order to distract from the state's new-found money troubles" (77). On this short-term basis, Kutz says the case for Popular Resource Sovereignty is not made.

This emphasis on the short term would not be surprising coming from a politician. Anyone trying to make major changes in, say, American or British law will confront short-termism at every step. Politicians in the West really do look mostly to the next election (or the next fundraiser), and if one asks about the national interests in the long term, a puzzled congressional staffer may look off into the middle distance and say, "I think the military or intelligence people do long-term."[6]

Philosophy, of course, can look not only to the short or even medium term, but also to the foreseeable future. And in the long term, as we know, the oil curse is bad for the people of the country where the oil is—major oil states outside the West are on average no richer, no freer, and no more peaceful than they were in 1980, while most of the oil states with accountable governments have avoided the worst resource-curse pathologies. If Clean Trade helped a transition to accountable governance in Petrostan in the medium term, its people would likely become better off. Why does Kutz rest his case against Popular Resource Sovereignty on the short term?

I suspect this is because Kutz is not at heart a consequentialist. A hint of this comes from his using the same kind of language as Stilz to denigrate "pragmatic" arguments, in contrast to non-consequentialist arguments of "principle." Another hint, which I will return to, is his puzzlement at the focus on resource trade at all, since it seems to him just one factor that can affect a non-consequentialist's traditional concern, which is income inequality within countries.[7] And the best way I can make sense of his focus on the short term in the Petrostan case is to frame his objection as saying that Clean Trade would violate non-consequentialist "side-constraints."

Kutz's argument seems to be that political action is morally disallowed if it will likely lead, in the short term, to increased repression and international adventurism by a foreign state. And yet, if this is non-consequentialism, it cannot be part of a responsible politics. The world as we have helped to make it is often bad; to help make it better, we must countenance that, in the short term, we may make it worse. Transitions, as history teaches us, can be very hard, even wretched. Statesmen know this, and political philosophers—if they are doing the philosophy of real political action—might keep the lessons of history in mind.

The fight of the American colonials to gain independence from Britain lowered their real incomes by almost 30 percent—and even twenty-five years after their victory, Americans' incomes were 20 percent below what they had been.[8] Was the American Revolution worth it? From our long-term perspective we can see why it was, but for decades the revolution brought real hardship to many who survived it. Or again, Abraham Lincoln fought America's Civil War to save the union and bring an end to slavery. Hundreds of thousands of deaths, whole regions devastated, cities burned to the ground, a gigantic national debt, a generation and more of economic dislocation—was it worth it? Short-term, side-constrained reasoning cannot say yes.

The transition away from effectiveness in resources will not have costs nearly as large as these. But as peoples struggle to wrest some control of their own countries away from the coercive actors that we are now empowering, there will surely be costs—both for them and for us. Philosophers who cannot countenance political action that will result in short-term suffering will have to find some way to reconcile themselves to perpetuating the greater miseries that they see around them in the present.[9]

Kutz's arguments for both "denizen rights" and cosmopolitanism also show his reluctance to follow through on arguments about consequences. His theory of agentic democracy leads him to commend resource trade on the basis that a country's denizens, not its citizens, should be in control of natural resources. "All those participating in the national project," he says, "have a claim on its resources, guest-workers and citizens alike" (83).[10]

Before discussing the pragmatics of this proposal, it is worth noting its weakness even in terms of principle. Kutz's "agentic democracy" theory is of the same form as recent non-consequentialist theories of national territorial control (of which Stilz's is a leading exemplar).[11] National territorial control, these theories say, is needed for a collective agent like a people or "all denizens" to accomplish a collective goal—in Kutz's case, to construct a shared political order.

What is notable about these theories of national territorial control is that while they may succeed on their own terms to justify national collective control over land, they all struggle to explain national collective control over the subsurface resources that are at issue in this book. These theories cannot simply assume that subsurface resources like oil should be controlled by groups smaller than humanity as a whole, since (as Kutz says) the cosmopolitan alternative for these resources is in theory quite attractive. But then whatever the national collective goal is said to be, it is evident that national collectives do not need control over subsurface resources to accomplish it. For collectives in countries like Japan, where there are no significant subsurface resources, are achieving their collective goals (like constructing a shared political order) at least as well as countries in which the collectives do control such resources. Whatever collectives need to do, they don't need domestic subsurface resources to do it. Kutz's form of argument has yet to produce a convincing rationale for national control over oil.

Turning now to expected consequences, Kutz's proposal of "denizen rights" faces dim prospects of success. Kutz's main moral concern appears to be the current exploitation of guest workers in oil-rich countries, but his proposal is unlikely to benefit even them much.[12] In a world where being resident in an oil-rich country becomes sufficient to be legally entitled to share in a country's oil wealth, we would likely see two things happening very quickly.

The first is that restrictions on new residents entering oil-rich states would be tightened.[13] The second is that these barriers would soon come to have legal revolving doors. National authorities would require any guest-workers already in the country to leave, and then invite guest-workers in only on condition they sign a contract transferring all of their future "denizen shares" of resource revenues to the state. Kutz's proposal has unpromising consequences, because its mechanism for transferring benefits away from those who currently have power is so easily evaded by those with the power.

Kutz's discussion of cosmopolitanism carries a similar unreality with it. Cosmopolitanism is, without doubt, a more attractive principle than Popular Resource Sovereignty from the perspectives of free human unity and of many theories of global justice. Yet, Kutz worries,

> if it were widely understood that Popular Resource Sovereignty institutions were a second-best to global justice, then it would be difficult to motivate citizens to fully support them; and citizens of resource-rich states might reasonably fear an ultimate trajectory of globalization. . . . Popular Resource Sovereignty institutions will be vulnerable to popular under-commitment unless they can be shown to represent a preferred model of justice.[14]

I must confess that this concern seems to me to retain, as they used to say, a whiff of the schoolman's lamp. The prospect seems remote that people worldwide will become seriously concerned that popular sovereignty is philosophically second-best to cosmopolitanism. And even if some do see it this way, Kutz's conclusion about their motivations to act does not follow.

Thomas Paine, for instance, famously believed in the common ownership of the earth.[15] Why then did he fight so hard for American independence, instead of going straight for universal implementation of his proposals for redistributive land taxes? Gandhi once said, "Nationalism is not the highest concept. The highest concept is world community. It is that kind of world community to which we have to attach ourselves."[16] How then could Gandhi have been motivated through the decades to struggle to free the Indian nation? The answer that both of these men would doubtless give would be a story of historical progress.

If there will ever be a cosmopolitan future, a world of Popular Resource Sovereignty is the best staging ground to reach it. Popular Resource Sovereignty shifts power over resources out of the hands of autocrats and armed groups into the hands of peoples, who will thereby become more democratically capable and who may, in time, freely join together to form a United Persons with ultimate control over the earth.[17] Whoever wills the ends must will the means, and for cosmopolitans this means Popular Resource Sovereignty.

We might also not forget that cosmopolitan principles of global justice are themselves merely "intermediate" between us and a still more ideal world in which these principles no longer solve a problem that anyone has. Having a fair share of the earth's rocks, muds, and gasses is (we hope) not a supreme value in anyone's life. Integrity, community, solidarity and love are much more plausible in that role. If cosmopolitans can say nothing more than that their principles for distributing rocks, muds and gasses will achieve "justice," then the question, which many philosophers today seem never to get around to, is why we should think that justice so understood is ultimately important in human affairs.[18]

Because he is focused on the traditional non-consequentialist concern of domestic income inequality, Kutz worries that Clean Trade is "irrationally selective." And he is correct that many factors beyond resource trade contribute to domestic unfairnesses in incomes. However, he is not correct, as we have seen, that the current system of trade has "strongly positive human development consequences for the least well off in those states."[19] And what he (and others) miss by attending to income patterns instead of to power is that Clean Trade is a core reform, which goes down to the causes of many other contemporary problems.[20]

To some it may seem that the resource curse is just one issue that people might care about. Political prisoners, free speech, women's rights, refugees, the arms industry, youth radicalization—these are all worthy causes too. But the deeper truth is that the problems in these areas are often the follow-on effects of unaccountable power in resource-rich states. *Blood Oil* and chapter 1 of this volume set out the evidence that oil states are worse for civil rights, political rights, and women's rights, that they have spread extremism around the world, that they are more often at war, that their wars have driven many to become refugees, and that they have provided a major stimulus to the production of highly destructive arms worldwide.

Of course, all of these issues also arise in states and regions that are not resource-rich. As always, resources aren't everything.[21] But they certainly are something. The next time you read a newspaper's-worth of reporting on these issues, check how often natural resources are part of the stories. Many of the world's most visible disorders are symptoms of an underlying imbalance of power, and treating the disease is the best way to ease these symptoms. This will not happen magically, or overnight. But the abolition of effectiveness for resources will reach down to the source of many future disorders, instead of merely reacting to them once they emerge.

Where Kutz and I are in furious agreement is that a positive campaign for the abolition of effectiveness can be effective for motivating change. We are both firmly in the realm of practical politics here, and while there is no need to give up other kinds of appeals, Kutz is right about the potential of efforts to show that "consumers can, through market choices, actually increase their well-being through wise petroconsumption: consuming the products they want, while at the same time generating positive political externalities by voting with dollars for morally clean petroleum."[22] I have had the same thought, and positive steps that consumers can take right now can be found on the Clean Trade website.

At the level of practical action, and at the level of long-term priorities, Kutz and I agree on much. We are both looking for positive actions to encourage the world further toward cooperation, stability, and peace. Whether he, and others like us, will make progress will, in the end, depend on how many of us there will be.

9

Reply to Stilz

Leif Wenar

John Stuart Mill declares that the object of *On Liberty* is "to assert one very simple principle, as entitled to govern absolutely the dealings of society with the individual in the way of compulsion and control." This is the principle of liberty, "that the sole end for which mankind are warranted, individually or collectively, in interfering with the liberty of action of any of their number, is self-protection."[1]

Were *On Liberty* published today, an academic review might concede that the liberty principle is a "good pragmatic principle" for our times. And yet, the review might protest, Mill had not tried to defend its "philosophical plausibility." Yes, Mill has shown the importance of his principle for furthering the most profound interests of people in our day. But still, the review might ask, what of the principle's *moral validity*? Even given its prominence in his book, how much could a *philosopher* like Mill really believe in this liberty principle?

In *Blood Oil*, and in chapter 1 of this book, I've argued that the justifications for rights over territory and resources are consequentialist in form. In the quizzical condition of today's academy, it can seem as though consequentialism is just a dismissible "pragmatism"—as though the great tradition of Bentham, Mill, and Sidgwick is not really philosophy at all. Stilz, for instance, seems uncertain as to whether a philosopher could really believe in Popular Resource Sovereignty. Her chapter devotes only a single paragraph to consequentialist reasoning, and nowhere brings itself even to mention that term.[2] The suggestion appears to be that consequentialism could not be a method for finding "morally valid" principles.

Stilz's chapter reflects a reluctance in some parts of the academy to let normative conclusions about politics depend on robust empirical premises. My own view is that this reluctance has little to do with moral validity, and more to do with over-specialization in today's academy. A fear of robust empirical premises would certainly have seemed strange to nearly all of the founders of Western political philosophy—and not only to the utilitarians, but to Hobbes, Locke, Rousseau, and Marx as well. These philosophers would agree that as long as we are concerned with (as Stilz says) "what we ought to do," a relentless attention to consequences will be part of the search for valid political principles.[3]

Here I'll argue that a non-consequentialist strategy like Stilz's, despite its subtlety and brilliance, cannot ground important rights like those of territorial control. As is typical in non-consequentialist arguments, the single values that Stilz relies on lack the specificity and the substance to ground the rights she seeks.

Stilz is looking to justify the territorial rights of peoples within a system of states. Her first positive step is to argue for a particular sub-right: for an individual claim-right to use an area as a permanent residence. She bases this positive argument on a single value: on individuals' strong interest in pursuing what she calls "located life plans."

> Inhabiting a particular geographical space plays a key role in residents' material subsistence and in their most important projects and relationships. Geography and climate may affect the economic practices people take up, making it difficult for them to reconstitute those in some very different place. Their religious, cultural, and recreational activities also often have territorial components. And people form personal bonds and enter work, religious, and friendship relations in part because they expect to remain spatially arranged in certain ways.[4]

Now as a consequentialist like Bentham would say, fulfilling people's existing expectations about major issues like where they will live is indeed of supreme importance for generating greater well-being. Yet these "existing expectations" are of little use to a non-consequentialist strategy like Stilz's. This is because everyone's existing expectations about where they will live, work, and play have been formed within the state system of control over territory. And the non-consequentialist legitimacy of the state system, and so of those expectations, is just what Stilz is trying to show.

Stilz needs to find a *transhistorical* interest in "located life plans" if she is to show the legitimacy of the state system without begging her question. Yet Stilz does not tell us how to identify this transhistorical interest, as separate from all existing expectations. I suspect that Stilz is attracted to "state of nature" reasoning partly as a tool for identifying such transhistorical human interests. I also suspect, as Rousseau said, that such reasoning will end up "transfer[ing] to the state of Nature ideas . . . taken from society."[5]

Insofar as we can identify any transhistorical interest in "located life plans," it is much weaker than what Stilz needs for her conclusions. In order to complete her argument for the system of territorial states, Stilz needs to prove that there is a right for specific individuals to reside in specific, proper-named places—for Belgians to live in Belgium, for instance, and for the French to live in France. But aside from special cases such as holy sites, most individual life plans require not living in a specific, proper-named place, but only a type of place. Dairy farmers need to graze their cows in some temperate place or other—not specifically in either Leuven or Lille. No surfer needs Malibu, but only some coastline with great waves.

Indeed, despite what Stilz says, one struggles to think of many life plans that require a person to be permanently located in any specific place at all. Some homes are mobile, truck drivers keep up their faith and their friendships while on the road, ever-more education happens in cyberspace instead of campus space. Whole communities—such as the Roma and the aptly named Travelers—fiercely defend their itinerant ways of life, and one suspects there would be many more such groups were it not for the rather suburban norms of our day.

More, the difficulties of a "single-value" strategy of arguing for a residency right, as Stilz does, would persist even if all of those objections could be met. Imagine that Stilz could in fact find what she needs to ground a right to remain on a specific piece of territory, which is a very strong transhistorical interest in pursuing one's life plans within some proper-named location. Then she would have proved too much. For if there were such a strong interest, then migration itself would become irrational, in any but the most extreme circumstances.[6] If relocation must harm vital life plans, then the American Dream of leaving for the frontier would always have become a nightmare, and the quest of so many to emigrate for love or work today would be a kind of madness.

The hazards of attempting a "single-value," non-consequentialist justification for important rights are equally evident in Stilz's second positive argument, for the collective rights of self-determination. This right she grounds in an individual interest in political autonomy:

> Unilaterally coercing others fails to respect them as rational deliberators. It leaves them unable to act independently, on the basis of their own sense of justice, to establish and comply with a political order they can affirm. Instead, they find themselves subjected against their will to institutions that fail to reflect their judgments and priorities. They are likely to find life within such an imposed order highly alienating. And they are unlikely to experience their social world as a cooperative system where they enjoy valuable relationships

with fellow-participants, or as a place where they can feel at home. These are significant harms. Avoiding these harms, in my view, tells in favor of recognizing collective self-determination.[7]

As *Blood Oil* emphasizes, collective self-determination is one weighty value within the argument for Popular Resource Sovereignty.[8] The mutual identification of so many millions of humans with their co-nationals is also one of the greatest and most surprising achievements of unity in our age. More, the denial of collective self-determination was also, as Stilz emphasizes, one of the outrages of colonial rule. Yet Stilz's specific argument for self-determination cannot credibly explain this right.

Self-determination in Stilz's sense is, after all, a recent phenomenon in the human experience, found at best in a few countries before World War II. Even in our own time, by Stilz's criteria it would appear that at least one-third of human beings do not enjoy the political autonomy that collective self-determination allows—including everyone living in China and the Middle East, and everyone in Africa. So, by Stilz's lights, all of these people have historically been, and are now, subject to "alien coercion" by their governments. Yet how plausible is it that all of these people, for all of those ages, and in all of these places now, have found their lives "highly alienating" and their social world as not "a place where they can feel at home"? Does Stilz have data to support her empirical claims?

As Joseph Raz once said, "Politicians, journalists, writers, etc., excepted, their right of free expression means little in the life of most people. It rightly means less to them than success in their chosen occupation, the fortunes of their marriages, or the state of repair of their homes."[9] And much the same can be said for other rights required for collective self-determination, like the right to vote. There is no doubt that these rights are today highly consequential—but this is not because lacking them damages a strong, eternal, and universal individual interest.

Indeed, Stilz herself admits that the interest against being subject to "alien coercion" is only weighty enough to ground *pro tanto* requirements. "If there is no other way to achieve the essentials of justice, security, and public order, the wrong of alien coercion may be trumped by its strongly beneficial effects."[10] Yet if this is all we get from this interest in the end, then we have lost the one resource that Stilz gave us to decry the illegitimacy of colonialism. For very many countries, even today, lack the essentials of justice, security, and public order. If being subject to "alien coercion" is only *pro tanto* wrong, it might be entirely legitimate for Niger now to be ruled once again from Paris—if French rule achieved these "essentials"—or for the Congo to be returned to the personal estate of the Belgian king. We seem not to have found the right form of argument to make a convincing case against colonial domination.

Blood Oil argues that the state system that allocates territories to national peoples is justified by the monumentally important human goods that this system produces: peace, prosperity, and freedom—and because we have scarcely any feasible idea of how we could reallocate power to do better. The book goes on to argue that the post-war reform that made national borders "force-proof" has improved the state system, because it appears to have contributed to the system producing ever more of these great goods, and indeed to producing the freest, richest, and most peaceful period in recorded human history.[11] While this consequentialist reasoning seems to me the most plausible—indeed, the obvious—justification for today's state system, it also appears to be missing from today's Anglophone philosophical literature on territory.[12] I suspect this is partly because many Anglophone theorists take the goods of the state system for granted—they take it for granted that electricity and fresh water will always come through their walls, while bombs never will.

Be that as it may, some contemporary theorists do seem unwilling to engage in realistic reasoning about consequences. In its single paragraph on the consequentialist argument, Stilz's chapter considers an alternative to the state system:

> Suppose that a world government were coercively imposed upon existing states in order to enforce every global citizen's right to an equal share of the earth's natural resources. No doubt the transition would be a rocky one, with much strife and resentment on the part of those subjected against their will. But Wenar allows that the use of coercive power can be "redeemed" if it facilitates a greater unity. Perhaps after several generations those living under this global order would develop new identities and allegiances as egalitarian world citizens, committed to freely sharing their resource wealth with one another. If so, then a common ownership rule might be preferable, on the free unity criterion.[13]

Perhaps—yet would you chance your child's life on it? Consider attempts in the twentieth century to effect radical transformations of identities and allegiances through the coercive imposition of egalitarian distributions: Stalin's Soviet Union, Mao's China, Pol Pot's "Democratic Kampuchea." These attempted transitions were certainly "rocky," in terms of uncontroversial values like peace, stability, and prosperity. Were they successful?

My view is that they were not, even in their own terms as transitions. And these were attempts at identity-transformation only at a national level, coercing relatively homogenous populations—not, as Stilz is imagining, at the global level, coercing a highly diverse humanity. Of course, as Stilz says, it is "difficult to predict what would happen, in the future, as a result of various possible institutional setups."[14] But that's not a problem with consequentialism. That is a permanent feature of our reasoning about what we ought to do.

Prudence mostly cautions against major upheavals in institutions. Battling great evils like slavery is an exception—as would be a case where some feature of current institutions is producing widespread suffering and injustice, where a principle that addresses the flaw is already widely supported, and where an institutional transition can be made without too much damage to other great goods. This, I've offered, is just our current situation with trade in natural resources, where effectiveness should be replaced with Popular Resource Sovereignty.[15] As both *Blood Oil* and Stilz's chapter notice, Popular Resource Sovereignty will come with costs as well as benefits.[16] The question of politics, as always, is whether its benefits outweigh its costs, given what other actions we might take.

Stilz's chapter does consider a reform for resources, which is an international resource tax intended to provide minimum welfare provision to the world's poor. "It is not obvious," Stilz says, that this reform would have to be imposed coercively from above. Rather, Stilz says, she does not see why it should be ruled out that proponents of this reform could instead create a global consensus "from the bottom up," through public persuasion and peaceful inducements.[17] Why not?

If this is meant as the beginning of a discussion on the relative merits of reforms of international institutions, then I look forward to it. Speaking in favor of reforms based on Popular Resource Sovereignty are the majorities of individuals in all regions who say they favor popular sovereignty, the declarations of leading politicians worldwide that resources belong to the people, and the major treaties under which 98 percent of the world population already live that say that national peoples should freely dispose of their natural wealth. What facts today favor a global consensus forming around an international resource tax remain to be seen.

As philosophers, we are all prone to the fantasy that if we can just offer a valid argument, a consensus might form around it to change institutions accordingly. But valid arguments are easy. Those who try to make real political change know that none of their reforms begin with a valid argument and end in "why not?" All of their days are filled with fierce debates over "how?" and "what then?"

Non-consequentialist arguments like Stilz's lack the resources to reach their desired conclusions. And any responsible proposal for institutional reforms must own its outcomes. By being allergic to robust consequentialist reasoning, some normative theorists are doing more than losing touch with the tradition of our greatest political philosophers. They are removing themselves from the common human project of thinking through, as Stilz puts it, "what we ought to do."

10

Reply to James

Leif Wenar

Aaron James is characteristically magnanimous. His chapter offers a crystal-line summary of my consequentialist case against effectiveness for natural resources—and then also gifts us a sparkling, practice-based deontological argument for the same conclusions. James's argument for Popular Resource Sovereignty is compelling in its own terms, and one would think the proper response would be thanks. For me to query James's generous gift may seem ungrateful in the extreme—like a man in choppy waters who, when thrown a line, calls up to ask whether it's made of a sustainable fiber.

Since James and I are reaching the same conclusions, many will want to know whether James's path is in fact an open, and perhaps even a better, methodological route to them. What I will question is the practice-based element in James's deontological approach, the development of which is one of his signal contributions to the philosophical literature.[1] I will interrogate this by examining James's practice-based arguments in their most developed form, which are for principles to regulate general international trade. With regret I will conclude that his practice-based methodology does not offer a clear path in political theory—or at least, many thorny problems block us from going that way.

James describes his practice-based method thus:[2]

> In this practice-based method of moral reasoning, we justify principles of justice for, and in part from, a social practice's distinctive structure, in light of the best (perhaps constructive) interpretation of its understood aims and organization. Principles of what we owe to each other are defended not simply by pure sociological interpretation, and not simply by pure moral argument, but rather by both, blended together in a suitable reflective equilibrium.

On this method, when theorizing a practice like international trade, we should first look for a sense of its nature and purpose—and one that is "firmly rooted in the understandings of its aims and organization that practitioners already share or can readily recognize. Evidence from widely shared assumptions within the practice . . . should be assigned special interpretive weight."[3] This "sociological interpretation" is the empirical, descriptive element in practice-based reasoning. This descriptive element about what practitioners actually believe about the practice will then be blended with pure moral arguments to reach principles of justice for regulating the practice.

Which political principles will emerge from applying such a "blended" method will depend on which sociological interpretation and which moral arguments a practice-based theorist decides to add to the mix. We can see already that what this method must avoid at all costs is "policy-based philosophy," where a theorist blends whatever mixture of the sociological and the moral will produce the political principles to which he had a strong prior commitment. In other words, the desired political results shouldn't be guiding the theorizing—else the theorizing won't be justifying those results.

James knows that he must be especially wary of the dangers of policy-based philosophy. For his prior commitments in politics are to an egalitarianism that most would regard as rather radical. And his book on international trade favors egalitarian principles of justice that are similarly radical.

For example, James's book endorses the highly progressive egalitarian principle that trading countries must distribute the gains of trade equally to all of their citizens who are affected by trade. And another of the book's principles can require that a rich country (like the United States) funds the social insurance scheme of a poorer country with which it trades (like Mexico), to ensure that the trade makes no individual's life-prospects worse in the poorer country (e.g., through unemployment).[4]

James is aware that, without an especially disciplined account of the reasoning with which he reaches these principles, his readers may worry that he has just chosen whatever theoretical horse looks best for pulling the egalitarian cart that he'd already bought. Yet can practice-based reasoning ever be so disciplined?

One may wonder, and going deeper into James's description of his own method for reaching principles for international trade raises doubts about the practice-based method as a whole.

International trade, James says in his book, is not merely a "social regularity" in which agents repeatedly coordinate their actions. Trade is a social practice, he says, where the agents involved coordinate their actions by a shared organizing purpose.[5] James says that after poring over two hundred years' worth of the writings of economists, he came to the view that the organizing purpose of international trade is *the augmentation of national incomes through specialization of labor.*[6] He claims that this purpose—"greater wealth of nations through division of labor"—is the understanding of international trade that, sociologically, its participants "already share or can readily recognize."

James then goes on to mix in pure moral argument, based on fairness, to argue that those who engage in the practice of international trade (so described) must respect his favored strong egalitarian principles of trade, like those just mentioned.

What I will query in this method is the "sociological" or descriptive element that James puts into his mix. Is the shared purpose of international trade, as its participants understand it, really the augmentation of national incomes through labor specialization? To test James's assertion, we need to scrutinize who the participants to this practice are meant to be—and indeed whether trade is a practice in James's sense at all.

Who, precisely, are the participants in international trade? James says that it is "countries as represented by their respective governments," and elsewhere "whole societies."[7] By contrast, James says that individuals in the market are not participants in the practice of international trade—individuals (and presumably corporations) are just buying and selling goods that cross borders, each for his or her own pleasure or profit. Exchange between individuals is just a "social regularity"; only trade between countries is a social practice that has a shared purpose.

Right away we run into problems with this description. If countries are the participants in this practice, as James says, then it must be countries that as a matter of sociological fact can "share or readily recognize" the point of the practice. Yet does America, or Mongolia, recognize the purpose of international trade as the augmentation of national incomes through the specialization of labor? Even if we are relaxed about ascribing cognitive states to countries, we will need a sophisticated story here. For if most of the individuals who make up a country are not engaged in the practice of international trade, but are just buying and selling, how then does the country itself come to have this extra belief about the purpose of international trade?

Polling of Americans shows that their grasp of basic economics often appears weak (we have no such polling of Mongolians).[8] Not having had the time or interest to study international trade, ideas like "the augmentation of national incomes through the specialization of labor" likely mean little to most Americans. But if the majority of Americans don't understand the economic theory of comparative advantage, how does the country believe in it? James says that the participants in international trade are "countries *as represented by their governments*," and it is true that some government officials understand comparative advantage. Yet how do these

officials with an understanding represent citizens without an understanding?

James most often speaks of "government officials" as those who participate in the practice of international trade. While "officials" are more plausible participants than "countries," we might also enquire about this. Charles
Beitz reminds us that the framers of the post-war trade regime saw its guiding purpose to be international peace, at least as much as international
prosperity.[9] And A. J. Julius raises the obvious possibility that each government is only trying to raise *its own* national income through trade, not the
income of all countries.[10] That would make governments more like individuals, merely buying and selling for their own profit, and not engaged in a
social practice with a common purpose.

More, it may well be that there is no single story about why officials of
different countries sign trade deals and otherwise engage in international
trade. Rich-country officials may sign trade deals with each other to increase
their own countries' growth; poor-country officials may agree to open their
markets to rich-country companies in exchange for development assistance
or security guarantees. Closer examination of the motives of officials may
make us wonder precisely which officials are meant to be believing in the
"wealth of nations" ideal that, James claims, defines the purpose of the
system.

James's answer is that *no official* need really believe in this ideal:

> A practice can be different from a mere social regularity if the aim that makes
> interpretive sense of its distinctive structure has sufficient "ideational"
> endorsement. . . . The basic aim of market reliance is developed and reinforced
> by the public arguments of economists and other worldly commentators, who
> have told us for over 200 years that freeing trade will augment the wealth of
> nations, in a relation of mutual benefit, in which, ideally, we all enrich our-
> selves together. The arguments catch on, and officials gradually choose to open
> borders. They do that for what may be all sorts of reasons, perhaps largely
> selfish, while mainly paying lip service to the larger goal of mutual national
> benefit, simply to publicly legitimate their decisions. . . . Invocation of the goal
> of mutual benefit, for perceived legitimacy, adds to its public recognition, and
> further shapes decisions about what can or cannot be publicly legitimated.
>
> In this way, as the practice of market reliance emerges, it counts as "having
> the aim of mutual national income augmentation." That is not because anyone
> must actually share that aim . . . but simply because that is the aim that ratio-
> nalizes the practice's distinctive structure, by having become part of the public
> ideology that shapes what decisions actually get made in its construction and
> maintenance.[11]

James has set out a formal model of how this process can work in the
abstract, which turns on a social perception that certain policies are reasonable.[12] Even in this formal model, the kind of coordination that James

describes becomes less likely as the agents involved are assumed to be more selfish, and to understand each other better. And James does not offer evidence that his formal model actually does apply to the case of international trade. So we might look more closely at what James would need to show to convince us that it does.

In the passage above, we ask this: *who* is it that thinks that *who* believes in this "public ideology" of free trade? The trade officials of one country are unlikely to believe that the trade officials of other countries believe that ideology—because these officials are engaged in hardball bargaining with each other all the time, each determined to achieve their maximum national interest. Of course, trade officials might know that the officials of some other countries legitimate their decisions to their own public by appealing to "free trade." But all of them know from long experience around the negotiating table that all trade officials will press hard for their own national advantage, whether this means freer trade or not. So while the officials of some countries might make ideological speeches, to show that the ideology in these speeches "shapes what decisions actually get made" would require showing that this ideology moves agreements toward different results than pure power-based bargaining would. And this James has not shown.

James might mean that it is *national publics* that come to believe the "public ideology" that trade augments the wealth of nations. But even beyond the point that Ricardian economics may not have sunk in for the average citizen, there is the separate question of whether it would make sense that the average citizen would embrace this ideology. How much do most citizens care about economic growth in other countries? Humanitarian emergencies aside, I would hazard that most citizens are largely indifferent—and in some cases even hostile—to growth in other countries. (Does the average American really want China to get economically stronger? What are such sentiments between most Indians and Pakistanis, or Iranians and Saudis?) And indeed, long-term polling shows that Americans are quite divided as to whether free trade agreements are even good *for America*.[13]

Recall that we are being "sociological" here—we are looking for the interpretation of the purpose of international trade that is "firmly rooted in the understandings of its aims and organization that practitioners already share or can readily recognize." Yet when we look at government officials and national publics, we need more evidence that James's "wealth of nations" understanding of the purpose of trade is decisive in shaping what decisions actually get made. The ideology of mainstream trade economists may in fact be playing no substantive role in these decisions.

Here is another possibility for explaining what happens in trade negotiations, which does not fit James's practice-based model. American trade officials often perceive that opening the markets of poorer countries will be good for American business and, when they do, they strongarm their poorer counterparts to open markets.[14] The trade officials of other countries know exactly what the American officials are doing (and they also know that sometimes Americans make ideological speeches). The trade officials of poorer countries open their markets not because they think that they, their own publics, or the American officials or the American public believe that free trade is "reasonable." They open their markets because the Americans force them to—the Americans offer "a deal they can't refuse."

This explanation has the virtue of simplicity, and there is some evidence to back it.[15] To show that his "lip service" model not only can but does apply to the trade regime, James will need to show that his model does better at explaining the phenomena than this simple explanation. James needs to provide the evidence that a widespread ideology explains what happens in international trade better than raw power does.

Finally, let me make one further point that also brings James's practice-based method into question. Even if James could shore up his "lip service" model, it seems that the descriptive element of his practice-based method will constrain the domain of principles that his moral arguments can reach. For even granting that some government officials do wholeheartedly endorse (or believe that others endorse) a "wealth of nations" purpose for the trade system, they must surely endorse it in a *reform-limiting* way. Maybe some officials today do endorse the global benefits of international trade, but it's not conceivable that officials today endorse the trade system *however its benefits are distributed within and between countries.*

How likely is it, for example, that American officials today endorse international trade understood as a practice that could possibly require the United States to pay for welfare benefits to Mexicans in Mexico? (And of course, the American public will not endorse, and would likely vigorously reject, any such understanding of trade.) Recall that James is stuck with a catholic, "sociological" conception of trade: he wants the "strong normativity" of addressing officials based on their own understandings of the trade system.[16] But that very understanding is incompatible with the highly egalitarian principles that James also wants. An American official, told that the trade system that he endorses requires America to fund Mexico's unemployment budget, would simply reply "that's not a trade system that I can endorse."

To bring this back to rights over natural resources—James beautifully summarizes the consequentialist case against the rule of effectiveness when he says that it should be replaced because it's a disaster that's driven many of the great evils of history, and that it can be replaced with acceptable costs. As he says, much of our confidence that effectiveness can be replaced comes from widespread acceptance of the principle of Popular Resource Sovereignty, which will replace it.

James's practice-based method looks good in his chapter, when it is supporting Popular Resource Sovereignty, which most people accept. Yet James means to be presenting a philosophical method that is also sturdy enough to drive down into people's actual beliefs and pry them into conclusions that they reject as yet, such as his highly egalitarian principles for international trade. And practice-based philosophy seems not to have the tensile strength to do that—a close look at the practice-based approach raises real questions about its rigor as a philosophical method. Consequentialism remains the one true faith of reform.

In conclusion, let me recognize that readers who are not academic philosophers may not care much about such debates over method. When informed that there is a flaw in international trade that turns the money from their everyday purchases into massive oppression, conflict, and corruption abroad—and into major threats to their families at home—most readers will say "let's fix that flaw." At least, let's fix it if it looks like we can do so without endangering other things that we care about, like peace and prosperity and good relations among the people of our own country.

This just shows that the best practical reasoning is about reaching the best future we can, thinking through the likely results of our actions and how our actions will affect the balance among the many things that have real value. My message in this book is that today we have a great opportunity—perhaps the best of our lifetimes—to act together to reach a better future. We can throw out a nonsensical rule, whose abolition in other domains has marked humanity's greatest moral progress for centuries, and which is now causing suffering and injustice and instability worldwide. We can replace that archaic rule with the modern rule that affirms the rights of ordinary people, and can do so in peaceful ways that will build trust between peoples, and that may even revive our own belief in the transformative power of principled democratic politics.

Insofar as there is any philosophical innovation here, it is only in grouping the many things that we know have value in our relations with each other under a single word, which is "unity." What is bad is cruelty and violence and domination and betrayal and neglect; what is good is honesty and compassion, reciprocity and community, cooperation and friendship, peace and trust. Calling this a "theory of unity" is just bringing together everything that we already know. "The free unity of humanity" is just a fancy phrase for what—you might consider—is already your vision of the best world.

Notes

FOREWORD

1. A. O. Scott, "Feeding Europe, Starving at Home," *The New York Times*, Aug. 3, 2005: http://www.nytimes.com/2005/08/03/movies/feeding-europe-starving-at -home.html (accessed May 22, 2018).

NOTES TO CHAPTER 1

1. This chapter covers many of the main points in Wenar, Leif. 2016. *Blood Oil: Tyrants, Violence, and the Rules that Run the World*. New York: Oxford University Press, in less than 10 percent of the length. Those looking for fuller exposition of any of the ideas in this chapter may find it useful to consult *Blood Oil*, which has an extensive index.

2. BBC Two. 2015. "World's Richest Terror Army." http://www.bbc.co.uk/ programmes/b05s4ytp (accessed February 13, 2017); McElroy, Damien. 2014. "Iraq Oil Bonanza Reaps $1 Million a Day for Islamic State." *The Telegraph*, July 11.

3. Solomon, Jay, and Nour Malas. 2015. "Qatar's Ties to Militants Strain Alliance." *The Wall Street Journal*, February 23.

4. Oxfam. 2017. "Yemen Cholera Worst On Record & Numbers Still Rising." https://www.oxfam.org/en/pressroom/pressreleases/2017-07-20/yemen-cholera -worst-record-numbers-still-rising (accessed April 15, 2018).

5. BBC News. "The 38-Year Connection Between Irish Republicans and Gaddafi." http://www.bbc.co.uk/news/uk-northern-ireland-12539372 (accessed February 12, 2017).

6. U.S. Department of State. "Country Reports on Terrorism 2016." https:// www.state.gov/j/ct/rls/crt/2016/272235.htm#IRAN (accessed April 15, 2018).

7. Wenar, Leif. "Blood Oil: How You Can Stop Funding Dictators." CNN. http:// edition.cnn.com/2016/03/16/opinions/wenar-blood-oil/index.html (accessed February 12, 2017).

8. Silverstein, Ken. 2014. *The Secret World of Oil.* London: Verso, chapter 2; World Bank. 2013. "Equatorial Guinea Overview." www.worldbank.org/en/coun try/equatorialguinea/overview (accessed November 26, 2014).

9. Maass, Peter. 2009. *Crude World: The Violent Twilight of Oil.* New York: Knopf, p. 32; UK Foreign and Commonwealth Office. 2003. *Human Rights: Annual Report.* London, p. 55; U.S. Department of State. 1998. *Equatorial Guinea Country Report on Human Rights Practices.* Washington, DC.

10. BP. 2017. *Statistical Review of World Energy.* London, p.8. In this section, "oil" means petroleum. The two other big hydrocarbons—coal and natural gas—are humanity's second and third largest sources of energy. Together these fossil fuels supply more than three quarters of the world's energy. In later sections, "oil" will sometimes refer to both oil and gas, as appropriate.

11. International Energy Agency. "Transport." http://www.iea.org/topics/ transport/ (accessed February 12, 2017).

12. Shah, Sonia. 2004. *Crude: The Story of Oil.* New York: Seven Stories, pp. 3–4; calculations corrected by Michael Tucker.

13. Bryce, Robert. 2013. "The Tyranny of Oil." *National Review*, March 11.

14. Adapting Oilandgasinfo.ca. 2014. "Products Made from Oil and Natural Gas." www.oilandgasinfo.ca/oil-gas-you/products/ (accessed January 21, 2015).

15. This chapter focuses on the political resource curses of authoritarianism, civil conflict, and corruption. A distinct literature discusses the (related) economic resource curse of slower growth. For a survey see Frankel, Jeffrey A. 2012. "The Natural Resource Curse: A Survey of Diagnoses and Some Prescriptions." www .hks.harvard.edu/centers/cid/publications/faculty-working-papers/cid-working -paper-no.-233 (accessed April 25, 2015).

16. Ross, Michael. 2012. *The Oil Curse: How Petroleum Wealth Shapes the Development of Nations.* Princeton: Princeton University Press, p. 1.

17. UNICEF. 2015. *Levels & Trends in Child Mortality.* New York, pp. 18–27.

18. Ross, Michael. 2014. "What Have We Learned About the Resource Curse?" ssrn.com/abstract=2342668 (accessed April 25, 2015).

19. Ross 2012, p. 1.

20. The list of countries marked on the map is from the combined Freedom House / Economist Intelligence Unit metric described in the second part of the chapter.

21. Results reported to this point in the paragraph are from the literature review in Ross 2014; "ever-higher proportion" from personal correspondence with Michael Ross, September 2015.

22. The exception to this trend is the oil state of Libya, where the authoritarian fell. But Libya was exceptional, because the rebels had NATO as their air force. Syria is the interesting intermediate case: Assad's oil revenues per capita when the revolt started were between the levels at which other authoritarian regimes survived and fell.

23. Economist Intelligence Unit. 2018. *Democracy Index 2017.* London.

24. Malaquias, Assis. 2001. "Diamonds Are a Guerrilla's Best Friend: The Impact of Illicit Wealth on Insurgency Strategy." *Third World Quarterly* 22(3): 311–25.

25. Data from personal communication with Michael Ross, September 2015.

26. Le Billon, Philippe. 2012. *Wars of Plunder: Conflicts, Profits and the Politics of Resources*. New York: Columbia University Press, pp. 15–16 and *passim*.

27. Buhaug, Halvard, Scott Gates, and Päivi Lujala. 2009. "Geography, Rebel Capability, and the Duration of Civil Conflict." *Journal of Conflict Resolution* 53(4): 544–69.

28. Lujala, Päivi. 2009. "Deadly Combat over Natural Resources: Gems, Petroleum, Drugs, and the Severity of Armed Civil Conflict." *Journal of Conflict Resolution* 53(1): 50–71; Lujala, Päivi. 2010. "The Spoils of Nature: Armed Civil Conflict and Rebel Access to Natural Resources." *Journal of Peace Research* 47(1): 15–28.

29. Weinstein, Jeremy M. 2007. *Inside Rebellion: The Politics of Insurgent Violence*. Cambridge: Cambridge University Press.

30. Data from personal communication with Michael Ross, June 2016.

31. Ross 2012, p. 1, updated in personal communication, June 2016.

32. Freedom House. 2018. *Freedom in the World*. Washington DC. For the civil wars that had over 1000 violent deaths in 2017, Uppsala Conflict Data Program. www.ucdp.uu.se (accessed April 15, 2018). For corruption, scores less than 20 on Transparency International. 2017. *Corruption Perception Index*. www.transparency .org/cpi (accessed April 15, 2018). For refugees, see World Bank. 2016. "Refugees by Country or Territory of Origin." https://data.worldbank.org/indicator/ SM.POP.REFG.OR?year_high_desc = true (accessed April 23, 2018). For hunger, see the Global Hunger Index. http://www.ifpri.org/topic/global-hunger-index (accessed June 1, 2018). For poverty, see James Cust quoted in *Business A.M.* 2018. "Share of the World's Poor Living in Resource-Rich Countries may Peak at 75% in 2030." https://www.businessamlive.com/share-of-the-worlds-poor-living-in-resource-rich -countries-may-peak-75-in-2030/ (accessed April 15, 2018).

33. Sanctions, which are active measures taken to cut off trade, show that countries' legal default is commercial engagement.

34. Law, James. 2014. "Democratic Republic of Congo: The Worst Place in the World to Be a Woman." http://www.news.com.au/lifestyle/real-life/true-stories/ democratic-republic-of-congo-the-worst-place-in-the-world-to-be-a-woman/news -story/e8ee02223f7ab6003314c77d70923fc8 (accessed February 12, 2017).

35. BBC News. 2016. "DR Congo Country Profile." http://www.bbc.co.uk/news/ world-africa-13283212 (accessed February 12, 2017). For the debate over the mortality figures, see *Science Insider*. 2010. "How Many Have Died Due to Congo's Fighting? Scientists Battle over How to Estimate War-Related Deaths." news .sciencemag.org/2010/01/how-many-have-died-due-congos-fighting-scientists -battle-over-how-estimate-war-related (accessed January 24, 2015). All reports agree that most excess deaths have been civilian and non-violent (for example, child deaths from disease and malnutrition).

36. *U.S. Executive Order 13566.* 2011.

37. U.S. Treasury. 2011. *General Order 5.*

38. The United States didn't recognize the rebels diplomatically until months later. Wan, William, and William Booth. 2011. "United States Recognizes Libyan Rebels as Legitimate Government." *Washington Post*, July 15.

39. Colgan, Jeff D. 2013. *Petro-Aggression: When Oil Causes War*. New York: Cambridge University Press.

40. Sloan, Stephen, and Sean K. Anderson. 2009. *Historical Dictionary of Terrorism.* New York: Rowman & Littlefield, p. 640; U.S. Department of State. 2015. "Country Reports on Terrorism." www.state.gov/j/ct/rls/crt/ (accessed February 12, 2017). South Yemen is a debatable case and so is omitted; its oil exports began halfway through its time on the list.

41. Lipton, Eric. 2010. "U.S. Intensifies Air Screening for Fliers from 14 Nations." *New York Times,* January 3.

42. Felter, Joseph, and Brian Fishman. 2007. *Al-Qa'ida's Foreign Fighters in Iraq: A First Look At The Sinjar Records.* U.S. Military Academy. West Point, p. 7.

43. Maass, Peter. 2009. *Crude World: The Violent Twilight of Oil.* New York: Knopf, p. 172. For reporting on this issue, see the views of the named scholars quoted in Shane, Scott. 2016. "Saudis And Extremism: 'Both the Arsonists and the Firefighters.'" *New York Times.* August 25.

44. For a genealogy of the Hijazi pan-Islamist ideology, see Hegghammer, Thomas. 2010. *Jihad in Saudi Arabia: Violence and Pan-Islamism since 1979.* Cambridge: Cambridge University Press. For a country-level survey, see Wilson, Tom. 2017. "Foreign Funded Islamic Extremism in the UK." Henry Jackson Society. London.

45. Freedom House. 2006. "Excerpts from Saudi Ministry of Education Textbooks for Islamic Studies: Arabic with English Translation." [no city], pp. 43, 103–6.

46. Weinberg, David Andrew. 2015. "Saudi Textbooks Propagate Intolerance." http://thehill.com/blogs/congress-blog/education/258583-saudi-textbooks -propagate-intolerance (accessed February 13, 2017).

47. Zakaria, Fareed. 2017. "How the Saudis Played Trump." *Washington Post,* May 25.

48. See, e.g., Armstrong, Karen. 2014. "The Deep Roots of Islamic State." *New Statesman,* November 21, 24–31.

49. Engel, Pamela. 2016. "CIA Director: The Middle East Is the Worst It's Been in 50 Years with 'Unprecedented' Bloodshed." *Business Insider UK.* February 10.

50. National Intelligence Council. 2012. *Global Trends 2030: Alternative Worlds.* Washington, DC; on the "youth bulge" in the Arab world, see *Economist.* 2016. "Look Forward in Anger." August 6.

51. New York Public Library. 2012. "The Abolition of the Slave Trade." http:// abolition.nypl.org/essays/us_slave_trade/ (accessed February 13, 2017).

52. Under Westphalia, states could also drive other states out of existence by conquering all their territory. As James Crawford once put it, "The law of nations was, in a sense, the codified law of the jungle." Crawford, James. 2001. "The Right to Self-Determination in International Law: Its Development and Future." In *Peoples' Rights,* ed. Philip Alston. Oxford: Oxford University Press, pp. 7–67 at p. 12.

53. Campbell, Greg. 2002. *Blood Diamonds: Tracing the Deadly Path of the World's Most Precious Stones.* Boulder: Westview.

54. The Kimberley Process. https://www.kimberleyprocess.com/en/about (accessed February 13, 2017).

55. Reuters. 2011. "Ex-President Clinton Backs Libya Intervention." March 25. Bush, George W. 2006. *Public Papers of the Presidents of the United States.* Book 1. Washington, DC: U.S. Government Printing Office, p. 1119; *Telegraph.* 2003. "Tony

Blair's Statement." March 17; Australian Government. 2010. "Prime Minister Transcript of Doorstop Interview, Geelong Hospital 7 May 2010." pmtranscripts.dpmc .gov.au/browse.php?did = 17284 (accessed February 1, 2015); Blount, Jeb, and Adriana Brasileiro. 2009. "Tupi Oil Imperiled as Price Drop Unravels Energy Plan." www.bloomberg.com/apps/news?pid = newsarchive&sid = aszdg.tiMLMs (accessed February 1, 2015); Rathborne, John Paul, and Eduardo Garcia. 2013. "Mexico Opens Up Its Energy Sector." *Financial Times*, August 12; John, Mark, and Kwasi Kpodo. 2010. "Ghana Bids to Break Africa's Oil Curse." www.reuters.com/article/ 2010/05/26/us-frontiers-ghana-idUSTRE64P1HU20100526 (accessed April 25, 2015); Norwegian Ministry for Petroleum and Energy. 2011. *An Industry for the Future—Norway's Petroleum Activities*. Oslo, p. 5; BBC. 2002. "Iran Wields Oil Embargo Threat." news.bbc.co.uk/1/hi/business/1912795.stm (accessed January 26, 2015).

56. Dalton, Russell, Doh Shin, and Willy Jou. 2008. "How People Understand Democracy." In *How People View Democracy*, eds. Larry Diamond and Mark Plattner. Baltimore: Johns Hopkins University Press, 1–15; Diamond, Larry. 2010. "Why Are There No Arab Democracies?" *Journal of Democracy* 21(1): 93–112.

57. *International Covenant on Civil and Political Rights*. 1966. 999 UNTS 171, Articles 1, 47; *International Covenant on Economic, Social, and Cultural Rights*. 1966. 993 UNTS 3, Articles 1, 25. A people's rights over its resources is the only right that each human rights treaty affirms twice.

58. UN Treaty Collection. 2013. *Status of Ratification of Human Rights Instruments as of February 13*. www.ohchr.org/Documents/HRBodies/HRChart.xls (accessed February 3, 2015). Though the language of the covenants and other treaties clearly express the principle of Popular Resource Sovereignty, the dominant legal interpretations of the treaties do not ascribe strong rights to peoples over their resources. These interpretations are dubious, but the fact remains that most major international actors do not accept that treaties impose international obligations to respect the rights of peoples over their resources against their own states. See Wenar 2016, chapter 12.

59. BP. 2017, p. 8, cross-referenced with the combined Freedom House/Economist Intelligence Unit metric described in the second part of the chapter. The figure for crude oil is 60%; for natural gas it is 50%.

60. Such indices are already in use. For example, the Millennium Challenge Corporation, a U.S. foreign aid agency, decides on eligibility for aid using an index based on several indicators. Millennium Challenge Corporation. 2015. "Report on the Criteria and Methodology for Determining the Eligibility of Candidate Countries for Millennium Challenge Account Assistance in Fiscal Year 2016." https:// www.mcc.gov/resources/doc/report-selection-criteria-and-methodology-fy16 (accessed February 13, 2017).

61. This metric combines the "Not Free" ratings from Freedom House. 2018. *Freedom in the World 2018* with the "Authoritarian" ratings from Economist Intelligence Unit. 2018. The list includes only states that are major exporters by the International Monetary Fund's definition: resources provide at least 20 percent of exports or fiscal revenues. International Monetary Fund. 2015. *The Commodities Roller Coaster: A Fiscal Framework for Uncertain Times*. Washington, DC, p. 21. (The

IMF list has been expanded to include Myanmar, Turkmenistan, and South Sudan, which also meet its definition. See the country reports by the MIT Observatory of Economic Complexity at http://atlas.media.mit.edu/en/ (accessed April 15, 2018). Central African Republic is also included: even though some official statistics do not report its (often illegal) diamond exports at all, other sources plausibly list diamonds as its top exports. See, for example, CIA. World Factbook. 2018. "Central African Republic." https://www.cia.gov/library/publications/the-world-factbook/geos/ct.html (accessed April 15, 2018).

62. U.S. Energy Information Administration. "Oil Imports and Exports" http://www.eia.gov/energyexplained/index.cfm?page = oil_imports (accessed April 15, 2018). The percentage is for 2016.

63. On the WTO, see Bartels, Lorand. 2015. "WTO Law Aspects of Clean Trade." https://papers.ssrn.com/sol3/papers.cfm?abstract_id = 2634567 (accessed February 13, 2017).

64. Lipton, Eric, David E. Sanger, and Scott Shane. 2016. "The Perfect Weapon: How Russian Cyberpower Invaded the U.S." *New York Times*, December 13.

65. UK Government. 2017. "Imports of Crude Oil & Petroleum Products by Country of Origin." https://assets.publishing.service.gov.uk/government/uploads/system/uploads/attachment_data/file/632678/DUKES_3.9.xls (accessed April 15, 2018).

66. Nick Butler, a former vice president of BP and the energy columnist for the *Financial Times*, was asked to evaluate the time and cost of North American and European transitions away from authoritarian oil and gas (personal communication, December 2014). Butler concluded that North American imports would present few problems: these could be switched away from authoritarian oil and gas in a matter of months. Europe could also make a quick transition for its oil. In these cases, imports could easily be substituted on the open trading market, while the oil excluded from Europe and North America could find ready buyers elsewhere. The hardest part of a transition will be European gas, because parts of Europe are heavily dependent on Russia for supply through pipelines. Even here, Butler predicted that supplies could adjust within a few years. Norway and other non-authoritarian countries would boost production, new pipelines would be laid, the European gas grid would be joined up, and more use would be made of underutilized import capacity for liquefied natural gas.

67. OPEC. 2017. *OPEC Annual Statistical Bulletin.* Vienna, Tables 5.3 and 5.7. Even with these 2016 figures, which do not register the later expansion of U.S. crude oil exports, non-authoritarian exporters already meet over 90% of the import demand of North America and all of Western Europe. (Because gas is primarily transported by pipeline, the overall balance of exports and imports is less meaningful. Yet the OPEC report [figures 9.4 and 9.5] shows that non-authoritarian gas exporters more than meet the import demands of North American and all of Western Europe.)

68. Lincoln, Abraham. "First Inaugural Address of Abraham Lincoln." http://avalon.law.yale.edu/19th_century/lincoln1.asp (accessed February 13, 2017). Lincoln said, "This country, with its institutions, belongs to the people who inhabit it."

69. Structuring trade policies with such conditionalities is already common. For example, the U.S. African Growth and Opportunity Act allows extra trade privileges to African countries that score higher on the rule of law, political pluralism, and anti-corruption indices.

70. de Tocqueville, Alexis. 2001. *Writings on Empire and Slavery.* Trans. and Ed. Jennifer Pitts. Baltimore: Johns Hopkins University Press, p. 199.

71. Kaufmann, Chaim D. and Robert A. Pape. 1999. "Explaining Costly International Moral Action: Britain's Sixty-Year Campaign Against the Atlantic Slave Trade." *International Organization* 53: 631–68.

72. Pew Research Center. 2011. "Muslim-Western Tensions Persists." www .pewglobal.org/2011/07/21/muslim-western-tensions-persist/ (accessed February 7, 2015); Carnegie Endowment. 2013. *US-China Security Perceptions Survey.* Washington, DC, p. 12.

73. Mathias Risse traces the idea of common ownership of the Earth from Grotius to contemporary philosophers like Hillel Steiner, Michael Otsuka, and Thomas Pogge in Risse, Mathias. 2012. *On Global Justice.* Princeton: Princeton University Press, pp. 89–129.

74. Many potentially worthwhile reforms—such as fighting illicit financial flows, or a carbon tax—might further egalitarian goals, but would also likely further humanitarian and utilitarian goals as well. The focus here is on reforms concerning resources that are more distinctively egalitarian.

75. Steiner, Hillel. 1994. *An Essay on Rights.* Oxford: Blackwell, pp. 269–73; 2011. "The *Global Fund*: A Reply to Casal." *Journal of Moral Philosophy* 8: 328–34.

76. Chris Armstrong, for instance, is enthusiastic about how much egalitarian good could be done with the oil-derived money in Abu Dhabi's sovereign wealth fund—while mentioning in passing only "concerted political intervention" as a means to make the rulers of Abu Dhabi hand some of that money over. Armstrong, Chris. 2017. *Justice and Natural Resources.* Oxford: Oxford University Press, p. 197.

77. For Clean Trade, the answers are "yes" to recession and friction, "no" to depression.

78. See Ignatieff, Michael. 2017. *Ordinary Virtues.* Cambridge: Harvard University Press.

79. Christiano, Thomas. 2011. "An Instrumental Argument for a Human Right to Democracy." *Philosophy & Public Affairs* 39: 142–76.

80. For a rich account of popular sovereignty in the creation of cosmopolitan agency, see Ypi, Lea. 2011. *Global Justice and Avant-Garde Political Agency.* Oxford: Oxford University Press, chapter 6.

81. To take a fanciful example, suppose that by the time common ownership becomes politically feasible, machines are doing all necessary labor and humans are eagerly spending as much time as possible in an infinite, shared virtual world, where their invulnerable, self-created avatars are fully sensorily engaged—and that they can create any art, music, or craft just by imagining it. How urgent will it then be to get to each person their share of the value of the Earth's natural resources?

82. One might say that no truly inspiring philosophical ideal could be the premise of a reality-television show.

83. Rawls, John. 1971. *A Theory of Justice.* Cambridge: Harvard University Press, p. 259.

84. Rousseau, Jean-Jacques. 1987. *On The Social Contract.* Trans. Donald A. Cress. Indianapolis: Hackett, p. 46.

85. Rawls 1971, pp. 178, 102.

86. Kant, Immanuel. 1998. *Groundwork of the Metaphysics of Morals,* ed. and trans. Mary Gregor and Jens Timmermann. Cambridge: Cambridge University Press, p. 45; substituting "realm" for "kingdom."

87. Mill, John Stuart. 2001. *Utilitarianism.* 2nd ed. Ed. George Sher. Indianapolis: Hackett, p. 33.

88. The subjective meta-rules ordering these multiple levels is again unity. A person should reason on these levels as will result in the greatest free unity.

89. Mill, John Stuart. 1989. *On Liberty and Other Writings.* Ed. Stefan Collini. Cambridge: Cambridge University Press, p. 14.

NOTES TO CHAPTER 2

1. In this chapter, I will focus almost exclusively on Clean Trade Acts; the Clean Hands Trust only emerges as an instrument after we have established the viability and desirability of conditioning trading relationships on the achievement of a decent standard of human rights.

2. Nor, to be fair, does Wenar himself; see, for instance, his discussion of Equatorial Guinea on 289–91. My intention in this paper is not so much to introduce ideas Wenar has not considered, but to emphasize how many and how complex the ways are in which the sanctions he imagines might go awry.

3. The precise impact of the sanctions is disputed. Some economists credit the sanctions with accelerating the pace of change; others note that the sanctions made the economy of the post-apartheid state worse than was desirable, and note that exogenous political factors contributed to the abandonment of apartheid as well. See Keller, Bill. 1993. "South African Sanctions May Have Worked, at a Price." *New York Times,* September 12.

4. Seay, Laura. 2012. "What's Wrong with Dodd-Frank? Conflict Minerals, Civilian Livelihoods, and the Unintended Consequences of Western Advocacy." Center for Global Development, Working Paper 284, January. The case is discussed in Rubenstein, Jennifer C., "Misuse of Power, Not Bad Representation: Why It Is Beside the Point that No One Elected Oxfam," 22(2) *Journal of Political Philosophy,* pp. 204–30.

5. Data as of Fall 2016, in a survey of 230,000 high school students. Available at http://www.doh.wa.gov/Portals/1/Documents/8350/160-NonDOH-DB-MJ.pdf.

6. For a good account of this, see French, Howard W. 2014. *China's Second Continent: How a Million Migrants Are Building a New Empire in Africa.* New York: Vintage.

7. Moyo, Dambisa. 2010. *Dead Aid: Why Aid Is Not Working and How There Is a Better Way for Africa.* New York: Farrar, Straus and Giroux, reprint edition.

8. Cole's words are from his Twitter account, and are cited in Robert Mackey, "African Critics of Kony Campaign See a 'White Man's Burden' for the Facebook Generation." *New York Times,* March 12.

9. Reiff, David. 2003. "Were Sanctions Right?" *New York Times,* July 27. It is

worth noting that the American leadership justified sanctions in terms similar to those used by Wenar: L. Paul Bremer argued that "Saddam and his cronies were taking money, stealing it, really, from the Iraqi people."

10. The Clean Trade Act is a sort of conditional sanction: make these reforms, or we will not engage in trading relationships with you. This conditional sanction is identical in form to the ones discussed above; both South Africa and Iraq, for instance, were offered tools with which to re-open trading relationships, once they had altered the activities (and, in the case of South Africa, the constitutional nature) of the state in question.

11. Mueller, John, and Karl Mueller. 1999. "Sanctions of Mass Destruction." *Foreign Affairs*, May/June.

12. Khan, Carrie. 2014. "Cubans Blame Their Woes on the U.S. Embargo." *NPR News*, December 20, available at http://www.npr.org/2014/12/20/372070447/cubans-blame-their-woes-on-the-u-s-embargo.

13. Diehl, Jackson. "Venezuela and the Eclipse of American Leadership." 2017. *Washington Post*, April 16.

14. Hence, the famous Soviet maxim: so long as they pretend to pay us, we'll pretend to work. This is discussed in Marcus, Naomi, "What's in It for Me, Comrade?" *Mother Jones*, October 1988.

15. Labott, Elise, and Phil Hirschkorn. 2005. "Documents: U.S. Condoned Iraq Oil Smuggling." *CNN News*, February 2.

16. Lewis, Barbara et al. 2012. "Insight: Canada's Oil Sand Battle with Europe." *Reuters*, May 12.

17. Hislop, Mark. 2017. "Would Alberta's Oil Sands Benefit From Sanctions Against Venezuela?" *Exploration and Production Magazine*, August 1.

18. Cooper, Helene. 2017. "Senate Narrowly Backs Trump Weapons Sale to Saudi Arabia." *New York Times*, June 13.

19. See the figures at http://priceofoil.org/thepriceofoil/corruption/.

20. Bowden, John. 2017. "Oil Companies Lobby against New Russia Sanctions." *The Hill*, July 4.

21. Davenport, Coral, and Eric Lipton. 2017. "How G. O. P. Leaders Came to View Climate Change as Fake Science." *New York Times*, June 3.

22. This doctrine was given its best articulation in *Banco Nacional de Cuba v. Sabbatino*, in which the Supreme Court of the United States refused to provide a forum in which Cuban nationals could contest the nationalization of their assets by the revolutionary government. *Banco Nacional de Cuba v. Sabbatino*, 376 U.S. 398 (1964). This case was controversial, and led to legislative responses that undermined its authority going forward.

23. *Sabbatino*, at 410.

24. Richard Holbrook, President Clinton's ambassador to the United Nations, described sanctions as filling a role between outright warfare and mere pressure: "What else fills in the gap between pounding your breast and indulging in empty rhetoric and going to war besides economic sanctions?" In Reiff 2003.

25. See, on this, Mahbubani, Kishore. 2009, *Can Asians Think?* Singapore: Marshall Cavendish, 4th ed.

26. My own discussion of these ideas can be found in *Justice and Foreign Policy* (Oxford: Oxford University Press, 2013).

27. Collier, Paul. 2009. "Development in Dangerous Places." *Boston Review*, July.

28. Easterly, William. 2009. "Response to Collier." *Boston Review*, July.

29. Wenar discusses this in several places, most notably in "Poverty Is No Pond," in *Giving Well: The Ethics of Philanthropy*, P. Illingworth et al., ed., (Oxford: Oxford University Press, 2010).

NOTES TO CHAPTER 3

1. Herbstreuth, Sebastian. 2016. *Oil and American Identity: A Culture of Dependency and US Foreign Policy.* London: I.B. Tauris.

2. Ibid., pp.18–39.

3. Klein, Naomi. 2016. "Let Them Drown: The Violence of Othering in a Warming World." *London Review of Books*, 38 (11), June 2, pp. 11–14.

4. Kirby, Jen. 2017. "Venezuelan President Nicolás Maduro Scoffs at Emperor Trumps Sanctions." *New York Magazine*, August 1. http://nymag.com/daily/intelligencer/2017/08/venezuelan-president-maduro-scoffs-at-emperor-trump.html (accessed 15 September 2017).

5. Data as of August 1999–July 2016. Available at https://www.levada.ru/en/ratings/.

6. Data as of March 2015. Available at http://www.levada.ru/en/2015/04/15/ukraine-crimea-and-the-sanctions/.

7. See, for instance, Goldenberg, Suzanne. 2014. "Fracking Is Depleting Water Supplies in America's Driest Areas, Report Shows." *The Guardian*, February 5. https://www.theguardian.com/environment/2014/feb/05/fracking-water-america-drought-oil-gas (accessed on 3 August 2017).

8. U.S. Environmental Protection Agency. "Draft Plan to Study the Potential Impacts of Hydraulic Fracturing on Drinking Water Resources." https://yosemite.epa.gov/sab/sabproduct.nsf/0/D3483AB445AE61418525775900603E79/$File/Draft + Plan + to + Study + the + Potential + Impacts + of + Hydraulic + Fracturing + on + Drinking + Water + Resources-February + 2011.pdf (accessed August 1, 2017).

9. U.S. Energy Information Administration. 2016. "Hydraulically Fractured Wells Provide Two-thirds of U.S. Natural Gas Production." May 5. https://www.eia.gov/todayinenergy/detail.php?id = 26112 (accessed August 13, 2017).

10. Meyer, Gregory. 2017. "US Shale Oil Output Remains Resilient Despite Rig Count Fall." *Financial Times.* January 12.

11. Bryant, Jason, Thomas Welton, and Johanna Haggstrom. 2010. "Will Flowback or Produced Water Do?" *E&P*. September 1. It is known from other research that the reuse of the water in the Marcellus Shale in Pennsylvania was estimated at 70 percent in 2011 with disposal of waste to municipal sewage plants decreasing sharply but the remaining volume was still large and toxic. Based on the knowledge of the chemical cocktails used in hydraulic fracturing, the EPA estimated the number of potential drinking water contaminants at several hundred.

12. Caulton, Dana R. et al. "Towards a Better Understanding and Quantification of Methane Emissions from Shale Gas Development." Proceedings of the National Academy of Sciences. http://www.pnas.org/content/111/17/6237.abstract; see also Patterson, Clark. 2014. "Unexpected Loose Gas from Fracking." *The Washington Post.*

April 14. https://www.washingtonpost.com/apps/g/page/national/unexpected -loose-gas-from-fracking/950/ (accessed July 20, 2017).

13. Howarth, Robert. 2014. "A Bridge to Nowhere: Methane Emissions and the Greenhouse Gas Footprint of Natural Gas." *Energy Science and Engineering,* vol. 2(2), pp. 47–60.

14. In 2015, a rule was introduced into the EPA's Greenhouse Gas Reporting Program to ensure that new fracking sites account for and capture the gas that escapes into the atmosphere during hydraulic fracturing. The rule was met with stiff opposition from the shale lobby, which called it a threat to the development of hydraulic fracturing in the United States. Even if the rule is not rescinded under President Donald Trump, whose administration has shown avid opposition to it, the problem remains that the EPA relies on self-reporting of the emissions data by industry participants. Given their vested interest in under-estimating emissions and in the absence of independent verification by EPA, a number of studies have claimed that methane concentrations in the atmosphere over shale wells are several times higher than the reported data (see, for instance, https://www.gpo.gov/fdsys/ pkg/FR-2014-12-09/pdf/2014-28395.pdf; https://www.ft.com/content/95f22ba8 -6028-11e7-91a7-502f7ee26895; https://www.scientificamerican.com/article/epa -moves-to-count-methane-emissions-from-fracking/; https://www.climatecentral .org/news/fracking-methane-emissions-catastrophe-17439).

15. "Shale Gas and EU Energy Security." 2014. European Parliament Briefing. December. http://www.europarl.europa.eu/RegData/etudes/BRIE/2014/542167/ EPRS_BRI(2014)542167_REV1_EN.pdf (accessed June 20, 2017).

16. "France Cements Fracking Ban." 2013. *The Guardian,* October 11. https:// www.theguardian.com/environment/2013/oct/11/france-fracking-ban-shale-gas (accessed June 20, 2017).

17. Grealy, Nick. 2016. "France, How Can You Square Your Ban on Fracking with the Import of Shale Oil?" *Energy Post,* August 29. http://energypost.eu/france-can -square-ban-fracturing-import-shale-oil/ (accessed June 21, 2017).

18. Beckman, Karel. 2016. "Dutch Government: Only EVs and Hydrogen Cars from 2035, Phase-out Natural Gas." *Energy Post,* December 8. http://energypost.eu/ dutch-government-evs-hydrogen-cars-2035-phase-natural-gas/ (accessed June 15, 2017).

19. McKinsey & Company. 2016. "Accelerating the Energy Transition: Cost or Opportunity? A Thought Starter for the Netherlands." September. http://www .mckinsey.com/global-themes/europe/accelerating-the-energy-transition-cost-or -opportunity (accessed September 2, 2017).

20. Press Information Bureau of the Government of India. 2017. "India Takes Giant Leap on Green Energy Targets." May 8. http://pib.nic.in/newsite/printrelease .aspx?relid = 161622 (accessed June 15, 2017).

21. *BP Energy Outlook 2017,* https://www.bp.com/content/dam/bp/pdf/energy -economics/energy-outlook-2017/bp-energy-outlook-2017.pdf (accessed June 10, 2017).

22. Aggarwal, Mayank. 2017. "Modi Government Achieves Only 19 Percent of 12,000-MW Solar Power Target in 2016–17." *LiveMint,* January 10. http://www .livemint.com/Industry/MyawHsvvqTE2IYIjCqj72O/Modi-govt-achieves-only-19 -of-12000MW-solar-power-target.html (accessed September 12, 2017).

23. See, for instance, Velentina Ruiz Leotaud, "Rare Earths: Battling China's Monopoly After Molycorp's Demise?" *Mining,* September 10, 2016. http://www .mining.com/rare-earths-battling-chinas-monopoly-after-molycorps-debacle/ (accessed September 12, 2017).

24. Quoted in Frik Els, "Canada Identifies Top Rare Earth Projects." *Mining,* June 29, 2014. http://www.mining.com/canada-identifies-top-rare-earth-projects -48319/ (accessed September 13, 2017).

25. U.S. Department of Energy. 2011. "Critical Materials Strategy." December. https://energy.gov/sites/prod/files/DOE_CMS2011_FINAL_Full. pdf (accessed September 12, 2017); European Commission. "Critical Raw Materials." https:// ec.europa.eu/growth/sectors/raw-materials/specific-interest/critical_en (accessed September 22, 2017).

26. Bradsher, Keith. 2010. "In China, Illegal Rare Earth Mines Face Crackdown." *The New York Times,* December 29. http://www.nytimes.com/2010/12/30/business/ global/30smuggle.html (accessed August 12, 2017).

27. Kaiman, Jonathan. 2014. "Rare Earth in China: The Bleak Social and Environmental Costs." *The Guardian,* March 20. https://www.theguardian.com/sustain able-business/rare-earth-mining-china-social-environmental-costs (accessed August 7, 2017).

28. Gee, Alastair. 2014. "The Rare-Earths Roller Coaster." *The New Yorker,* May 22. http://www.newyorker.com/business/currency/the-rare-earths-roller-coaster (accessed August 12, 2017).

29. Research and Markets. 2017. "Research Report on Rare Earth Industry in China, 2017–2021." March. https://www.researchandmarkets.com/research/ wrlvv9/research_report

30. Bradsher, Keith. 2010. "Amid Tension, China Blocks Vital Exports to Japan." *The New York Times,* September 22, 2010. http://www.nytimes.com/2010/09/23/ business/global/23rare.html?mcubz = 3 (accessed June 22, 2017).

31. Liu, Hongqiao. 2017. "As China Adjusts for 'True Cost' of Rare Earths, What Does It Mean for Decarbonization?" *New Security Beat,* Wilson Center, March 21, 2017. https://www.newsecuritybeat.org/2017/03/china-begins-adjusting-true-cost -rare-earths-decarbonization/ (accessed September 3, 2017).

32. "Rare Earth Metals Electrified China's Illegal Mining Clean-Up." 2017. *Bloomberg News.* September 11. https://www.bloomberg.com/news/articles/2017 -09-07/rare-earth-metals-electrified-by-china-s-illegal-mining-clean-up (accessed September 12, 2017).

33. "Research Report on Rare Earth Industry in China."

34. LNG from Sakhalin-2 was not developed by a Russian company but taken over by Gazprom. By contrast, Yamal LNG has been developed by Novatek and Russia now has experience in launching these complex projects. Sanctions were in part aiming to precluding Russia from developing LNG.

35. Government of the Russian Federation. 2003. *Energeticheskaya Strategiya Rossii na period do 2020 goda* [Energy strategy of Russia to 2020], p. 16. http:// www.energystrategy.ru/projects/ES-28_08_2003.pdf, p. 4.

36. Security Council of the Russian Federation. 2015. *Strategiya natsional'noy bezopasnosti Rossiyskoy Federatsii do 2020 goda* [National security strategy of the Russian Federation up to 2020], sections ii.9 and ii.12. http://kremlin.ru/acts/bank/ 40391 (accessed January 10, 2017).

37. "Putin: Novye sanktsii SShA—obespechenie svoikh ekonomicheskikh interesov s 'osobym tsiniszmom' " [Putin: New US sanctions—guarding its own economic interests "with particular cynicism"]. *Tass*, July 27, 2017.

38. EIA data reported in Andrew Follett, "China Now Number One Customer for US Oil," May 4, 2017. http://dailycaller.com/2017/04/05/china-now-number -one-customer-for-us-oil/ (accessed February 5, 2017).

39. Jopson, Barney, Demetri Sevastopulo, and Ed Crooks. 2017. "Trump Looks to Lift LNG Exports in US Trade Shift." *Financial Times*, June 22, 2017.

40. "Biden Says US 'Embarrassed' EU into Sanctioning Russia over Ukraine." *RT*, October 3, 2014. https://www.rt.com/usa/193044-us-embarrass-eu-sanctions/ (accessed August 5, 2017).

41. Gazprom, June 8, 2017. http://www.gazprom.com/press/news/2017/june/ article335985/ (accessed September 1, 2017)

42. For excellent background on this, see Mikkall E. Herberg, "Energy Competition and Energy Cooperation in Northeast Asia," in Kong, B. and Tae, H. Ku. 2015. *Energy Security Cooperation in Northeast Asia*. Abingdon, UK: Routledge, 12–37.

43. Hessian Ministry of Development, Transport, Urban and Regional Development. 2008. "Application of Nanotechnologies in the Energy Sector." August. www.hessen-nanotech.de (accessed August 1, 2017).

44. "China Claims Breakthrough in Mining 'Flammable Ice,' " May 19, 2017. http://www.bbc.co.uk/news/world-asia-china-39971667 (accessed June 23, 2017).

NOTES TO CHAPTER 4

1. Wenar, Leif. 2016. *Blood Oil: Tyrants, Violence, and the Rules that Run the World*. New York: Oxford University Press. I shall mainly be referring to the current volume's chapter 1.

2. I say "roughly" because, for reasons briefly discussed later, a somewhat inegalitarian distribution may, for familiar incentive reasons, provide a better flow of welfare.

3. That is, goals shared between Aristotelian/Millians, and Rawlsians. Wenar's overall philosophical posture appears to be that of a Millian indirect utilitarian, who believes that Rawlsian nation-state structures of justice provide the best way of achieving the goals of the former. At the same time, he says that he believes Popular Resource Sovereignty can be supported by a range of different philosophical positions, and thus enjoys the status of an object in a Rawlsian overlapping consensus of reasonable views.

4. America received about 4.7 percent of its total petroleum demand from Saudi Arabia in 2017, 346 million barrels of oil, or 6.8 billion gallons of gasoline; this amounted to 9 percent of total petroleum imports. U.S. Energy Information Administration, www.eia.gov (accessed May 21, 2018).

5. See generally Krasner, Stephen. 1999. *Sovereignty: Organized Hypocrisy*. Princeton, N.J.: Princeton University Press, for an account of sovereignty that recognizes its operational limitations while also ceding it some space in international organization. Krasner terms the specific form of sovereignty at issue when a home regime vouchsafes resources sales to the international market "interdependence

sovereignty" (p. 4). We can think of it more generally as one of the strands or sticks in the bundle of sovereign rights, to which Wenar has brought important attention.

6. Kant, Immanuel. 1795. "Perpetual Peace: A Philosophical Sketch"; Rawls, John. 1993. *The Law of Peoples*. Cambridge, MA: Belknap Press. Kant and Rawls both limit their claims of the virtues of the state system to a network of republican, or at least minimally human rights-respecting, states.

7. And such stability can come at the international price, as Wenar argues, of providing a means of support for international terrorism.

8. Of course, some might regard international stability, consistent with much weaker human rights protection, as consequentially justified. Such a position is, in fact, the status quo. To the extent that the position is not simply one of Realism, placing a substantially higher value on the stability benefits to the resource-purchasing state, it would be grounded in a claim that trade engagement leads to welfare and rights gains by the resource-rich nation. But I think Wenar has effectively disposed of that argument.

9. Hubbard, Ben. 2015. "Saudi King Unleashes a Torrent of Money as Bonuses Flow to the Masses." *New York Times*. February 19.

10. For Rawls, a society counts as decent if it is non-aggressive, human rights respecting, attendant (though not necessarily equally) to the interests of all its citizens, and "consults" with its citizens, even though it need not be democratically accountable. *Law of Peoples*, pp. 64–67. Petrostan is Rawls's "Kazanistan" plus oil wealth.

11. Wenar 2016, p. 26.

12. Surprisingly, the United States has a much higher ratio of foreign aid to energy revenues, of nearly 62 percent of governmental receipts given to aid, thus retaining 38 percent of these revenues for 6 percent of global population. However, Norway does contribute a far greater proportion of its total gross national income to foreign aid than the United States, at 1.05 percent versus .28 percent. Data from Norskpetroleum.no, http://www.norskpetroleum.no/en/production-and-exports/exports-of-oil-and-gas/; the World Economic Forum, https://www.weforum.org/agenda/2016/08/foreign-aid-these-countries-are-the-most-generous/; Trading Economics, https://tradingeconomics.com/; and the U.S. Energy Information Association, https://www.eia.gov/ (accessed October 4, 2017).

13. Presumably any efficiency-constrained principle of global distributive justice might permit oil-housing states to retain a somewhat greater national share, in order to incentivize production and extraction.

14. See Charles Beitz for the ur-argument for a Global Difference Principle resting on a global Original Position argument. Beitz, Charles. 1979. "Bounded Morality: Justice and the State in World Politics," *International Organization*, 33: 405–24.

15. "According to [Popular Resource Sovereignty], anyone who sells off a country's resources must be accountable to the owners of the resources—to the citizens." Wenar 2016, p. 22.

16. In 2014, Saudi Arabia had roughly 27 million residents, 8.5 million of whom were non-citizens. Estimates of unauthorized residents range from 2 to 5 million, presumably in addition; this would make the non-citizen/citizen ration closer to four in ten. https://en.wikipedia.org/wiki/Demographics_of_Saudi_Arabia, accessed October 4, 2017.

17. In Germany and the United States, for example, legal and non-legal noncitizen residents are about 7–8 percent of total population. Sources: Pew Research Center. "Five Facts about Illegal Immigration," http://www.pewresearch.org/fact-tank/2017/04/27/5-facts-about-illegal-immigration-in-the-u-s/ https://www.dhs.gov/immigration-statistics/population-estimates/LPR; U.S. Department of Home land Security. "Estimates of the Legal Permanent Resident Population," https://www.dhs.gov/immigration-statistics/population-estimates/LPR; Eurostat. "Migration and Migrant Population Statistics," http://ec.europa.eu/eurostat/statistics-explained/index.php/Migration_and_migrant_population_statistics. Sources accessed September 30, 2017.

18. Wenar could, of course, add normative constraints on the citizen control requirement of Popular Resource Sovereignty, such that control only counts if access to citizenship is sufficiently broad. But that would be just to concede that citizenship is doing no independent normative work.

19. See, e.g., Baubock, Rainer. 2007. "Stakeholder Citizenship and Transnational Political Participation." *Fordham Law Review* 75: 2392.

20. In my *On War and Democracy* (Princeton, NJ: Princeton University Press, 2016). I call the ideal "agentic democracy."

21. These paragraphs draw loosely on both my arguments in *On War and Democracy* and the theory of collective action I put forward in *Complicity: Ethics and Law for a Collective Age* (New York: Cambridge University Press, 2001).

22. I am not trying to suggest that, with respect to all forms of real or resource property, collective communal ownership is the normative default. That may or may not be true. But the specific characteristics of oil and gas resources, given the size of the relevant fields, are such that it is hard to imagine a principled defense of exclusive private control over windfall discoveries, much less revenue capture by officials of resources lying in public lands. (I recognize the conventional practice does treat the former as justified.)

23. For discussion, see Waldron, Jeremy. 1988. *The Right to Private Property.* New York: Oxford University Press, chapter 10.

24. Hart, H. L. A. 1955. "Are There Any Natural Rights?" *Philosophical Review* 64: 255.

25. My hesitancy on whether a global claim might be contradicted stems from the concern that states without natural resources also have a claim to self-realize, and it may be that a global natural resource tax, à la Pogge, is a reasonable way to meet the interest of other peoples.

26. There will still be difficult problems with particular cases, for instance the claim made on resources by someone who has been a foreign national white collar executive, working for years in-state. I assume that such cases can be handled by treating his or her salary as the channel by which they profit from the state's resources.

27. See, e.g., Nagel, Thomas. 2005. "The Problem of Global Justice." *Philosophy & Public Affairs* 33: 113–47.

28. I do not mean to exclude the possibility that culturally defined and collectively acting peoples might exist across state borders, thus raising questions about the claims of extraterritorial group members to resources found on only one side of the border.

29. See chapter 8, "Humanitarian Intervention and the New Democratic Holy Wars."

30. According to the 2016 UN Human Development report, Saudi Arabia ranks thirty-eighth overall in its Human Development index (the United States is tenth and the United Kingdom sixteenth) http://hdr.undp.org/en/2016-report (accessed May 21, 2018).

31. The analogy to blood diamonds is especially weak in a case like this, since conflict diamond sales were never, to my knowledge, beneficial to any but the warlords who seized them.

32. Wenar 2016, pp. 333–34.

33. Reports of contemporary slavery in the Pacific fishing industry, whose products are used in U.S. pet foods, have generated attention and change. Slavery still retains a charge.

34. In 2017 the United States consumed nearly four times as much Canadian oil as Saudi oil.

NOTES TO CHAPTER 5

1. For these criteria, see Wenar, Leif. 2016. *Blood Oil: Tyrants, Violence, and the Rules that Run the World*. New York: Oxford University Press, pp. 227–29 and 235–38.

2. Wenar 2016, p. 286.

3. See the International Covenant on Civil and Political Rights and the International Covenant on Economic, Social, and Cultural Rights. ttp://www.ohchr.org/EN/ProfessionalInterest/Pages/CCPR.aspx

4. Wenar 2016, pp. 202–05.

5. Moore, Margaret. 2015. *A Political Theory of Territory*. Oxford: Oxford University Press, p. 174.

6. Nozick, Robert. 1974. *Anarchy, State, and Utopia*. New York: Basic Books, p.178.

7. As Chris Armstrong puts it, improvement-based claims are "best responded to by granting not full and exclusive rights over all the natural resources in a territory, but an appropriate share of the income from the relevant resources." See Armstrong, Chris. 2017. *Justice and Resources*. Oxford: Oxford University Press, p. 133.

8. Grotius, Hugo. 2005. *The Rights of War and Peace*. Indianapolis: Liberty Fund, p. 455. Grotius's views are complex: he held that in some countries, only the right of jurisdiction has been occupied, leaving foreigners free to come and take, for example, unused land, while in other countries both the rights of jurisdiction and property have been occupied, prohibiting any outside appropriation of land or goods in the area. I leave aside this complication here.

9. Grotius 2005, pp. 432–33.

10. Pufendorf, Samuel. 1934. *De Jure Naturae et Gentium*. Trans. W. A. Oldfather. Oxford: Clarendon, pp. 570–71.

11. Vattel, Emer D. 2008. *The Law of Nations*. Eds. Kapossy and Whatmore. Indianapolis: Liberty Fund, p. 213.

12. Vattel 2008, p. 302. More recent theories of territorial rights have articulated

a similar distinction between property-like or "exclusionary" rights and rights of territorial jurisdiction or "control." See Simmons, A. John. 2016. *Boundaries of Authority.* Oxford: Oxford University Press, pp. 5, 93, 187.

13. Stilz, Anna. 2013. "Occupancy Rights and the Wrong of Removal." *Philosophy and Public Affairs,* 41(4): pp. 324–56.

14. Grotius 2005, pp. 426–27.

15. Pufendorf 1934, p. 536.

16. See Schrijver, Nico. 1997. *Sovereignty over Natural Resources: Balancing Rights and Duties.* Cambridge: Cambridge University Press, pp. 20–24.

17. Schrijver 1997, chapter 7.

18. Hume, David. 1978. *A Treatise of Human Nature.* Eds. L. A. Selby-Bigge and P. H. Nidditch. Oxford: Clarendon, pp. 484–513.

19. Freeman, Samuel. 1991. "Property as an Institutional Convention in Hume's Account of Justice." *Archiv für Geschichte der Philosophie,* 73, pp. 20–49.

20. Baldwin, Thomas. 1992. "The Territorial State." In *Jurisprudence: Cambridge Essays,* Eds. Hyman Gross and Ross Harrison. Oxford: Clarendon.

21. See Korman, Sharon. 1996. *The Right of Conquest.* Oxford: Clarendon Press.

22. See Wenar's lead chapter in this volume, pp. 44–49, and Wenar 2016, pp. 362–64.

23. See Moore 2015, p. 183, for a similar example.

24. Wenar 2016, p. 362.

25. Risse, Mathias. 2012. *On Global Justice.* Cambridge: Harvard University Press, p. 111.

26. See Pogge, Thomas. 1994. "An Egalitarian Law of Peoples." *Philosophy and Public Affairs,* 23:3, pp. 194–224; 2008. "Eradicating Systemic Poverty: A Brief for a Global Resources Dividend." In *World Poverty and Human Rights.* Polity; and 2011. "Allowing the Poor to Share the Earth." *Journal of Moral Philosophy* 8, pp. 335–52.

27. Steiner, Hillel. 1994. *An Essay on Rights.* Oxford: Blackwell, p. 236; and "Territorial Justice and Global Redistribution." In G. Brock and H. Brighouse, eds., *The Political Philosophy of Cosmopolitanism.* Cambridge: Cambridge University Press, p. 35.

28. Armstrong 2017, chapter 3.

29. See also Casal, Paula. 2011. "Global Taxes on Natural Resources." *Journal of Moral Philosophy* 8, pp. 307–27.

30. Wenar 2016, p. 351.

31. Schrijver 1997, p. 52.

32. Wenar 2016, p. 354.

33. I develop a more extended account in other work. See Stilz, Anna. 2016. "The Value of Self-Determination." *Oxford Studies in Political Philosophy* 2, pp. 98–127.

34. See Moore 2015, p. 175, for a similar argument.

35. Grotius 2005, p. 433.

NOTES TO CHAPTER 6

1. Wenar, Leif. 2016. *Blood Oil: Tyrants, Violence, and the Rules that Run the World.* New York: Oxford University Press; "Beyond Blood Oil," this volume, hereafter "this volume."

2. On the general idea of "structural equity," along with its application to international economic affairs, see my *Fairness in Practice: A Social Contract for a Global Economy*. 2012. New York: Oxford University Press, 2012, chapter 5.

3. Ruggie, John Gerard. 1993. "Territoriality and Beyond: Problematizing Modernity in Relations." *International Organization*, 47, 1 (Winter): 139–74. Ruggie writes (p. 151): "The distinctive feature of the modern system of rule is that it has differentiated its subject [i.e., the organization of human collectivities] collectively into territorially defined, fixed . . . mutually exclusive [functionally similar, political centralized] enclaves of legitimate [and supreme] dominion." He adds: "As such, it appears to be unique in human history," especially in contrast to the territorially fluid medieval order, and anything yet to emerge in its place.

4. Even "sovereignty" as a default legal standing hardly means that states are equal in capability or functioning in real practice. We can agree with Stephen Krasner in *Sovereignty: Organized Hypocrisy* (Princeton: Princeton University Press, 1999) that conventional models of legal sovereignty are unrealistic. We can also agree with David A. Lake in *Hierarchy in International Relations* (Ithaca: Cornell University Press, 2009) that power relations are often shaped not simply by coercion but by special authority relations (e.g., as between the United States and Mexico, and Nicaragua and both the United States and Mexico).

5. That practices of recognition are central to the territorial order is suggested by Ruggie 1993, p. 162.

6. Though for realists such as Kenneth Waltz, in *Theory of International Politics* (Reading: Addison-Wesley, 1979), powerful state incentives of self-help are created by the state system's effective operation. "Self-help" is the system's expectation. I resist Waltz's view on practice-based grounds in my *Fairness in Practice*, chapter 3, at pp. 82–87.

7. Such governance-by-argument may well amount to what Krasner (Ibid.) calls an "organized hypocrisy," because states routinely violate the norms they say they affirm. But the ideational affirmation that lip service perpetuates means that people worldwide are more or less generally organized, in a generally governed system, all the same.

8. Bull, Hedley. 1977. *The Anarchical Society: A Study of Order in World Politics*. London: Macmillan, pp. 8–10.

9. In this section and below, I draw from my "Authority and Territory," in *Sovereignty and the New Executive Authority*, Ed. Claire Finklestein and Sharon Lloyd (Oxford University Press, forthcoming). I follow Abram Chayes and Antonia Handler Chayes, *The New Sovereignty: Compliance with International Regulatory Agreements* (Cambridge: Harvard University Press, 2009), in seeing the real practice of sovereignty rights as "cooperative sovereignty."

10. This is consistent with degrees of "cooperativeness" and perhaps corresponding degrees of stability in different settings. How cooperative a group is may depend on such varying factors as: how widely a social purpose is actually endorsed; whether and to what degree people personally intend to comply, and for what reasons; whether people are motivated by moral concerns; and whether to what degree people also have genuinely shared intentions, joint commitments, or shared identities, etc.

11. Both forms of interpretation—"catholic" and "protestant"—can be "constructive," albeit to different degrees. Yet while a relatively protestant method offers greater latitude for defending an expansive list of aims or principles, both are constrained by interpretive charity, which may fall well short of our own best, free-standing ideas of justice. A "constructive interpretation" is still an interpretation of a state system that is anyway there, rather than a pure moral recommendation about how things ought to be, ideally speaking. On the pros and cons of catholic and protestant methods of constructive interpretation, see my "Why Practices?" *Raisons Politiques* 51, August (2013); and "Replies to Critics," *Canadian Journal of Philosophy*, 44, 2 (2014).

12. In this practice-based method of moral reasoning, we justify principles of justice for, and in part from, a social practice's distinctive structure, in light of the best (perhaps constructive) interpretation of its understood aims and organization. Principles of what we owe to each other are defended not simply by pure sociological interpretation, and not simply by pure moral argument, but rather by both, blended together in a suitable reflective equilibrium. See James, Aaron. 2005. "Constructing Justice for Existing Practice." *Philosophy and Public Affairs* 33(3); James 2012, chapter 1; James 2013; and James 2014.

13. Dworkin, Ronald. 2013. "A New Philosophy for International Law." *Philosophy and Public Affairs* 41 (1), pp. 17–20.

14. See Dworkin 2013 for this orientation to the problem and several of the following examples.

15. Scanlon, T. M. 1998. *What We Owe to Each Other*. Cambridge: Harvard University Press.

16. James 2012, p. 154.

17. On the other hand, I take even absolute burdens to be morally relevant only because of how they compare to the burdens upon others in action for their mitigation. I do draw a contrast between two comparative notions of fairness, "structural equity" and "equity of fortune," the latter being essentially normative, the former not. See my "Fortune and Fairness in Global Economic Life," *Journal of Moral Philosophy*, 14(3) (2017): 270–90.

18. A word of acknowledgment: I am enormously grateful and indebted to Leif Wenar's work and to our extensive stimulating and fruitful discussions over many years.

NOTES TO CHAPTER 7

1. Wenar, Leif. 2016. *Blood Oil: Tyrants, Violence, and the Rules that Run the World*. New York: Oxford University Press, p. 101.

2. Blake, this volume chapter 2.

3. Blake's invocation of *Sabbatino* and the Act of State doctrine is not apt here. This doctrine is largely one of judicial deference to the "political branches" of government (which are the branches that would enact and enforce Clean Trade legislation). More, as with laws on the sovereign immunities of foreign states, courts distinguish between what those states do in their sovereign and in their commercial capacities; selling oil abroad is clearly the latter. See Born, Gary, and Peter Rutledge.

2011. *International Civil Litigation in United States Courts,* 5th ed. New York: Wolters Kluwer, chapter 3.

4. Christopher Kutz, in chapter 4 of this volume, uses this language as well.

5. Blake, this volume, chapter 2.

6. Wenar 2016, pp. 294–97.

7. Blake, this volume, chapter 2. A recent study disputes the child-death number that Blake cites. Dyson, Tim, and Valeria Cetorelli. 2017. "Changing Views on Child Mortality and Economic Sanctions in Iraq: A History of Lies, Damned Lies and Statistics.'" *BMJ Global Health* 2.2: 1–5.

8. The case is only used only to critique Blake's method, not to comment on the realities of Iraq: it does not preserve many features of the Iraq sanctions, such as the no-fly zones or the failed Oil-for-Food program; nor of course does it parallel the West's years of political support for Saddam.

9. Seay, Laura. 2012. "What's Wrong with Dodd-Frank? Conflict Minerals, Civilian Livelihoods, and the Unintended Consequences of Western Advocacy." Center for Global Development, Working Paper 284, January, p. 15.

10. UN Security Council, "Letter Dated 8 August 2017 from the Group of Experts on the DRC." S/2017/672/Rev.1 (August 16, 2017), p. 1.

11. Kock, Dirk-Jan and Sarah Kinsbergen. 2018. "Exaggerating Unintended Effects? Competing Narratives on the Impact of Conflict Minerals Regulation." *Resources Policy* https://doi.org/10.1016/j.resourpol.2018.03.011 (accessed April 16, 2018).

12. Enough Project. 2017. "Progress and Challenges on Conflict Minerals: Facts on Dodd-Frank 1502." http://bit.ly/2y8dOAR (accessed October 1, 2017). Gold is still a concern in the eastern Congo, and those who care about the Congo will want to attend closely to what will happen next on cobalt.

13. Commercial firms like Lloyd's and intelligence agencies like the CIA monitor oil tankers, a task recently made much easier by satellites. See Wenar 2016, p. 409 ft. 2. Blake's concerns about bias in metrics of accountability are mentioned in Wenar 2016, p. 285.

14. Wenar 2016, pp. 272–74, 325–26.

15. The Iran shipping sanctions are explored more in Wenar, Leif, and Giannakis Kouris. 2018. "Shipping Policy to Fight the Resource Curse." *Global Policy* 9(2), pp. 184–92.

16. Drezner, Daniel. 2015. "Targeted Sanctions in a World of Global Finance." *International Interactions* 41.4, pp. 755–64; Farzanegan, Mohammad. 2013. "Effects of International Financial and Energy Sanctions on Iran's Informal Economy." *SAIS Review of International Affairs* 33.1, pp. 13–36.

17. Atkinson, N. 2014. "Iran Battles Sanctions, Low Oil Prices and Tough Asian Competition, Lloyd's List Maritime Intelligence." https://lloydslist.maritimeintelligence.informa.com/LL048952/Iran-battles-sanctions-low-oil-prices-and-tough-Asian-competition (accessed November 20, 2016).

18. U.S. Government Accountability Office. 2013. "IRAN: U.S. And International Sanctions Have Adversely Affected the Iranian Economy." [GAO-13–326]. http://www.gao.gov/assets/660/652314.pdf (accessed November 22, 2016).

19. Maloney, Suzanne. 2015. "Un-sanctioning Iran: What the Nuclear Deal

Means for the Future of Sanctions." http://brook.gs/2hti04W (accessed November 22, 2016); Cimino-Isaacs, Cathleen et al. 2015. "The US-Iran Nuclear Deal and the Effectiveness of Economic Sanctions." http://bit.ly/2huHK16 (accessed October 20, 2017); Bazoobandi, Sara. 2013. "What's Driving Iran's Shift?" http://bit.ly/2hsvnT3 (accessed October 12, 2017).

20. Thirarath, Itt. 2016. "China's Crude Oil Imports from Iran." http://bit.ly/2hrLOPA (accessed October 17, 2017).

21. The shipping sanctions would have limited application to one major case, Russia, whose petroleum is transported mostly through pipelines.

22. Blake, this volume, chapter 2.

23. It will be easy for Norway or Brazil to enact laws banning authoritarian oil imports—for they import almost no authoritarian oil at all.

24. Wenar 2016, pp. 269–71.

25. U.S. Energy Information Agency. "U.S. Household Spending for Gasoline Is Expected to Remain Below $2000 in 2017." www.eia.gov/todayinenergy/detail.php?id=33232 (accessed October 30, 2017).

26. Hussain, Yadullah. 2014. "New Emissions from Canada's Oil Sands 'Extremely Low,' Says IEA's Chief Economist." *Financial Post*, November 27. A 2014 study by the U.S. Congressional Research Service found that Canadian oil sands crude is 9–19 percent more emission-intensive, well-to-wheels, than an average barrel of Middle Eastern sour. Lattanzio, Richard. 2014. "Canadian Oil Sands: Life-Cycle Assessments of Greenhouse Gas Emissions." CRS 7-5700, p. 23.

27. Ross, Michael, and Eric Voeten. 2015. "Oil and International Cooperation." *International Studies Quarterly*, pp. 1–13 at 10.

28. Crooks, Ed. 2016. "Gas Wasted by Oil Industry Flaring on the Rise." *Financial Times*, December 13 (flared gas per barrel list).

29. On such projections more generally see Milanovic, Branko. 2016. *Global Inequality*. Cambridge: Harvard University Press, chapter 4.

30. Wenar 2016, pp. 308–11.

31. World Bank. "GDP Per Capita PPP." http://bit.ly/2hnCjAS (accessed October 30, 2017).

32. Deloitte Insights. "Ageing Tigers, Hidden Dragons." http://bit.ly/2hnY1Vq (accessed October 30, 2017).

33. Brooks, Stephen, and William Wohlforth. 2016. "The Once and Future Superpower." *Foreign Affairs* (May/June).

34. Council on Foreign Relations. 2017. "China in Africa." http://on.cfr.org/2hlsWSj (accessed October 29, 2017).

35. Lekorwe, Mogopodi et al. 2016. "China's Growing Presence in Africa Wins Largely Positive Popular Reviews." *Afrobarometer* 122. http://bit.ly/2holiXr (accessed October 29, 2017).

36. See Wenar 2016, chapters 1 and 2.

37. See Wenar 2016, p. 183, the first paragraph of the Chinese constitution.

38. Mehdiyeva has helpfully pointed out in personal correspondence that the United States could subsidize the cost of hydrocarbons for China in the same way as it could for Europe, and that China would favor a longer tapering period in order to be able to fulfil existing contracts with Russia and the Central Asian energy exporters.

39. Mill, John Stuart. 2001. *Utilitarianism*, 2nd ed. Indianapolis: Hackett, pp. 31–32.

40. Lincoln, Abraham. 1860. "Cooper Union Address." http://bit.ly/2hw476l (accessed October 13, 2017).

NOTES TO CHAPTER 8

1. Wenar, Leif. 2016. *Blood Oil: Tyrants, Violence, and the Rules that Run the World*. New York: Oxford University Press, pp. 112–13; this volume, chapter 1.

2. U.S. Department of State. 2017. "US-Taiwan Relations," http://bit.ly/ 2zD4K8d (accessed October 12, 2017).

3. Ibid.; "Taiwan Relations Act," 22 USC 48, emphases added.

4. As stated by the European Economic and Trade Office in Taiwan, "The EU pursues a 'One China' policy and recognizes the government of the People's Republic of China as the sole legal government of China. However, it recognizes Taiwan as an economic and commercial entity." 2017. "Taiwan and the EU," http://bit.ly/ 2hnu1ZQ (accessed October 15, 2017).

5. Mazzetti, Mark and Ben Hubbard. 2016. "Rise of Saudi Prince Shatters Decades of Tradition." *New York Times*. October 16.

6. This conversation actually happened. (Congress of course passes laws that affect the long term all the time, but that says nothing about why members of Congress vote as they do.)

7. Kutz, this volume, chapter 4.

8. Lindert, Peter, and Jeffrey Williamson. "America's Revolution: Economic Disaster, Development, and Equality." http://bit.ly/2zCd1Jz (accessed October 16, 2017).

9. The best question I've ever gotten when speaking on the reforms I advocate is whether I would still press for them were it my own life that would be sacrificed in the transition to a better world. My answer is, of course yes.

10. Kutz, this volume, chapter 4.

11. See the illuminating surveys of contemporary non-consequentialist theories of territory in Armstrong, Christopher. 2017. *Justice and Natural Resources*. Oxford: Oxford University Press; and Stilz, Anna. (forthcoming.) *Territorial Sovereignty*, chapter 1.

12. Many white-collar guest-workers in Saudi Arabia and other Gulf monarchies live quite well indeed (the next time you're on a posh Greek island, ask around about who is filling the nightclubs). And while the conditions of laboring guest-workers in the Gulf is a serious moral concern, it is unlikely the most serious one even in its domain. These foreign workers know what they're signing up for, and often travel great distances to reach their jobs in the Gulf. They are, if one wants to put it this way, some of the best-off exploited workers in the world. We should certainly press for their exploitation to be reduced, but that is not the same as advocating a fundamental shift in the international system solely for their sakes.

13. And perhaps not just in the Middle East. A Canadian prime minister might be elected on the promise to "build a wall" along Canada's southern border to keep out Americans, whose oil revenues-per-capita are only one-fifth as high.

14. Kutz, this volume, chapter 4.

15. Paine, Thomas. 1797. "Agrarian Justice." http://bit.ly/2hqRngZ (accessed October 15, 2017).

16. Mahatma Gandhi Foundation. "Mahatma Gandhi and One World," p. 8, http://bit.ly/2hqVFoz (accessed October 15, 2017).

17. Wenar 2016, pp. 350–53.

18. Wenar 2016, pp. 353–55.

19. Kutz may be misled by his examples like Saudi Arabia's relatively high score on the Human Development Index. It should first be remembered that one-third of this index is simply average national income, which of course reveals relatively little about the fate of the worst off. More importantly, the real question is how well off the worst-off Saudis could expect to be given the country's enormous oil wealth. This the index does not measure.

20. I suspect a correlation between the political resource curse and income inequality. However, we cannot do a rigorous study—many major resource-cursed states withhold their data on incomes. Government opacity is yet another dimension of the curse.

21. Wenar 2016, pp. xxvi–xxvii.

22. Kutz, this volume, chapter 4.

NOTES TO CHAPTER 9

1. Mill, John Stuart. 1989. *On Liberty*. Cambridge: Cambridge University Press, p. 13.

2. See also Armstrong, Chris. 2017. *Justice and Natural Resources*. Oxford, UK: Oxford University Press. Armstrong also described Popular Resource Sovereignty as merely a "pragmatic" principle.

3. Stilz, this volume, chapter 5.

4. Stilz, this volume, chapter 5.

5. Rousseau, Jean-Jacques. 1997. *The Discourses and Other Early Political Writings*. Trans. Victor Gourevitch. Cambridge, p. 132.

6. In her forthcoming book, Stilz makes it explicit that her case for a right of territorial occupancy does not rest on the badness of coerced removal, but on the goodness of staying in one place for the pursuit of one's life plans.

7. Stilz, chapter 5, this volume.

8. Wenar, Leif. 2016. *Blood Oil: Tyrants, Violence, and the Rules that Run the World*. New York: Oxford University Press, chapter 10.

9. Raz, Joseph. 1994. *Ethics in the Public Domain*. Oxford: Clarendon Press, p. 39.

10. Stilz, this volume, chapter 5.

11. Wenar 2016, pp. 160–63.

12. Sidgwick appears to be the last major figure in the Anglo-American tradition to give a consequentialist justification for territorial rights.

13. Stilz, this volume, chapter 5.

14. Stilz, this volume, chapter 5.

15. There is one error in Stilz's otherwise admirable summary of my analysis of

Popular Resource Sovereignty. I do not say that a people's territorial jurisdiction makes the people the original owner of a country's resources. The conceptual distinction between popular jurisdiction and popular ownership is made on *Blood Oil* p. 203, and the arguments for popular ownership thereafter do not rely on jurisdiction.

16. This is true even of a more qualified version of Popular Resource Sovereignty than Stilz discusses. *Blood Oil* does not argue for an unqualified version of this principle that would say that Bolivians can for trivial reasons refuse a mineral needed to stop climate change. But the precise qualifications to the principle don't matter here, for Stilz would be quite correct to say that Popular Resource Sovereignty in any form will have costs, especially compared to any feasible cosmopolitan alternatives.[17]

17. Stilz, this volume, pp. 101–2.

NOTES TO CHAPTER 10

1. As James says, practice-dependent and practice-independent deontological arguments may justify different principles. James, Aaron. 2012. *Fairness in Practice.* Oxford: Oxford University Press, p. 50; James, Aaron. 2014. "Reply to Critics," *Canadian Journal of Philosophy* 44(2), pp. 286–304 at 290–92. Here we focus specifically on the former. Whether consequentialism or deontology is superior is too large an issue for us here; it would lead us to how unity theory combines what's most attractive in both.

2. James, chapter 6, this volume, footnote 12; see also James, Aaron. 2013. "Why Practices?" *Raisons Politiques* 51, pp. 43–62.

3. James 2012, pp. 57–58. This is, at least, the mode of interpretation of a practice that is relevant if we are looking for principles that are "normative for us" (*Fairness in Practice*, p. 48).

4. James 2012, pp. 203–04. James does qualify these principles, which makes them somewhat less radical than described above.

5. James 2012, pp. 37–38, 167–68; James 2014, p. 294.

6. James 2012, p. 167; James 2014, p. 290.

7. James 2012, pp. 40, 96.

8. For example, a large, opt-in poll of Americans found that while most adults did understand basic "everyday" concepts like money and investment, most did not seem to understand what it means when GDP goes up. Markow, Dana and Kelly Bagnaschi. 2005. "What American Teens and Adults Know About Economics," National Council on Economic Education brief, http://bit.ly/2xPtMiY (accessed September 1, 2017).

9. Beitz, Charles. 2014. "Internal and External," *Canadian Journal of Philosophy* 44(2), pp. 225–38 at 232–33.

10. Julius, A. J. 2014. "Practice Independence," *Canadian Journal of Philosophy* 44(2), pp. 239–54 at 240–41.

11. James 2014, pp. 294–95.

12. James, Aaron. 2016. "How Cynical Can Ideal Theory Be?" *Journal of International Political Theory*, pp. 1–16.

13. Pew Research Center. 2017. "Support for Free Trade Agreements Rebounds Modestly, but Wide Partisan Differences Remain." April 25, http://pewrsr.ch/2xQXItG (accessed September 1, 2017).

14. Here "America" could also stand for a larger subset of countries, say the traditional "Quartet" that also includes the EU, Japan, and Canada.

15. Even within the formal trade regime of the GATT, a leading history of major agreements shows that most have been made "in the shadow of power," especially American power. Barton, John H., et al. 2006. *The Evolution of the Trade Regime.* Princeton, N.J.: Princeton University Press, p. 206. It might also be noted that in this telling of history, America has generally used its power to push for freer trade, which American officials have both endorsed ideologically and have seen as in America's interests. To demonstrate that free-trade ideology has itself shaped trade agreements, James would have to show many instances where American and other officials supported free trade even when doing so went against their perceived national interests—and history does not appear to show this.

16. James 2014, p. 291.

Index

abolition, of effectiveness, 14–15, 18, 26, 140
abolitionism, 86
abuses, of human rights, 38
accountability, 7, 15–16, 23–24, 108
Act of State doctrine, 45–46, 165n22
Africa, 14, 37, 146; China and, 40–41, 64, 69, 121, 128
agentic democracy, 80–81, 138
alien coercion, 100–102, 146
America. *See* United States
apartheid, 1, 14, 39
Arab Spring, 8, 10, 134
Arctic, 58, 65
Asian market, 62–68
associational deontology, 116
associative obligation, 108, 113, 114, 116, 117
associative sovereignty, 175n12; associative obligations with, 108, 113, 114, 116, 117; normative with, 112–13; perspective of, 113; problems with, 113–14
authoritarian hydrocarbons, 54, 70; alternative market for, 60; banning of, 56, 57; import reduction of, 64, 71; sanctioning of, 53, 58, 67
authoritarian import-dependence, 21
authoritarianism, 12; civil conflict, corruption, and, 5–7, 158n15;

killing and displacement of people with, 51
authoritarian oil, 20, 21, 52, 56, 60, 67, 162nn66–67
authoritarian states, 3, 5–6, 6, 14, 89, 158n20, 158n22; Russia, 62; sanctions against, 52, 53–54, 124
autocrats, 1, 8, 21–22, 53, 76, 170n7
autocrats to alternatives plan, 126, 127
autonomy, 99–100

Baathist government, sanctions against, 41, 164n9
black market, 40, 41
blood diamonds, 86–87, 123, 172n31
borders, 83, 95, 102, 147
boycotts, 51–52, 84–85, 86, 136
BP Energy Outlook 2017, 61
Brazil, 20, 22, 125, 177n25
Bush, George W., 3, 16

Canada, 44, 52, 59, 126
carbon dioxide, 59, 71
catholic view, of state system, 111, 175n11
Central Asia, 53, 69
chemical weapons, in Syria, 2
China, 19, 20, 89, 146, 147; Africa and, 40–41, 64, 69, 121, 128; Clean Trade Act relating to, 22, 40–41, 55; Clean

Trade cooperation of, 69–71,
125–29, 178n40; ecological degradation caused by, 64, 127; green
energy impact on, 60, 61–62; human
rights and, 47; labor in, 47; market
dependence on, 62–64; One China
policy, 134, 135, 178n4; United
States and, 40
Chinese Communist Party, 129
citizens: control of, with Popular
Resource Sovereignty, 79–80; guest-
workers and, 83, 171n26; non-
citizens and, 80, 171n17
Clean Hands Trust, 18, 20–21, 37, 55,
64, 102, 164n1
Clean Trade, 60, 61, 77, 137, 141; China
cooperation with, 69–71, 125–29,
178n40; climate goals with, 127;
costs associated with, 125–26; countries with, 20–21, 23, 55, 64; future
of, 69–71; implementation of, 52,
55, 57, 59; income inequality and,
140, 179nn19–20; moral legitimacy
of, 67; motivation for, 74; policies of,
23, 25, 31, 34, 52, 53, 54, 57, 64–65,
83–84, 89, 120; political acceptability of, 55; popular control
requirement of, 80, 171n18; popular
sovereignty and, 130; reforms with,
125–26, 129; results of, 69; sanctions
relating to, 52, 53, 54, 55, 57, 58, 62,
67–69, 85–86, 121–25
Clean Trade Act, 18–19, 37, 106, 164n1;
China relating to, 22, 40–41, 55; as
economic sanctions, 41–42, 165n10;
framework for, 23; global human
rights impacted by, 42–44; incentives
for, 44; international relations with,
47; legislation for, 20, 21–22, 125;
with malignant regime, 38; Public
Power Spectrum with, 23–24,
162n69; reform with, 22–23, 25, 31,
34–35, 39–41, 127, 177n24; relationship between states impacted by,
45; Rules of Engagement with, 23; as
tool, 44, 49; touchstones for, 25

Clean Trade Boycott, 136
Clean Trade states, cartels for, 123–24
clientelism, 54
climate: change in, 1, 3–4, 21, 59, 86,
96, 168; Clean Trade goals with, 127;
geography and, 93
climate, energy and: authoritarian
import-dependence relating to, 21;
issues with, 21; Paris climate change
agreement, 21; Russia cyberespionage, 21
coalbed methane, 58, 59
coercion, 10, 15, 17, 34, 84, 97, 147;
alien, 100–102, 146; non-moralized
baseline with, 121–22; political, 100
coercive actors, 5, 18, 27, 29, 33; power
of, 1, 7, 15
collective agency, 81–83, 171n22,
171n25
collectively authorized agents, 99
collective ownership, 116–17
collective resource control, power of
complicity and, 73–88
collective self-determination, 90, 91,
97–99, 101, 103, 108, 145–46
common ownership: of Earth, 26–27,
97, 139, 163n73; of humanity, 91;
legitimacy problem with, 98; philosophical issues of, 26–27, 30,
163n73, 163n81; self-determination
and, 101, 103
complicity: consumer, 86; international,
77; petrocomplicity, 86; power of,
73–88; psychology of, 87
complicity-based campaign, 87
Congo, 1, 10, 123
consequentialism, 74, 107, 143–44,
147, 155
constitutive social norms, 109–10,
174nn4–5
consumerism, 53, 86, 172n34
consumption: of energy, 53, 77; ethical
sourcing of, 73; First World, of petroproducts, 73; of oil, 4; wrongness of,
74
cosmopolitanism: costs of, 28–30, 75,
78, 163n74, 163n76; Popular

Resource Sovereignty and, 78–79, 80, 83, 138–39, 170n13
costs and trust, with resource curse, 24–26
counter-power norm, 106
country, people of, 89; international conventions with, 90, 94–98; jurisdiction with, 90; natural property rights of, 90, 91–94; ownership with, 90; self-determination of, 90, 97, 98–103; sovereignty of, 90
Crimea, annexation of, 44, 57, 62, 65, 67

Darfur genocide, 2, 136
demagogic populists, 130
democracies, 29, 80–81, 84, 138
democratic legitimacy, 80
Democratic Republic of Congo, 39
democratization, 8
Denizen Rights Sovereignty, 80–81, 83
denizens, 80, 84, 87; non-denizens and, 81, 83; rights of, 133, 138–39
deontological cast: mitigation with, 115–16; obligations with, 115–16; resource curse relating to, 114–17, 175n17
deontology, 84, 108, 116. *See also* practice-based deontological arguments
Department of Energy, U.S., 62
diamonds, 14–15, 52; blood, 86–87, 123, 172n31
diplomatic recognition, 133
dirty trade, bad men and, 37; conclusions, 48–49; international relations, 45–48; oil-importing states, 42–45; oil-producing states, 38–42
distributions, 30–31, 78, 150
distributive justice, 1, 80
diversity, 75, 169n3
Dodd-Frank Act, 39
domain, 92
domestic property rules, 95, 105, 107
drugs, criminalization of, 40
Dutch energy plan, 61

Earth: common ownership of, 26–27, 97, 139, 163n73; as livable environment, 95
ecological degradation, by China, 64, 127
economic sanctions, 39; Clean Trade Act as, 41–42, 165n10; people killed by, 41
The Economist, 8, 19, 44
EEZs. *See* Exclusive Economic Zones
effectiveness, 135; abolition of, 14–15, 18, 26, 140; choice of, 11, 122–23, 127, 128, 129, 130, 131; "Might Makes Right" relating to, 9–11, 14, 18, 19, 24, 26, 29, 35, 51; for natural resources, 130; Popular Resource Sovereignty and, 120, 133, 148, 179n15, 180n16; principle of, 89; reform of, 17–18, 127; risk of, 127, 131; as systemic cause of resource curse, 9–11, 14–15, 17–18. *See also* rule of effectiveness
effectiveness-based trade, in resources, 51–52
egalitarianism, 147, 150
energy: climate and, 21; consumption of, 53, 77; Dutch energy plan, 61; oil as source of, 4; renewable sources of, 4, 21, 71; rise of consumerism in, 53. *See also* green energy
energy sovereignty, 71
energy trap, of West: boycotts relating to, 51–52, 84–85, 86; future for Clean Trade, 69–71; green energy problem, 60–64; makers of their own destiny, 64–69; monetary sacrifices relating to, 52; moving sacrificial places to West, 57–60; trading with resource-disordered states as, 51, 56; US versus them, 54, 55–57
environment: costs relating to, 52, 54, 57, 58, 59, 60, 62; of Earth, 95
environmental degradation, 52, 127
Equatorial Guinea, 20–21, 85
ethical narcissism, 73

ethical sourcing, of consumption, 73
ethnic cleansing, 14
Exclusive Economic Zones (EEZs), 94–95
exports: failed oil-exporting states, 6, 158n20; failed resource-exporting states, 6, 158n20; global, of Russia, 65, 168n34; of oil, 5, 37, 66, 125
extractive industries, 38, 39

failed oil-exporting states, 6, 158n20
failed resource-exporting states, 6, 158n20
fake news, 45
first occupancy principle, 91–93
First World consumption, of petroproducts, 73
Five-Year Plan, for Rare Earth Industry, 64
flammable ice, 71
force-proof borders, 95, 102, 147
foreign sovereignty, 110
fossil fuels, 54, 55–56, 61, 126
fracking, 52, 59, 60
Freedom House, 19, 44, 161n59
free trade, 153
free unity of humankind, 91, 96–97

Gaddafi, Muammar, 2, 11, 12, 134
gasoline, 39, 59, 60, 179n14
genocide, 1, 2, 14, 122, 136
geography, climate and, 93
geostrategy, 127–28
global deposits, of rare earth metals, 62
global economy, 31, 81
global exports, of Russia, 65, 168n34
global human rights, 42–44
global injustice, reduction of, 69
global institutions, reform guidelines for, 1
global justice, 140
global petroleum markets, 73
global principle, of Popular Resource Sovereignty, 16–17, 18, 22, 26, 27, 29–30
global problem, of resource curse, 1
global resource distribution, 78

global resource divided (GRD), 97
Global Resource tax, 101
global spread, of Islam fundamentalism, 12, 160n44
GRD. *See* global resource divided
green energy, 64, 69, 71; China impacted by, 60, 61–62; Dutch energy plan relating to, 61; fossil fuels impacted by, 61; implementation cost of, 60; India impacted by, 61–62; innovations for, 70; oil and gas reduction relating to, 60; rare earth metals impacted by, 54–55, 60–63, 70
greenhouse gas problem, 59, 167n14
Green Movement, 8
green technologies, 54
guest-workers, 83, 138–39, 171n26, 179n14

humanity, 31, 79; common ownership of, 91; free unity of, 91
human rights: abuses of, 38; China relating to, 47; Clean Trade Act impact on, 42–44; evaluation of, 44; global, 42–44
Human Rights Covenants, 1966, 94
Hussein, Saddam, 2, 9, 11, 12, 41, 122
hydraulic fracturing, 52, 59–60; water impact on, 58, 166n11
hydrocarbons: access to, 52; demand for, 54; depletion of, 52; rising price of, 57; unconventional, 59. *See also* authoritarian hydrocarbons
hydrocarbons-rich regions, of Russia, 65
hydrocarbons society, 52

imperialism, of United States, 56, 125
incoherence, 106–8
income inequality, 140, 179nn19–20
India, green energy impact on, 61–62
internalization, of norms, 42–43
international commerce, 106
international complicity, 77
international conventions, with people of country, 90, 94–98
International Energy Agency, 70, 127

international law, of territory, 95, 113, 133

international relations: Act of State doctrine impact on, 45–46, 165n22; Clean Trade Act and, 47; dangerous work with, 49; juridical authority with, 45; law of politics with, 46; moral pathway to, 47; political interference impact on, 45–46; Popular Resource Sovereignty impact with, 48; property-holder, refusal to engage with, 45–46; resource sovereignty with, 47; sanctions relating to, 46, 48, 165n24; between states, 45; unilateral power with, 47; virtues displayed with, 48

international trade: flaw in, 155; government officials relating to, 152; in oil, 51; participants in, 151–52, 180n8; principles of, 150–52; public ideology relating to, 153; sociological perspective of, 153

international treaties, 89–90

intervention, 13, 46, 49, 86

Iran, 2, 13, 124, 136, 177n22

Iraq, 2, 3, 9, 13, 122, 136

Iraq-Syria conflict, 2

Irish Republican Army, 2

ISIS, 1, 2, 9, 12, 22, 87, 136

Islam fundamentalism, global spread of, 12, 160n44

Islamic Jihad, 2

juridical authority, 45

jurisdiction: with people of country, 90; right of property and, 91–92; territorial, 109

Kant, Immanuel, 76

Kimberly Process, 16

kleptocracy, 37, 106, 114, 115

Law of Peoples (Rawls), 76

laws: of diplomatic recognition, 133; international, of territory, 95, 113, 133; mineral-tracing, 123; natural resources relating to, 9–10; of

overture, 95; of politics, 46; of resource curse, 1; of United States, 9–10, 159n38; world natural resource law, 9–11, 14, 18, 19, 74–75, 76

legislation, for Clean Trade Act, 20, 21–22, 121

legitimacy, 67, 80, 98–99

Libya: conflicts in, 2, 8, 9–10; oil from, 10, 13, 134, 136

LNG, 55, 66–68

lobbies, for oil, 44

located life plans, 93, 144–45

long-term contracts, 68

magnets, 70

malignant regime, 38

marijuana, 39–40

markets, 40, 41, 60, 62–68, 73

Marshall Plan, 126

methane emissions, 58, 59

Middle East, 8, 12, 22, 37, 55, 118, 146; as oil-producing region, 6, 14, 17, 56, 126–27, 128

"Might Makes Right" (MMR), 77, 79, 88; effectiveness relating to, 9–11, 14, 18, 19, 24, 26, 29, 35, 51; for oil, 35, 51, 121; transition away from, 24, 26; as world natural resource law, 9–11, 14, 18, 19, 74–75, 76

military force, over-the-horizon guarantees of, 47–48

Mill, John Stuart, 143

mineral-tracing law, 123

mitigation, 115–16

MMR. *See* "Might Makes Right"

moral character, of oil-importing states, 42

moral claim, to natural resources, 95, 96, 117

moral legitimacy, of Clean Trade, 67

moral pathway, to international relations, 47

moral validity, 143

moratorium, on production, 59, 60

Muslim communities, 12

nanotechnologies, 70–71
National Intelligence Council, U.S., 14
National Security Strategy of Russian
    Federation to 2020, 66
Natural Duty of Justice, 112
natural property rights, of people of
    country, 90; challenges to, 92–93;
    domain relating to, 92; first occu-
    pancy principle, 91–93; with
    generations, 94; located life plans
    relating to, 93, 144–45; territorial
    rights, 91, 143, 173n12, 172nn7–8
natural resources, 1, 8; effectiveness for,
    130; laws relating to, 9–10; MMR
    relating to, 9–11, 14, 18, 19, 74–75,
    76; moral claim to, 95, 96, 117;
    ownership of, 74–75, 78, 80; private
    property rights of, 74–75, 82;
    purchase of, 120–21; world natural
    resource law, 9–11, 14, 18, 19,
    74–75, 76. *See also* oil
natural rights, 94, 115–16
neocolonialism, 48
non-citizens, 80, 171n17
non-moralized baseline, with coercion,
    121–22
Norway, 78, 125, 170n12, 177n23

oil, 3, 60, 107, 158n10; as cause of
    violence, 13; conflicts over, 8;
    consumption of, 4; curse of, 120;
    demand for, 43–44; dependence on,
    52; as energy source, 4; exportation
    of, 5, 37, 66, 66, 125; failed oil-
    exporting states, 6, 158n20; half
    world trade in, 17; international
    trade in, 51; in Iraq, 2, 9, 13, 136; in
    Libya, 10, 13, 134, 136; lobbies for,
    44; MMR for, 35, 51, 121; money
    from, 7; power with, 8, 12–13; price
    increase of, 53; propositions about
    purchase of, 37–38, 164n2; sale of,
    120–21, 175n3; smuggling of, 123;
    spills, 58; stolen, 47; uses for, 4
oil-importing states, 44–45; moral char-
    acter of, 42; sanctions relating to, 42,

43; with tyrants, 42–43; virtuous
    agency of, 42–43
oil-producing regions, 38, 40–42;
    extremism from, 120; Middle East, 6,
    14, 17, 56, 126–27, 128; sanctions
    against, 39, 164n3; Saudi Arabia, 5,
    13, 17, 68, 75, 79, 169n4, 170n16,
    172n30
One China policy, 134, 135, 178n4
On Liberty (Mill), 143
Orientalism, 56
outsiders only focus, 122
ownership: collective, 116–17; of
    natural resources, 74–75, 78, 80;
    with people of country, 90; popular,
    80; resource, 107; supreme, 92. *See
    also* common ownership
ownership *vel non*, 80

Paris climate change agreement, 21
PEPFAR, 126
Permanent Sovereignty over Natural
    Resources, 94
"Perpetual Peace" (Kant), 76
Petro-Aggression, 11
petrocomplicity, 86
petroconsumption, 141
petrocrats, 8, 11, 129
petrodollars, 51
petroleum, 2, 73, 76, 84–85, 86
petroproducts, First World consumption
    of, 73
Petrostan, 77, 84–85, 133, 136–37
philosophical issues: common
    ownership, 26–27, 30, 163n73,
    163n81; Cosmopolitanism costs,
    28–30, 75, 163n74, 163n76; distri-
    butions, 30–31; unity theory, 31–35
point source resources, 5
policy-based philosophy, 150
political acceptability, of Clean Trade,
    55
political activism, 39
political agency, 84
political authority, of territorial
    division, 109
political coercion, 100

political economy, 7–9, 129
political interference, in international relations, 45–46
politics: law of, 46; of resource curse, 1
popular ownership, 80
Popular Resource Sovereignty, 74, 96, 103, 125, 129; alternatives to, 133; citizen control relating to, 79–80; consequentialism and, 143–44; Cosmopolitanism and, 78–79, 80, 83, 138–39, 170n13; effectiveness and, 120, 133, 148, 179n15, 181n16; as global principle, 16–17, 18, 22, 26, 27, 29–30; international relations impacted with, 48; international treaties support of, 89–90; language of, 17, 161n58; meaning of, 16; Petrostan relating to, 136–37; practice-based deontological arguments with, 154–55; property rights relating to, 11, 17–18, 21–22, 75, 82–83, 85, 87; resource curse, 16–17; SDTR and, 77; superiority of, 133; violations of, 17
popular sovereignty, 18, 22, 29, 33, 34, 130
power, 31, 47; of coercive actors, 1, 7, 15; counter-power norm, 106; with oil, 8, 12–13; over resources, 120; superpower, 42, 66, 128
power of complicity, collective resource control and, 73–88
practice-based deontological arguments, 149–51, 180n1, 180n3, 181nn14–15; formal model of, 152–53; lip service model of, 154; Popular Resource Sovereignty impact on, 154–55
practice-based theory, 108
principles, 76; consequence and, 74; of effectiveness, 89; first occupancy, 91–93; global, of Popular Resource Sovereignty, 16–17, 18, 22, 26, 27, 29–30; of international trade, 150–51; of liberty, 143
property, rule of, 106

property-holder, refusal to engage with, 45–46
property rights, 91–92; with natural resources, 74–75, 82; with Popular Resource Sovereignty, 11, 17–18, 21–22, 75, 82–83, 85, 87; private, 74–75, 82. *See also* natural property rights, of people of country
pro tanto, 100–101, 146
protestant view, of state system, 111, 175n11
public accountability, as structural solution, 15–16
public ideology, international trade and, 153
Public Power Spectrum, 23–24, 162n69
Putin, Vladimir, 2, 3, 11–12, 57

al Qaeda, 2, 12, 136

radioactive contamination, 63
rare earth metals, 54–55, 60–61, 127; dependence on, 70; global deposits of, 62; leverage of, 63–64; process of, 63; renewable technologies use of, 62–63; shortages of, 62; wastewater and, 63
rational deliberators, 99
Rawls, John, 76
Rawlsian society, 77, 170n10
Realism, 170n8
Realist principle of sovereignty, 76
realist view, of state system, 109, 174nn6–7
reforms, 1; with Clean Trade, 127–28, 131; with Clean Trade Act, 22–23, 25, 31, 34–35, 39–41, 127, 177n24; of effectiveness, 17–18, 129
refugee crisis, in Syria, 2
renewable sources, of energy, 4, 21, 71
renewable technologies, 62–63
resource curse, 120, 125, 136, 140; analysis of, 2–18; of authoritarianism, civil conflict, and corruption, 5–7, 158n15; global problem of, 1; law, economics, and politics of, 1;

politics for, 1; results of, 8; slavery relating to, 1
resource curse, analysis of, 2; effectiveness relating to, 9–11, 14–15, 17–18; oil is everywhere, 3–5; Popular Resource Sovereignty, 16–17; public accountability as structural solution to, 15–16; resource-cursed states, political economy of, 7–9; as systemic, 5–7; West failed strategies, 12–14; West relating to, 11–12
resource curse, policies for lifting of: Clean Hands Trusts, 18, 20–21; climate and energy, 21; conflict with, 23; costs and trust, 24–26; disqualified states relating to, 19, 161n61; index of indices, 19, 161n60; resource-dependent states relating to, 19; strategies for, 21–23; supporting accountability above line, 23–24. *See also* Clean Trade Act
resource curse, remedy for, 105; associative sovereignty, 112–14, 175n12; counter-power norm, 106; deontological cast, 114–17, 175n17; incoherence and its resolution, 106–8; state system, as social practice, 108–12; theory relating to, 117–18
resource-cursed states, 7–9, 22, 31
resource-dependent states, 19
resource-disordered states, 51, 56
resource-exporting states, failed, 6, 158n20
resource justice, to oppressed people, 52
resource-rich states, 8–9, 11, 56, 112
resources: accountability for, 108; effectiveness-based trade in, 51–52; global distribution of, 78; multinationals, 14; ownership of, 107; point source, 5; theft of, 85. *See also* natural resources; Permanent Sovereignty over Natural Resources; Popular Resource Sovereignty
resource sovereignty, 40, 47, 53, 69

"right rights," 98–99
rights: of denizens, 133, 138–39; natural, 94, 115–16; of people, 117; of property, 91–92; territorial, 91, 145, 173n12, 172nn7–8. *See also specific rights*
Rousseau, Jean-Jacques, 30, 31, 33, 81, 144
rule, of property, 106
rule of effectiveness, 111–12, 121, 154; end of, 53, 69, 71, 114, 115, 116; of states, 15, 51, 105–6, 110, 114–15, 117; weakening of, 52, 107–8, 115, 116
Rules of Engagement, 23
Russia, 13, 55, 57, 136; as authoritarian state, 62; cyberespionage of, 21; global exports of, 65, 168n34; hydrocarbons-rich regions of, 65; Sabine Pass LNG terminal impact on, 66–67; sanctions against, 65–69, 73–74; U.S. competition with, 66; U.S. crude oil exports to, 66

Sabine Pass LNG terminal, 66–67
sacrificial places, 54, 55–56, 57–60
sanctions, 10, 56, 159n33; against authoritarian hydrocarbons, 53, 58, 67; against authoritarian states, 52, 53–54, 124; against Baathist government, 41, 164n9; Clean Trade relating to, 52, 53, 54, 55, 57, 58, 62, 67–69, 85–86, 121–25; economic, 39, 41–42, 165n10; international relations impacted by, 46, 48, 165n24; against Iran, 124, 177n22; oil-importing states relating to, 42, 43; against oil-producing states, 39, 164n3; people killed by, 122, 176n8; against Russia, 65–69, 73–74; trade, 84; by United States, 124; West imposition of, 13
Saudi Arabia, 12, 77, 80, 85; as oil-rich country, 5, 13, 17, 68, 75, 79, 169n4, 170n16, 172n30
Saudi Salafism, 12

SDTRs. *See* Sovereign-Determined Transfer Rights

security and peace, of state system, 110–11, 174n10

self-determination: alien coercion with, 100–102; autonomy with, 99–100; collective, 90, 91, 97–99, 101, 103, 108, 145–46; common ownership and, 101, 103; incentives with, 102; justice relating to, 98–99; legitimacy relating to, 98–99; of people of country, 90, 97, 98–103; rational deliberators with, 99; respect for, 102–3; value of, 100–1

shale, 52, 54, 57, 58, 59

short-termism, 136–38, 178n7, 178n10

slavery, 17, 28, 86, 110, 114, 148; end to, 29, 33, 53, 137; resource curse relating, 1; trade in, 9, 14, 15, 24, 35, 48, 106, 130

smuggling, of oil, 123, 176n13

The Social Contract (Rousseau), 31

sociological perspective, of international trade, 153

Sovereign-Determined Rights of Purchase, 135

Sovereign-Determined Transfer Rights (SDTRs), 76–77, 83, 133, 135, 169n5, 170n8

sovereignty, 27, 78, 110; of country, 90; Denizen Rights Sovereignty, 80–81, 83; energy, 71; permanent, 94–96; Permanent Sovereignty over Natural Resources, 94; popular, 18, 22, 29, 33, 34, 130; Realist principle of sovereignty, 76; resource, 40, 47, 53, 69. *See also* associative sovereignty; Popular Resource Sovereignty

Soviet propaganda, 43, 165n14

Soviet Union, 2, 147

states, rule of effectiveness of, 15, 51, 105–6, 110, 114–15, 117

state sovereignty, 110

State Sponsors of Terrorism list, 11–12

state system, as social practice, 108; aims of, 110–12, 174n10; catholic view relating to, 111, 175n11; constitutive social norms of, 109–10, 174nn4–5; protestant view relating to, 111, 175n11; realist view of, 109, 174nn6–7; security and peace relating to, 110–11, 174n10

stolen goods, 89

structural equity, 117

superpower, 42, 66, 128

supreme ownership, 92

Syria, 2, 13, 136

systemic curse, of resources, 5–7

technologies, 54, 62–63, 70–71

territorial control theory, national, 138

territorial division, of political authority, 109

territorial jurisdiction, 109

territorial occupancy, 145, 179n6

territorial order, 82

territorial rights, 91, 145, 172nn7–8, 173n12

territory: conquest of, 95; international law of, 95, 113, 133

theories: of justice, 98–99; of legitimacy, 98–99; national territorial control, 138; practice-based, 108; for resource curse remedy, 117–18; unity, 35, 155. *See also* unity theory

trade, 123–24, 136; even distribution of gains of, 150; free, 153; with resource-disordered states, 51, 56; sanctions with, 84; in slavery, 9, 14, 15, 24, 35, 48, 106, 130. *See also* Clean Trade; Clean Trade Act; dirty trade, bad men and; international trade

Treaties of Westphalia, 108, 110, 160n52

Trump, Donald, 3, 44, 67

Ukraine, 65

unaccountable power, 7

UNCLOS. *See* UN Convention on the Law of the Sea

unconventional hydrocarbons, 59

UN Convention on the Law of the Sea (UNCLOS), 94–95
unilateral power, 47
United Nations General Assembly, 90, 94
United States: China and, 40; imperialism of, 56, 125; laws of, 9–10, 159n38; Libya and, 10; Russia competition with, 66; sanctions imposed by, 124
unity theory, 35, 155; as consequentialist, 34, 164n88; free, 32–33; freedom of, 33; humanity relating to, 31; maximum, 32
Universal Declaration of Human Rights, 106

US, them versus, 54, 55–57
US-Taiwan Mutual Defense Treaty, 134
US-Taiwan Relations Act, 134–35

virtuous agency, of oil-importing states, 42–43

wastewater, 63
water, 58, 63, 166n11
wealth of nations, 153
West, 1–3; failed strategies of, 12–14; military action of, 13; perceptions of, 24–25; resource curse relating to, 11–12; sanctions imposed by, 13. *See also* energy trap, of West
world natural resource law, 9–11, 14, 18, 19, 74–75, 76

About the Authors

Leif Wenar is the author of *Blood Oil: Tyrants, Violence, and the Rules that Run the World.* His work has been featured in *The New York Times, The Wall Street Journal, The Los Angeles Times, Foreign Affairs,* CNN, and the playbill for the White Light Festival at Lincoln Center.

Wenar holds the Chair of Philosophy and Law at King's College London. After graduating with honors from Stanford he was briefly Karl Popper's research assistant, and then went to Harvard to study with John Rawls. At Harvard he wrote his qualifying thesis on Karl Marx's theory of history, he taught Justice for Michael Sandel, and wrote his doctoral dissertation on property rights with Robert Nozick. He is a co-editor of *Hayek on Hayek: An Autobiographical Dialogue* and of *Giving Well: The Ethics of Philanthropy.*

He has been a Laurance S. Rockefeller Fellow and a Visiting Professor at Princeton's University Center for Human Values, and also a Visiting Professor at the Princeton Department of Politics. He has been a Visiting Professor at the Stanford Center on Ethics and Society, and the William H. Bonsall Visiting Professor in the Stanford Department of Philosophy. He has been a Faculty Fellow at the Center for Ethics and Public Affairs at The Murphy Institute of Political Economy, a Visiting Fellow at the Australian National University School of Philosophy, and a Fellow of the Program on Justice and the World Economy at the Carnegie Council on Ethics and International Affairs.

Michael Blake is Professor of Philosophy, Public Policy, and Governance at the University of Washington. Until 2016, he was the director of the UW's Program on Values in Society. He received his bachelor degree in Philosophy and Economics from the University of Toronto and a PhD from Stanford University. He obtained some legal training at Yale Law School before running away to become a philosopher. He is jointly appointed to the Department of Philosophy and to the Daniel J. Evans School of Public Affairs.

Aaron James is Professor of Philosophy at the University of California, Irvine. He is author of *Fairness in Practice: A Social Contract for a Global Economy*, many academic articles in ethics and political philosophy, and several popular books. He has been an ACLS Burkhardt Fellow, a fellow at the Center for Advanced Study in the Behavioral Sciences, Stanford University, Visiting Professor of Philosophy at New York University, and a visiting scholar at Australia National University.

Christopher Kutz joined the Jurisprudence and Social Policy Program at Boalt Hall in 1998. Before joining the Berkeley faculty, he clerked for Judge Stephen F. Williams of the U.S. Court of Appeals for the District of Columbia. Since his appointment at Berkeley, he has been a Visiting Professor at Columbia and Stanford law schools, as well as at Sciences Po University in Paris.

Kutz's work focuses on moral, political, and legal philosophy, and he has particular interest in the foundations of criminal, international, and constitutional law. His book *Complicity: Ethics and Law for a Collective Age* (Cambridge University Press, 2000) addressed the question of individual moral and legal responsibility for harms brought about through collective and corporate activity. His 2016 book, *On War and Democracy* (Princeton University Press), addresses the collision between democratic values and the ethics and laws of war; it addresses both questions of when democratic states can engage in war, such as for purposes of humanitarian intervention, and what limits democratic commitments place on their means, such as torture and drone strikes. In addition, he has written on issues of the metaphysics of criminal responsibility, social welfare obligations, national responsibilities to mitigate climate change, humanitarian ethics, and political legitimacy. He teaches courses in criminal law and moral, political, and legal philosophy.

Kutz's publications include "The Collective Work of Citizenship," *Legal Theory* (2002); "Justice in Reparations: The Cost of Memory and the Value of Talk," *Philosophy & Public Affairs* (2004); "The Difference Uniforms Make: Collective Violence in Criminal Law and the Law of War," *Philosophy & Public Affairs* (2005); "The Lawyers Know Sin: Complicity in Torture," in *The Torture Debate in America*, ed. Karen J. Greenberg (2006); "Secret Law and the Value of Publicity," *Ratio Juris* 22: 197–217 (2009); "Democracy, Defense and the Threat of Intervention," in *Justifying National Defense*, eds. Cécile Fabre and Seth Lazar (2014); and "How Norms Die," *Ethics and International Affairs* (2014).

Dr. Nazrin Mehdiyeva is Academic Visitor at St Antony's College, Oxford University, and an independent geopolitical and energy consultant working with international institutions and energy majors. Nazrin specializes in energy security and geopolitics. The subject of her special interest is the interrelationships between political decision-making and hydrocarbons production and exports. Her primary regions of specialization are Russia and Eurasia, but she also works on the global dynamics of oil and gas, covering the United States, Australia, and the Middle East. She has recently held a number of senior positions in the private sector and is a regular contributor to the debate on the future of European energy security. Nazrin holds DPhil in International Relations from Oxford University and MPhil in Russian and East European Studies. Nazrin regularly publishes articles in academic and industry journals, and her book *Power Games in the Caucasus* was published by I. B. Tauris in 2011. Her current interest focuses on Russian energy strategy and foreign policy, on which she is writing her latest monograph.

Anna Stilz is Laurence S. Rockefeller Professor of Politics and Human Values at Princeton University. Her first book, *Liberal Loyalty: Freedom, Obligation, and the State*, was published by Princeton University Press in 2009. She is currently finishing a second book, titled *Territorial Sovereignty*. This project tries to articulate moral principles for demarcating state boundaries and investigates the limits of a state's justified power within these boundaries. She is also interested in related questions concerning the status of indigenous peoples, historic injustice, colonialism, and theories of property. She is an associate editor for *Philosophy & Public Affairs*.